The Making of a Transnational Community

Bancroft Dissertation Award Recipients

1972 Carol Berkin   Jonathan Sewall: Odyssey of an Anglo-American Conservative

1973 Paul Edmund Beard   Bureaucratic Politics and Weapons Innovation: A Study of Development of the ICBM

1974 Jacquelyn Dowd Hall   Revolt Against Chivalry: Jessie Ames and the Women's Campaign vs. Lynching

1975 Thomas Dublin   Women at Work: The Transformation of Work and Community, Lowell, Mass., 1826–60

1976 Elizabeth P. McCaughy   Wm. Samuel Johnson: Loyalist and Founding Father

1977 Viviana A. Zelizer   The Development of Life Insurance in the U.S.: A Sociological Analysis

1978 Daniel M. Hausman   A Philosophical Inquiry into Capital Theory

1979 Jonathan Haas   The Evaluation of the Prehistoric State Toward an Archaeological Analysis of Political Organization

1980 Catherine Ann Barnes   Journey from Jim Crow: The Desegration of Southern Transit, 1937–65

1981 Thomas Brown   Politics and Statesmanship: A Study of the American Whig Party

1983 James D. Wallace   Early Cooper and His Audience

1985 Eugenia Georges   The Causes and Consequences of International Labor Migration from a Rural Dominican Sending Community

The Making of a
Transnational Community

*Migration, Development, and
Cultural Change in the Dominican Republic*

EUGENIA GEORGES

COLUMBIA UNIVERSITY PRESS New York

As a manuscript this book was awarded the Bancroft Dissertation Award by a committee of the faculty of the Graduate School of the Arts and Sciences of Columbia University.

Columbia University Press
New York   Oxford
Copyright © 1990 Columbia University Press

Library of Congress Cataloging-in-Publication Data

Georges, Eugenia.
  The making of a transnational community : migration, development, and cultural change in the Dominican Republic / Eugenia Georges.
  p. cm.
Includes bibliographical references.
ISBN 0-231-07096-9
1. Dominican Republic—Emigration and immigration—Case studies.
2. United States—Emigration and immigration—Case studies.
3. Dominicans (Dominican Republic)—United States—Case studies.
4. Working class—Dominican Republic—Case studies.
5. Dominican Republic—Social life and customs—Case studies.
6. Dominican Republic—Rural conditions—Case studies.
I. Title.
JV7395.G46   1990
304.8'097293—dc20   89-28628
                      CIP

Casebound editions of Columbia University Press books are Smyth-sewn and printed on permanent and durable acid-free paper

Printed in the United States of America
c 10 9 8 7 6 5 4 3 2 1

To the memory of Chris and Eugenia Peltier, with love

Contents

Contents

Acknowledgments

Living in New York, and more particularly in Morningside Heights, as a graduate student, I became aware early on of the importance of Dominicans among new immigrants to the city. Two summers of fieldwork in the Dominican Republic heightened my interest in Dominican migration and led to the idea for this study. Where I settled among the many villages with heavy emigration to the United States was largely the result of a conversation with the Dominican sociologist Wilma Weisz, who suggested, on the basis of her own research, that I visit the western Sierra. It was a suggestion that led me to the community that is the focus of this study, and one I have not regretted following.

As villagers have struggled to confront the economic and political hardships that have befallen their communities over the last several decades, they have devised sometimes ingenious, often extralegal ways of improving their life chances. To avoid the possibility of any detrimental consequences of this study, I refer to the community that is its focus by the pseudonym of Los Pinos. I also have changed most of the local place names and all names of local people, and, where appropriate, I have altered some critical identifying features, such as occupation.

I was very fortunate to receive the hospitality and generous assistance of many, if not most, Pineros. That a study of this nature was completed at all attests to the remarkable tolerance of the people of Los Pinos. Many had understandable misgivings and doubts about my purposes, doubts which, had they been justified, might conceivably have jeopardized their undocumented friends and relatives in the United States. I am deeply grateful for the tolerance, patience and friendship that so many offered to me. One of the great personal advantages that the study of U.S.-bound migration afforded me was the ability to continue friendships once I returned. These friendships have enriched my life and work in many ways.

My acceptance by many Pineros undoubtedly was encouraged by the offering, at the suggestion of several community members, of an English course at the local school. This course was largely taught by a linguist, Larry Krute, who accompanied me in the field. I appreciate the energy he devoted to this project as well as his support of the research in general. The course turned out to be very popular and made it possible to get to know many people quickly in a pleasant and informal way.

Many Dominicans outside of Los Pinos helped me in countless ways to complete this study. Dr. Frank Moya Pons was unstinting in his support, without which this project would have been a much more difficult undertaking. Affiliation with the Fondo para el Avance de las Ciencias Sociales provided many research advantages and I am grateful to Frank and to Jeanette Canals for always making me feel welcome there. I am also very grateful to Dr. Javier and Belgica Peña for their advice and hospitality during my visits to Santiago, to Dr. Rafael Yunén for encouragement and making it possible for me to use the facilities of the Universidad Católica Madre y Maestra, and to Drs. Julio Cross Beras and Amiro Pérez Mera for edifying discussions, suggestions, and orientation. Diane Rocheleau, Victor Montero and Melvyn Martin helped me enormously in making sense of aerial photographs of the region. I wish to thank them and also to express my gratitude to Blas Santos and to the National Cartographic Institute for making these photographs available to me. I owe a special debt of gratitude to Lic. Mercedes Morales de Liz, former Director of the Data Bank of the National Statistics Office (ONE), who allowed me fullest use of the Data Bank for weeks at a time and offered me the run of her house in Santo Domingo.

This study has benefited in every stage from the sound advice, support, and friendship of Lambros Comitas, who taught me much about the Caribbean and about fieldwork. I am profoundly indebted to him for his unwavering encouragement and for the perceptive direction he gave me at various stages of this project. I also received valuable suggestions from Conrad Arensberg, Charles Harrington, and Libbet Crandon. In putting the local context of Los Pinos into broader theoretical perspective, I have relied heavily on the work of Alejandro Portes. I am also appreciative of the encouragement he gave at an early stage of this study. Marty Murphy, Brian Ferguson, and Karin Tice took the time to read and comment on the manuscript. Their comments and suggestions, together with those of an anonymous reviewer, have helped me a great deal to focus the work. Along the way, I additionally have benefited from conversations with Rob Wasserstrom, Jerry Murray, Max Castro, Diane Rocheleau, and John Roy, and from the support of Bar Levy, Ernie Alleva, and Lisa Leizman. Sarah Mahler and Bob Warren provided me with statistical information on current Dominican immigration and Eric Larson was generous with information from his analyses of the 1981 Dominican National Census. All, of course, are absolved of responsibility for any misstatements or errors of fact. I also wish to thank Jane Lang for typing the several drafts of the conclusion and for her enthusiasm for the project. Louise Waller was a meticulous editor.

I owe a great and varied debt to my family. My sister Danae Georges visited me in the field and helped me computerize the village censuses and complete the statistical analysis. She also edited several versions of the manuscript. More than anything else, the tireless encouragement and support I received from her, my mother Naffe Georges, my husband Bob Etnyre, and my grandparents, to whom this book is dedicated, helped me see this project through.

The fieldwork upon which this study is based was made possible by grants from the Institute of Latin American and Iberian Studies, Columbia University; the National Institute of Mental Health (F31 MH 08167); and the Inter-American Foundation. I especially wish to thank Liz Veatch for her many kindnesses. A first version of this study was written while I was the recipient of a predoctoral fellowship from the American Association of University Women. I am very grateful to all of these institutions for their generous financial support without which this project would not have been possible.

The Making of a Transnational Community

Introduction

Over the past two decades, women and men from the Dominican Republic have formed a sizable current in the international flow of migrants to the United States. Some 300,000 to 500,000 people—between 5 and 8 percent of that country's 1981 population—have come to work and live in the United States. Especially since the mid-1960s, these Dominicans have played an important role in supplying labor to the expanding low-wage sectors of cities of the northeastern United States, most notably to New York City, where the majority settle. Their concentration in New York is such that, after Puerto Ricans, Dominicans now represent its second largest Hispanic population.

This large and highly directed movement of people is by no means an isolated phenomenon, but rather part of an increasingly integrated worldwide flow of labor and capital that has occurred since World War II. Just as capital has become increasingly transnational, invested and accumulated on a world scale, so labor has become increasingly mobile, following capital from the underdeveloped to the developed capitalist nations of the world, or to enclaves of growth within the underdeveloped nations.

To be sure, immigrant labor has been of significance to the economic development of the United States at several points in its history. Unlike preceding waves, however, the geographic origins of this latest influx reflect a major shift in flow from east to west in the first half of this century to south to north in recent decades, a shift promoted in part by the passage of the Immigration Act of 1965. The 7.5 million legal immigrants admitted to the United States between 1960 and 1979 are predominantly from Asia, Latin America, and the Caribbean (Houstoun, Kramer, and Barrett 1984:922). Possibly another 3.0 to 3.5 million undocumented immigrants also resided in the

1

United States by 1980 (Warren 1988). Nor is the United States the only industrially advanced nation to receive large numbers of immigrants. Labor migration has involved millions of people in every part of the world. Beginning in the 1950s, some 20 to 30 million people migrated from the Mediterranean basin to northwestern Europe as temporary "guest" workers (Castles 1984:1, Rogers 1985:3). After the 1973 rise in oil prices, immigration to OPEC countries also increased dramatically. By 1975, some 3 million immigrants were found in the Gulf states and Libya, and after that this number may have doubled (Abu-Lughod 1982:450).

This heavy traffic in people has had significant implications for both the areas of migrants' destination and the regions from which they migrate. In the United States, the new immigration has dramatically increased cultural diversity within a relatively short period of time. It has led to the formation of new ethnic and multiethnic communities in many cities and to the emergence of enclaves of economic and social mobility for some immigrant groups such as the Cubans and the Koreans. It has also exacerbated and helped reinforce the tendency toward segmentation of the United States labor market into a primary "core" of workers, largely citizens, who enjoy certain benefits that are absent in the insecure and low paid "secondary" sector in which immigrants tend to cluster. Politically as well as economically, it has thrown into sharp and invidious relief the differential status of citizen and noncitizen. And it has rekindled nativism among some sectors of the population and led to policy debates that touch on the very nature of community and polity in the United States.

This book is specifically concerned with the less well-studied sending side of the migration continuum and offers a close-range view from the migrants' communities of origin. It is an anthropological study of how United States-bound migration from a village in the Dominican Republic, Los Pinos, and from its surrounding countryside, has been initiated, organized, and articulated with larger social and economic processes through time. It is also an ethnographic account of the various consequences of international migration for those who remain in Los Pinos. Specifically, the following central questions have informed this study: What are the essential characteristics of documented and undocumented migrants to the United States, and why do they migrate? What are the consequences of intensive migration for the local society in general and its economic development in particular? Has international migration significantly enhanced social mobility and altered local social structure? Have gender relations and the status of women changed as a consequence of migration? Finally, what has been the ideological and cultural impact of migration on those still in the community? The specific questions guiding the research derive from the prinicpal issues currently debated in the growing body of theoretical and empirical literature on the causes and consequences of international labor migration.

THE THEORETICAL FRAMEWORK

The study of migration has been approached from two major theoretical perspectives, the *equilibrium* and the *structural-historical* approaches. Although neither is monolithic, it is possible to discern a broad set of features common to each. Generally speaking, equilibrium models focus on individual migrants, their characteristics, and the decisions they make in response to "push" and "pull" factors emanating from the sending and receiving societies. In rural areas, population growth, dwindling and deteriorating land resources, low wages, and high unemployment help push potential migrants out of their home communities. At the same time, comparatively higher wages in the advanced industrial countries exert a strong pull that attracts those who decide they will come out ahead by leaving their communities behind. While the congeries of push and pull factors marshaled to explain migrant behavior may be drawn from different levels of analysis, the ultimate locus of explanation is the cost–benefit calculus of individuals. Indeed, within this perspective, neoclassical economic theories of rational choice sound the dominant chord. The equilibrium approach to the study of migration has been thoroughly critiqued in recent years (Bach and Schraml 1982; Nikolinakos 1975; Wood 1981; 1982). Ultimately, the problem with equilibrium theories, as Portes and Bach (1984:6) summarize, is "not that they fail to identify important forces, but that they do not take into account the changing historical contexts of migration."

Adherents of the equilibrium model have often viewed international migration as providing largely positive results for sending societies (Friedlander 1965; Griffin 1976; Hume 1973; Rose 1969; Spengler and Myers 1977). The movement of population from poor to rich nations and the counterflow of migrants' remittances and savings back to their home communities have been seen as means to equilibrate the distribution of strategic resources globally, and hence to lessen inequality and promote economic growth. For the society as a whole, postulated benefits included the relief of unemployment through the export of surplus labor, the infusion of financial capital, especially in the form of foreign exchange, and the repatriation of human capital when migrants returned with new skills and attitudinal innovations, the latter typically in short supply in sending societies in the process of economic development.

In contrast to equilibrium models, structural-historical approaches explicitly address the nature of the connections between sending and receiving societies and propose more effectively integrated explanations of international labor migration. Grounded in Marxist political economy, these approaches situate the migration process in the context of a global capitalist system (Amin 1974; Cheng and Bonacich 1984; Emmanuel 1972; Petras 1980; Portes 1978). The imperialistic expansion of this system has distorted the development of underdeveloped or peripheral areas and, in the process, has dislocated people from traditional economic pursuits. Simultaneously, the demand for cheap labor to maintain capitalists' rates of profit has increased. As a result of these complementary pressures, people migrate from peripheral areas undergoing social and economic transformation to labor in the advanced industrial economies of the core. In the process, they fill a vital role for core employers: not only do they cheapen labor in the competitive secondary sector of the economy where they tend to cluster, but their presence also drives down wages in general and hampers workers' solidarity and organization (Castells 1975; Castles and Kosack 1973).

The structural-historical analysis of the consequences of international migration for sending regions leads to pessimistic conclusions (Castles and Kosack 1973; Rhoades 1978, 1979; Sassen-Koob 1978; Weist 1979). Specifically, because migration siphons off the most productive members of the community, it leaves important gaps in the labor force; it converts erstwhile producers in the sending society into consumers, thereby reducing the supply of food and agricultural exports; and it produces inflation, both via increased demand for imports and decreased domestic output of food. Migration also can lead to ideological dependency and lack of interest in local economic development efforts even when opportunities present themselves (Reichert 1981).

A central question for those who adopt a structural-historical approach is the specific nature of the mechanisms that operate to cheapen labor in the periphery and create the value appropriated by core capitalists through the migration process (e.g., Amin 1974; Burawoy 1976; Castles and Kosack 1973; de Janvry 1981; Meillassoux 1972, 1981; Portes and Walton 1981; Rey 1973; Wallerstein 1979; Wolpe 1972). One approach that has been especially influential for anthropologists attempting to address this question is that of Claude Meillassoux (1972, 1981). Meillassoux's relevance lies in the theoretical significance he gives to the domestic community, the traditional unit of anthropological study, while situating it within the larger context of imperialism (Kearney 1986:342ff.; Marx 1986:17). We may take Meillassoux's work as a useful point of departure to examine the role of the sending community in lowering the labor costs for core capitalists.

Briefly, Meillassoux posits an international division of labor wherein the rural areas of peripheral regions specialize as exporters of labor to the core, that is, the industrially advanced countries. Within this global system, one of their functions is inexpensively to produce, or more accurately, reproduce, labor. According to Meillassoux (1981:97), "it is by preserving the domestic sector which is producing subsistence goods [within these labor-exporting communities], that imperialism realises and, further, perpetuates primitive accumulation." That is, by relegating the reproduction of labor to those areas of the world considered to be essentially precapitalist—where market relations are not dominant and unpaid household labor fulfills most subsistence requirements—the average cost of rearing a worker is reduced. A hidden transfer of value takes place when workers leave the periphery, which has born the costs of raising them, and then migrate to the core. Furthermore, after their peak productive energies are spent, migrants are repatriated to the periphery, which must then assume the costs of supporting this aged population. In short, migrant communities are seen as the nurseries and nursing homes for cheap labor. In a similar vein, Burawoy (1976) has argued that with migration, the function of labor renewal (reproduction) becomes physically and institutionally separated from the process of labor maintenance. The former is relegated to peripheral sending regions where the cost of living is lower, while the latter is now conveniently located near sources of employment. The result is lower wages for core employers.

At the theoretical level, the structural-historical perspective has been criticized for its "lurking functionalism" and high degree of abstraction (Rapp 1983; see also Bach and Schraml 1982; de Janvry 1981; Portes and Walton 1981; Shanin 1978). As it is often presented, the international division of labor between labor-importing and labor-exporting regions is too neat, too static. Shanin (1978:283), for instance, has observed that the model of capitalism underpinning this approach tends to "over-rationalization or 'hyper-intentionality.' " Complementing and reinforcing the rational calculations of core capitalists is the assumption of a "passive periphery." The resulting functional fit between labor-importing core and labor-exporting periphery tends to overstate the stability of the system (cf. Nash 1981:398–99). Neither can such a model adequately accommodate the unanticipated results of migration, such as the spontaneous migration of dependents to live with their families (Castles 1984:14), or the emergence of ethnic enclaves and the proliferation of immigrant-owned enterprises that provide an alternative route of economic and social integration for some groups of new immigrants to the United States (Portes and Bach 1984; Waldinger 1985). Thus, where the equilibrium perspective rests heavily on the voluntarism of individuals to explain migration and ignores the pattern of constraints imposed by the larger context, the structural-historical approach commits the opposite error: migrants are subsumed into the broad analytic category "labor," scanting in the process the "rich consciousness which people bring to their relations of production and reproduction" (Rapp 1977:322). For peripheral regions in general, but particularly for their rural areas, a fine-grained analysis of the process of social differentiation through time, particularly of local-level class formation, is often lacking. Often absent too is an on-the-ground examination of intermediate processes—of the "organized flow" of rural society in which actors are linked to each other over time and across space through their activities and their networks (Vincent 1977).

In addition to these theoretical objections, empirical exceptions to the structural-historical perspective recently have begun to accumulate. While recognizing the general validity of the model, Portes and Walton (1981:12), for example, note that the precapitalist sector, which is charged with shouldering a portion of the costs of reproducing and maintaining cheap labor for core employers, is identified almost exclusively with subsistence agriculture in rural areas. They point out (p. 15, 73–75) that in much of the periphery, this segment of the population is rapidly diminishing. For Latin America, de Janvry (1981) has provided a powerful analysis of the decline of the rural sector, the origins of which he situates in the contradictions of peripheral capitalist development. Specifically, rural poverty and stagnant food production result from peripheral capitalists' need to keep food prices down in order to ensure the low cost of wage labor. Cheap labor, in turn, is essential to the production of exports that are competitive on the world market. Rural poverty is also a result of capitalist penetration of the countryside, which has accelerated the process of semiproletarianization which began as a response to demographic pressure on a restricted and deteriorating land base. Semiproletarianization—a worker's simultaneous dependence on non-waged production in the subsistence sector on the one hand and on temporary wage labor within the capitalist industrial or agro-industrial sector on the other—is an inherently unstable condition. For both ecological and economic reasons, the subsistence base of the semi-proletariat eventually will be destroyed, thereby ensuring the persistence of a labor surplus and outmigration.

The Dominican Republic is no exception to the general trend toward rural disintegration. Between 1965 and 1984, rural population decreased from 65 percent to 45 percent of the total population (World Bank 1986:240). During the 1970s, when U.S.-bound migration climbed steadily, production of all food staples, with the exception of rice, remained stagnant or decreased (Encarnación 1982:27). A comparison of 1970 and 1981 Dominican national census data reveals the extent of decline in agricultural employment. In 1981, approximately 24 percent of the labor force, or 428,045 people, was employed in the agricultural sector, compared to about 46 percent, or 551,617 people, in 1970 (Larson 1987a:75). Underscoring the extent of this decline is the fact that nearly three-quarters of Dominican smallholding agriculturalists also must rely on wage labor and crafts to supplement their income from farming (Duarte 1980:180). Clearly, it appears that in the Dominican case, as well as for many other areas in Latin America, the agricultural sector is increasingly incapable of filling its theoretical mandate to reproduce migrant labor inexpensively and to support these workers once their productive energies are spent (see also Deere and Wasserstrom 1980; Deere and de Janvry 1981).

Other empirical limitations beset the global applicability of Meillassoux's model and the structural-historical perspective. Specifically, many of the proposed benefits to core employers rest on the assumed temporary nature of migration. Rotation of migrants between their core communities and their communities of origin is essential to the continued functioning of the domestic community. This is because, in the face of disintegrating pressures, the domestic economy can persist only if migrants continue to contribute to basic subsistence activities. Migration may take other forms, however, with distinct consequences. Over two decades ago, Gonzalez (1961) recognized that different types of migration—seasonal, temporary, recurrent, continuous, and permanent—would have differing implications for the family organization of rural communities. Since then, Amin (1974), Graves and Graves (1974), Watson (1975), and others also have underscored the importance of duration of migratory absences as a variable conditioning the consequences of migration for sending regions. Further, as migratory streams mature, temporal patterns may shift: in Western Eurpoe before 1975, the great majority of guestworkers were solitary males who intended to return to their communities of origin. Since that date, European migration has entered a phase of family immigration, as the "expectation that superfluous labour units would quietly pack up and go away has proved fallacious" (Castles 1984:4).

Meillassoux's model is restricted also in that the temporary migration it describes is the temporary migration of men. For what underwrites the international division of labor for Meillassoux, as for Burawoy and others, is a division of labor by gender. That is, the model assumes that women generally remain in the domestic or precapitalist sector as nonwaged reproducers of workers, while men migrate to core countries to sell their labor. In effect, then, women's nonwaged "housework" activities in the periphery help subsidize the reproduction of cheap immigrant labor and produce the value appropriated by capitalists in the core. Apposite to the specific context of Africa, where Meillassoux conducted his fieldwork, as well as to the Middle East and pre-1975 Europe, this model is most helpful in the analysis of temporary male labor migration.

But, as is increasingly recognized, "birds of passage are also women" (Morokvasic 1984). Indeed, the massive new immigration to the United States—by far the largest single international flow—has been dominated by women (Houstoun, Kramer, and Barrett 1984:908–909). Spurred by the strong demand for women workers in the competitive secondary sector of the United States economy and changes in immigration law favoring family reunification, the migration of women and their children has outstripped that of men over the last several decades. Indeed, between 1960 and 1979, approximately 54 percent of all documented migrants to the United States were women, and women and children together represented 67 percent of the total flow (p. 922). Obviously when a woman leaves the home community and takes a job in the United States, her nonwaged productive services are no longer available to her household. When she leaves dependents behind, these unpaid services may become commodified to a greater or lesser extent depending upon the specific demographics of each household. The cost of child rearing to the household would then be increased. In addition, when women bear and/or rear children in their new migrant communities, it is the core, not the domestic community, that must bear the social costs of reproduction (for example, education). Thus, when women migrate in substantial numbers, the functional division of labor between sending and receiving societies, although applicable initially, would be modified over time.

In the Western Hemisphere, the most important exception to this general pattern of the new immigration has been Mexico. With the longest land border shared by a peripheral nation and a core nation, Mexico is undoubtedly the most thoroughly studied sending country in the world and represents a popular prototype of the new immigration to the United States. In a recent introduction to the subject, Jones (1984:1) counted more than one hundred articles and twenty monographs dealing with United States-bound migration from Mexico, a fact no doubt related to the demographic and geopolitical importance of this migrant stream. Migrants from Mexico are predominantly men. Historically, they have traveled to the United States to fill the demand for temporary unskilled agricultural labor in the Southwest, California, and elsewhere and have returned to their home communities after the harvest season. In recent years, this pattern has begun to change. The migration of women has increased, and many migrants settle in urban areas and work in manufacturing and services for extended periods of time. Nonetheless, the general contours of the Mexican migrant stream readily conform to Meillassoux's model (Cornelius 1976; Mines 1984; Reichert and Massey 1979; Weist 1973, inter alia). Very likely, the well-documented example of Mexican labor migration has helped affirm the general applicability of the model to North American students of migration. It may also have helped obscure the basic demographic significance of women's migration to the United States.

Dominican immigrants to the United States, as we shall see in greater detail in the following chapter, differ from Mexicans and resemble more closely other new immigrants from Latin America, the Caribbean, and Asia. The majority are women (Gurak and Kritz 1982:16; Pérez 1981:19; de los Santos et al. 1981). Most work year-round at low and semiskilled manufacturing and service jobs in New York City and other large cities of the Northeast (Grasmuck 1984a; Pérez 1981:20; Gurak and Kritz 1982:18), and they may spend relatively long periods of time away from their home communities (Kritz and Gurak 1983:Table 1). If Dominican women migrate in numbers equal to or greater than men, and if both are absent from their home communities for many years, then the consequences both for their receiving areas and their home communities should differ from those predicted by the Meillassoux model.

In this book, I argue that although the structural-historical perspective provides a valuable framework for identifying the political and economic forces that condition migration at the macro level, the concrete process of migration becomes intelligible only when adequate attention is paid as well to intermediate processes operating on the ground: the organization of households, the composition of networks, and the local formation of classes and class segments. In this study, migration from Los Pinos is continually assessed in the context of Dominican state policies and the broader constraints of the world system in which the republic is enmeshed. Thus, although the community is my locus of study, it is not the sole unit of analysis.

A focus on the community, however, makes possible an understanding of the nature and texture of the social relationships that link the community to the world system and of people's cultural responses to that system. From this perspective, "communities are . . . spatial precipitates of yet larger social relations, termini of worldwide economic, social, political and cultural patterns within which localities are embedded. They simultaneously exhibit patterns which are regionally rooted and also reflect the larger world" (Ross and Rapp 1981:58–59). Through the movement of people over time, the networks that link them across space, and the flow of capital in the form of remittances and savings, migrant communities like Los Pinos are bound in a concrete and complex fashion to core regions like the United States.

THE RESEARCH SETTING: LOS PINOS

The fieldwork for this study was carried out in the rugged northwestern spur of the Central Mountains of the Dominican Republic, a region known as La Sierra (see map). The focus of the study was the village of Los Pinos and its surrounding countryside. Visits to several migrant communities indicated that Los Pinos was broadly typical of many other Sierran villages with intensive international migration. Among the features that it shared with other villages are rapid population growth, changes in land use patterns, the decline of local employment opportunities, and a history of unequal exchange with urban centers of the republic.

At the same time that Pineros were migrating in large numbers to the United States, the Dominican Republic and Los Pinos along with it were experiencing the multiple effects of rapid and intensive modernization. To assess the impact of migration on a community, however, it is essential that the changes observed be associated directly with the migration process (FAO 1984:197). Because other processes also resulted in transformations, comparison of Los Pinos with a nonmigrant community was one way of teasing apart changes related to United States migration from those that were unrelated. During the

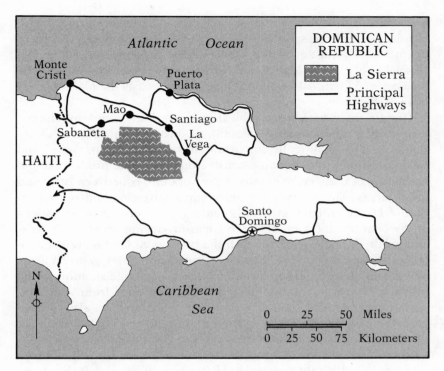

MAP: La Sierra Region, Dominican Republic

sixteen months I spent in the field in 1980 and 1981, I lived in Los Pinos, but I often visited the surrounding countryside to gather such comparative information and to learn more about the nature of the relationships among villages. As a result of this reconnaissance, I selected one village with a low level of United States-bound migration, El Guano, for more intensive comparative study. El Guano's population of 170 people relies heavily on agriculture and handicraft production for its livelihood. Only 3 of its 30 households had a migrant member residing in the U.S. at the time of fieldwork. Thus, although the main focus of the study was the international migrant community of Los Pinos, comparative information drawn from El Guano and other communities helped elucidate the causes and consequences of international migration.

The region of La Sierra in which Los Pinos is located falls within the north central province of Santiago. For nearly a century, this province has been a major source of internal migrants to other parts of the republic. Since the 1960s, it has been the site of intensive migration to the United States as well (Castro 1985; Gonzalez 1970; Hendricks 1974; Pessar 1982a). The province encompasses two very distinct ecological zones: the Cibao Valley, the long and fertile watershed between the Central and Northern Mountain Ranges, and the pine-covered Central Mountain Range, which boasts the highest peaks in the Caribbean.

Despite their stark geographical contrast, both zones are characterized by a predominantly peasant, or own-account, pattern of agriculture. The historically important trinity of tobacco, coffee, and cacao continues to dominate as cash crops. Early on, production and marketing of these crops created a network of ties between rural and urban areas. The processes of agro-industrialization and concentration of landholdings that in this century transformed other regions of the country, most notably the sugar-producing areas of the east and south, did not greatly disturb the traditional land tenure system of Santiago province. It is likely that long-standing ties to urban areas and the autonomy and somewhat enhanced economic standing of the province's rural population provided a springboard from which international migration could be launched. Such appears also to have been the case among European immigrants to the United States at the turn of the century: those areas of Italy, Transylvania, and Slovakia with the highest rates of emigration were also those in which property was least highly concentrated (Barton 1975). Similarly, it appears that in Mexico, too, communities and regions most heavily involved in United States migration tended to be "neither the poorest nor the most marginal" but rather, those "areas of traditional agriculture which have the stronger or more long-standing ties with the urban network" (Rivière d'Arc 1980:189).

With a population of about one thousand in 1981, Los Pinos was the seat of its *sección*, the smallest administrative and political unit in the republic. The sección of Los Pinos had a total area of 100 square km and encompassed some twenty villages. As administrative and political center of its sección, Los Pinos housed the post office, police station, jail, clinic, and high school that served the surrounding countryside. Secciones in turn are grouped into *municipios*, roughly equivalent to counties in the United States. Los Pinos was one of over forty secciones that fell under the jurisdiction of a municipio seat, La Sede. To the west of Los Pinos lay the provincial capital of Santiago de los Caballeros. With its population of 250,000, it was the premiere city of the north, and the second largest of the republic. Los Pinos was connected to La Sede and Santiago by a spottily paved but nonetheless heavily trafficked road constructed during the regime of Rafael Trujillo (1930–1961) and repaired from time to time with loose gravel. Under these conditions, the winding drive to Santiago took two or more dusty and dangerous hours. Accidents were common.

At an altitude of 580 meters, Los Pinos rests in the narrow river valley formed by the Los Pinos River, really a stream that might disappear altogether during a dry spell. Wending its way through the eastern part of the village, this river was the village's washbasin and principal source of water for domestic purposes. Its water was never drunk. Because Los Pinos had no pipe-borne water, potable water had to be hauled from the nearest clear water river, 5 km to the east of the village. Los Pinos had electricity since 1977.

Los Pinos' cool and dry climate made it a comparatively healthy community by national standards. Malaria and schistosomiasis, serious health problems in the western and eastern regions of the republic, were virtually absent in the Sierra. Among children, the most common diseases were diarrhea and parasitosis. Nutritional status varied according to the economic level of the household, but in general, severe malnutrition was uncommon. A survey of 446 children under five years of age conducted in several Sierran villages in 1980 found the "incidence of moderate and severe malnutrition to be less than expected" (Smith 1981:11); only 12.3 percent of Sierran children surveyed were moderately to severely malnourished, as compared to 21 percent to 31 percent nationally (p. 1).

The precise boundaries of Los Pinos were difficult to draw, and notions of where the village ended and neighboring villages began varied from person to person and depended on the circumstances. However, all Pineros recognized a division of their village into two major sections, with several named subsections. One was the village itself, a line settlement strung along either side of the road that connected it with La Sede and Santiago. Brightly painted houses, shops, and bars were densely packed together on the main road and its two spurs, one leading to the pine forest known as La Loma to the north, the other penetrating the vast hardwood forests to the south. At the east end, and entrance, of the village were found the cockfight pit, the site of Sunday matches that drew crowds of men from throughout the sección; the concrete six-bed rural clinic completed by the government of Antonio Guzmán in 1980; the modern, airy social club of Los Pinos to the construction of which migrants contributed substantially; and the large concrete church, also built with the help of migrants. Situated at the west end was Los Pinos' primary and secondary school complex, completed in 1974. Since most villages offered only three to five grades, Los Pinos' school attracted many children from throughout the sección.

All buildings, except for two new migrants' houses, were of a single story. Houses varied in size and building materials according to wealth and occupation. The most prosperous shopkeepers and some school teachers had large concrete houses with mosaic floors and flat concrete or pitched corrugated zinc roofs. The rest of the houses were made of pine boards, with floors of wood, cement, or dirt and roofs of zinc sheets or palm thatch. Houses of pine boards displayed varying degrees of finish which also varied with wealth. They might be constructed of the rough outer layer of the trunk (*costanera*) or of smoothly planed planks, often painted blue, pink, yellow, or green. Migrants' families lived in houses of all types, but in general, those who had been in the United States for many years had built large and modern houses, well-stocked with a variety of amenities.

The other half of Los Pinos, informally known as Los Pinos Abajo, lay directly to the south of the village's center. Characterized by a dispersed settlement pattern, Los Pinos Abajo was the site of most of the community's agricultural land. Cultivated fields were few, however. Indeed, viewed from a distance, the rolling hills of Los Pinos Abajo looked like vast, closely tended lawns, an impression created by the overgrazing of grass by cattle. Only an occasional agricultural plot provided a rough patch on the smooth surface of the landscape. Farming households resided on their landholdings, their houses typically situated along the ridge lines of foothills. The houses were connected to each other by a maze of dirt paths traversed by people, burros, mules, and motorcycles. Because land was divided equally among all heirs, neighbors tended to be siblings and the offspring of siblings. Such geographic clusters of kin daily engaged in a variety of exchanges: food, labor, child care, school texts, information, and gossip, among many others.

Although a sizable proportion of Los Pinos' population still practiced agriculture, few Pineros were full-time agriculturalists. There were several factors that limited the cultivation of crops. Soil quality was perhaps one of the most significant. Like the Sierran region as a whole, Los Pinos was characterized by stony soils of low fertility, recommended use for which, according to the United States Department of Agriculture system of classification, was other than agriculture (Antonini, Ewel and Tupper 1975:17). Developed on metavolcanic parent material, Los Pinos' soils were shallow, friable, sandy loams of poor quality. Seasonally heavy rains coursing down Los

Pinos' steep and largely deforested slopes had resulted in severe erosion. The friable, fragile structure of this thin soil, which lost its integrity with repeated plowings, exacerbated Los Pinos' serious erosion problem.

A second limiting factor was water. Because irrigation was lacking, agriculture in Los Pinos was entirely dependent on rainfall. *Conucos*, fields in which short-cycle crops were cultivated, were cleared of brush, fired, and planted to coincide with the rains. Rainfall followed a bimodal pattern, dividing the yearly calendar into two seasons, *invierno* (winter) and *verano* (summer). As its annual average temperature of around 30°C did not fluctuate dramatically, the seasons in Los Pinos were distinguished primarily by the amount of rain that fell. Although verano was the rainy season, heavy precipitation generally occured only in May. During invierno, which lasted from late November to April, rainfall was scarce. Crops were planted in May and again in October and November when a steady cool drizzle, known as *El Norte*, fell almost continuously. Although rainfall exhibited a bimodal pattern over the long term, large variation in rainfall might be experienced from year to year. Rain did not reliably fall during the critical planting months of May and October, and droughts were not uncommon.

About a dozen principal crops were regularly cultivated in Los Pinos. Major cash crops included peanuts, beans, tobacco, and cowpeas. Sweet potatos and sweeet manioc were the most important subsistence crops, and corn was grown for human and animal consumption. Significant tree crops grown for domestic use included plaintain, banana, oranges, lemons, and coffee. Of these, coffee was by far the most important, and the backyard plantation supplied all or part of the household's annual needs.

Because of Los Pinos' low altitude[1] coffee was not a commercial crop in the village, although an occasional hundred-pound bag might be sold to a local shopkeeper. Short-cycle commercial crops such as peanuts were frequently intercalated with crops that have longer growing seasons, such as sweet manioc and plaintain. Conucos were typically lined with cowpea shrubs. This inventory was a greatly reduced sample of the crops grown in the past in Los Pinos; completely gone were the varieties of peas, onions, tomatoes, garlic, sesame, and leafy vegetables once common.

Although risk was a pervasive feature of Pinero agriculture, re-

---

1. Commercially important coffee zones were all found at altitudes of 800 m or greater (SEA 1978).

turns were low even in good years. Agricultural productivity in the Sierra as a whole was 21.4 percent lower than the national average (Secretaria de Agricultura 1978). When Los Pinos was compared with the most fertile regions of the republic, such as the Cibao heartland, its low productivity was even more pronounced. Agronomists with experience in both areas told me that average yields for selected crops were two to three times greater in the Cibao Valley than in Los Pinos.

The technology of crop production remained virtually unchanged from the community's earliest days. Inexpensive loan capital for agricultural production and technological improvements in Los Pinos was scarce. Until the recent establishment of a regional development project nearby, extension services were virtually nonexistent. With all virgin and even secondary forest long destroyed, fields were fallowed for progressively shorter periods. New plots were cleared from scrub and bush using ax, machete, and fire. Fields were plowed by one of three professional plowers (*bueyeros*) in the village who owned steel plows and teams of oxen. Agriculture remained completely unmechanized. Chemical fertilizers were used by only 2 percent of households. Organic methods were virtually absent. Fertility of fields was maintained solely through fallowing, a method that had become increasingly inadequate in recent years. Ideally, conucos cleared on hill slopes were cultivated for one year and left to fallow five to eight years; plains were cultivated for one or two years and might be fallowed in pasture for two to five years before being plowed once again. In practice, however, brief grass fallows of only six months to a year had become widespread. After a few seasons of such intensive use, overworked plots had to be abandoned for several years in the hope that they would eventually regain sufficient fertility to be cultivated once again.

Livestock production evaded some of the more severe constraints limiting agriculture in Los Pinos. Pigs, goats, and chickens could be valuable supplementary sources of food and cash, and nearly all households raised one or the other of these small animals.[2] Cattle, however, were economically far and away the most important livestock raised. Their importance was evident from the fact that in 1981, eight times more land in Los Pinos was devoted to pasture than to short-cycle and tree crops combined. Cattle-raising techniques were considerably more advanced than those used in agriculture. Improved breeds with high meat yields, such as Zebu, had been intro-

2. Just before I arrived in Los Pinos, the Ministry of Agriculture had waged an all-out battle against African porcine disease in the republic. All pigs in Los Pinos, as elsewhere, had been destroyed by the time I arrived.

center or in Los Pinos Abajo, were linked to each other by ties of kinship, both real and fictive, as well as by the bonds of friendship and neighborliness. Just four surnames, those of the earliest settlers, accounted for some three-quarters of the village's households and attested to a high level of village endogamy. At dinnertime, children, especially adolescent males, could be found at the table of any of several relatives scattered throughout the village.

Households were the elementary units of social and economic cooperation in Los Pinos. Migration had a strong effect on household organization and was directly responsible for the great diversity in household composition observable in the community. The cultural ideal was the stable nuclear family, but only a minority of households were composed of both spouses and their offspring. Ideally, families were patrifocal, with husbands and fathers the principal decision makers and breadwinners. Here, too, practice departed from the ideal: nearly one-third of all households were headed by women. By necessity, many women responsible for the maintenance of their households could not conform to cultural expectations that restricted women to domestic activities and to the hearth. A few of the older men of some economic means maintained two or more households at the same time. This practice appeared to have been more common in the past, when abundant land made it easier for a man to provide for more than one family.

Above the level of the household, the basis of kinship was the personal kindred. This personal kindred was ego-centered and bilateral in nature: that is, it was composed of persons who were related to a specific individual both on the mother's and father's sides. Personal kindreds also included fictive or ritual kin (godparents, godchildren) and affines. Ties with the latter often were maintained even after the separation of spouses. These personal kindreds, as Whitten (1965) has noted for Ecuador, "are only apparent when functioning" (p. 140). In Los Pinos, the contours and composition of these kindreds became visible in the process of organizing a migration, mobilizing economic activities, performing life-cycle rituals, and on other occasions.

Pinero personal kindreds were not confined to the community but extended beyond local, and often beyond national, boundaries. A common strategy for some families was to send "branches" to the cities of the republic or the United States to secure contacts with diverse sectors of the national and world economy. This resulted in what has been called the "stem kindred": a form of social organization that functions corporately to unite and consolidate the interests of the kindred in the pursuit of survival or socioeconomic mobility (Walker

1972:103; see also Arizpe 1982:21; Garrison and Weiss 1979; Whitten 1965:139).

Personal kindreds in turn formed part of larger networks of social ties founded on friendship, neighborliness, and patronage. Friendship might reinforce and activate ties between kin, but it might also create new bonds between nonkin. The strength of the friendship ties was expressed in terms of the degree of *confianza*, "a Latin American native category that denotes mutual readiness to engage in reciprocal exchange" (Lomnitz 1977:4). Friendships marked by confianza tended to occur between social equals of the same sex and age grade and were characterized by an ongoing exchange of a variety of favors, information, goods, and services. Physical propinquity tended to foster such exchanges, which were culturally reinforced by ideals of neighborly behavior. Patron–client relations also were marked by ongoing exchanges, but the actors here were separated by a degree of social distance and such exchanges were generally unequal.

Life in Los Pinos had a daily rhythm, broken only during the patron saint's fiesta in April, at Christmastime, and on a few other important holidays. In the early morning, shortly after dawn, farmers walked or rode their mules to their fields. The jitneys, *públicos*, which daily made the four-hour trip to the capital city of Santo Domingo went from house to house to pick up their passengers. Pineros were already queuing in front of the butcher shop to buy from the limited supply of beef for their noonday meal; others were buying rice, beans, cooking oil, and other staples in one of the village's sixteen *pulperías*, or grocery stores. People from the other villages in the sección arrived on foot or on mule or horse to shop and pick up their mail. Later in the morning, other públicos began to ply the route between Los Pinos and La Sede and Santiago. Each day, several Pineros and others from the surrounding communities traveled into La Sede, the municipio seat, to obtain copies of their birth or marriage certificates and to have inaccurate certificates corrected, or into Santiago to have these documents certified in the courthouse. Securing these documents and seeing that they were in good order might take several trips, but they were essential first steps in the United States resident visa application process and had to be made by everyone attempting legal entry into the United States. Such traffic was one of the mainstays of the local público drivers.

By noon, the village was quiet and appeared deserted, as Pineros ate their noonday, and largest, meal of rice, beans, and for some, meat; some took a siesta afterward. Around three or four o'clock in the afternoon, the pace of activity quickened once again. Many people returned to the center of the village to make the purchases for the simple evening meal—chocolate or coffee, eggs, bread, and plaintains or manioc. Those who had gone to town in the early morning began to return, often laden with purchases from the large stores of the capital and Santiaigo. Farmers returned from their fields and headed to the Los Pinos River to bathe. After the evening meal, many families watched Mexican or Argentinian soap operas on the single television station received in the village; many without television sets viewed these serials in the house of a neighbor who did own one. Young men strolled up and down the street and ultimately congregated at the main intersection, where they told jokes with the village nightwatchman until midnight. Other men, often including male migrants vacationing in the village, gathered in one of the three bars, where drinking and socializing might continue until three or four in the morning, accompanied by the loud music of the jukeboxes.

METHODS

Anthropological fieldwork in a village entangled in a meshwork of extralegal activities that often cut across households and kindreds had to be approached with patience. It was natural that someone asking specific and personal questions about migration to the United States would be regarded with suspicion. Further, international migration was not the only activity important to Pineros' livelihood that sometimes pulled them beyond the pale of the law. Given these circumstances, the frank friendliness I often encountered never failed to astonish me. Besides the villagers' own remarkable forbearance, several factors helped me to be able to undertake a study of this nature. Offering a service requested by Pineros themselves such as the English course taught in the evenings was certainly crucial. The course was attended by adults as well as by older children and spilled over into informal socializing, tutoring sessions, and the like. Since most Pineros viewed knowledge of English as a way to help them to cope better with their future life in New York, or as a means to a more desirable job in the republic, the course was generally regarded as a valuable contribution to the community. Also of importance, I feel, was the fact that I took my time in trying to unravel the manifold tangles of villager's migration stories, longer, indeed, than I had originally intended. As I established friendships over the course of the fieldwork, I was often called on to help people with the paperwork for their visa petitions. I accompanied some to the United States

Consulate in Santo Domingo, wrote letters of support for others I had gotten to know well, and tried to interpret consular correspondence when meanings were unclear. Such activities allowed me to demonstrate my good will toward people's migration projects and, of no less importance, to reciprocate in some measure the good will that was so often shown to me. I was also very fortunate that no one was deported from the United States while I was in the field (nor, for that matter, for several years after I completed the study). Well into my stay, I learned that this fact was often adduced by my supporters as evidence that I was not a spy for the Immigration and Naturalization Service.

I used a variety of methods during the course of fieldwork. Observation of and participation in community activities took place continually. Unstructured interviews with Pineros were conducted in their homes and fields and in grocery stores, shops, and bars. I spent many hours talking in the kitchens of Pinera women, while shelling, roasting, and drinking coffee. Interviews also were conducted with United States migrants who returned to vacation in Los Pinos; with internal and "permanently" returned United States migrants living in Santo Domingo and Santiago; and with key individuals in those two cities whose activities affected the lives of Pineros (United States consular officials, bankers, industrialists, administrators, and others). Oral histories were obtained from many older Pineros, both individually and in group sessions in which three or four people gathered for free-wheeling discussions of the specific topics I introduced. Published and unpublished materials written on the Dominican Republic, including archival materials, also were consulted. Information garnered during visits to many other migrant communities during the course of my fieldwork, including a month spent in the eastern Sierra, helped me to place Los Pinos in the context of the region.

To complement the qualitative data obtained from observation and interviews, I censused both Los Pinos and El Guano. The census, which I conducted with the help of assistants after a year's residence in the field, was designed to generate quantitative information on differentiation among households in terms of their composition, migratory experience, access to strategic resources, income, and other variables. Information on income was supplemented by the collection of detailed budgets from six households over the course of a year, as well as by intensive budgetary interviews with many other households.

Obviously however, a census could not include households that had migrated from the community in their entirety. Nor could it be trusted to provide accurate information on such sensitive subjects as legal status of migrants. To gain a more complete understanding of the demographic, social, and economic characteristics of migrants, both documented and undocumented, I compiled a roster of all Pineros who had ever migrated to the United States. Through interviews with kin, friends, and neighbors, a few key characteristics of migrants were ascertained. Elaboration and cross-checking of the roster took place over most of the course of fieldwork. International migrants were identified through family geneologies and through inspection of aerial photographs to locate "disappeared" households. Aerial photographs of Los Pinos had been taken in 1958, just before large-scale migration to the United States began, and again in 1967 and 1980, only two months before I came to live in the community.

Once enlarged, these photos provided me with a detailed picture of the community at several points in time. They also aroused a keen interest in many Pineros which resulted in fruitful discussions that greatly facilitated analysis of changes in land tenure and land use over time. Photo inspection also enabled me to reconstruct the boundaries of the intact landholdings of the early twentieth century and to gain a sense of spatial relationships and the geographical clustering of kin in the village through time.

ORGANIZATION OF THE BOOK

In addition to this introduction, which outlines the principal issues addressed and introduces the community and the methods used to study it, the book comprises seven chapters. Chapter 1 looks at the general contours of Dominican migration at the national level and situates this migration within the context of national development over the last century. In chapter 2, I trace the history of Los Pinos itself, from its founding in the mid-nineteenth century to the onset of intensive United States-bound migration in 1961. Discussion of the social and economic development of the village in this chapter provides the background to an examination of the factors promoting the first wave of migration. Chapter 3 describes the migration process as it evolved over the last two decades and provides a quantitative description of the principal social, demographic, and economic characteristics of Pinero documented and undocumented migrants to the United States. It also introduces the reader to the nonmigrant community of El Guano and explores the question of why some villages become international migrant communities and others do not. Chapters 4 and 5 examine the impact of migration on the local economy and on economic development. Chapter 4 analyzes Los Pinos' economy and explores the consequences of international migration for the creation of jobs and the distribution of income. The differential impact on women and men of migration-related changes in the structure of local economic opportunities is examined. The agricultural system of Los Pinos—the effects of migration on agricultural production, land tenure, and the use and distribution of land—are discussed in chapter 5. Los Pinos is compared to El Guano in an attempt to control for significant variables and thus to ensure greater confidence in the assessment of which effects are strictly attributable to the migration process. Chapter 6 focuses on the social structural and cultural changes that have resulted from migration. The consequences of migration for the family and the issue of the social mobility of migrants' households and of return migrants are considered. In chapter 7, the research is summarized and placed in the context of what is known of the consequences of United States migration for the republic as a whole and of the patterns prevailing in other sending regions.

CHAPTER 1
Patterns of Peripheral Development and Labor Migration

The causes of contemporary international labor migration from the Dominican Republic can be traced to the beginning of the republic's incorporation into the world economy in the late nineteenth century, and more specifically to its increasing dependence on the United States over time. In the first section of this chapter, I describe the evolution of Dominican society and economy over the last century in order to situate U.S.-bound migration in its historical and political-economic context. In the second section, patterns and processes of Dominican migration are examined. The final section provides a profile of what is presently known of the general socioeconomic and labor force characteristics of Dominican migrants to the United States.

PATTERNS OF DOMINICAN DEVELOPMENT: AN OVERVIEW

For much of the nineteenth century, the Dominican Republic was a scarcely populated backwater, with relatively little movement on or off the island. Demographic stagnation reflected economic and social decline from a more prosperous colonial period left behind long ago. In 1871, the vast majority of the estimated population of 150,000 to 200,000 lived in the countryside. The virtual absence of an internal labor market and the abundance of land fostered a self-sufficiency bordering on autarky (Hoetink 1982:5–6). Social and economic differences between people appear to have been minimal. The number of large landholders was small and much of the national territory lay uncultivated. The social historian H. Hoetink (1982:6) has suggested

25

that during this period of decline Dominican life was characterized by a "democratization" which reflected the general leveling of society.

This period of stagnation and isolation ended rather abruptly during the last quarter of the nineteenth century, when Dominican society entered a period of rapid social and economic transformation. Economic growth was led by foreign investment in large-scale sugar production for the world market. Cuban sugar planters fleeing the disruptions caused by the first Cuban war of independence (1868–1878) provided the initial catalyst to growth. Bringing with them skills and capital lacking locally, these planters migrated to the nearby island of Santo Domingo in search of new investment opportunities. North American investors, Europeans, and Puerto Ricans soon followed suit. In the south and east, their investments established typically capitalist enterprises producing for a world market (Cassá 1980:160). Peasants displaced by these new enterprises supplied part of the needed labor and were joined in the canefields by immigrants from the British islands and Haiti. High world prices for sugar and resultingly high profits also led to the appearance of a new local elite. Composed partly of Dominican and partly of immigrant planters and merchants, this elite reinvested its growing sugar profits in the cultivation of other export crops, such as coffee and cacao, as well as in cattle ranching. Demand for land rose sharply as a consequence, leading to a substantial increase in land values (Gleijeses 1978:11; Hoetink 1982:10). Especially in the sugar-producing regions of the south and east, foreigners often acquired large tracts of land for sugar cultivation through false titles and coercion. This practice resulted in the emergence of an increasingly proletarianized labor force dependent on sugar cultivation and caused intense local resentment (Hoetink 1982:11).

The process of consolidation of landholdings was further expedited by the U.S. military occupation of Santo Domingo in 1916. Debts incurred by a series of Dominican presidents had brought the republic close to bankruptcy by the end of the nineteenth century. To ensure repayment and to forestall action by European creditors, President Theodore Roosevelt induced the Dominican government in 1905 to sign a decree placing Dominican customhouses and their revenues under U.S. control (Moya Pons 1980:444). Political instability in the following years and a growing desire to assert U.S. hegemony in the Caribbean resulted in full-scale U.S. military intervention in 1916 (Calder 1984:5ff.). Occupation of the Dominican Republic, which lasted until 1924, was thus the culmination of years of interference in the republic's internal affairs. It was also another step toward the expansion of U.S. influence in the Caribbean basin and indeed in the Pacific and the Far East, after the Spanish-American War of 1898 (p. xii).

One of the most significant changes promulgated by the occupation government was the Land Registration Act of 1920. This act effectively facilitated and reinforced the expansion of U.S.-owned sugar plantations (Calder 1984:240; del Castillo and Cordero 1980:57). When intense local opposition and a guerrilla war against the American presence finally succeeded in ending the occupation in 1924, sugar companies controlled nearly a quarter of all agricultural land, 80 percent of which was owned by U.S. interests (Gleijeses 1978:18). At the same time, restrictions on foreign investment were also put into effect. European, particularly German, capital previously had been of considerable significance to the republic's economy. The restrictions imposed by the occupation government, and others put into effect as a consequence of the First World War, significantly diminished the influence of European finance capital (Calder 1984:240; del Castillo and Cordero 1980:52). Simultaneously, dependence on North American capital increased.

Another creation of the occupation government, the Tariff Act of 1920, also favored U.S. exporters. This act enabled the United States to become the leading source of industrial and food imports to the republic, to the detriment of local producers. The Dominican historian Frank Moya Pons (1980:492) notes that the incipient local industries of the preceding period had been thwarted during the occupation, and he calculates that Dominican industrialization was retarded by some twenty years as a consequence. The occupation thus established the conditions for the dominance of U.S.-manufactured goods, a dominance that would increase in succeeding years.

The eight years of U.S. occupation also led to some important cultural, social, and political changes. The occupation government undertook ambitious public works projects which linked remote regions of the rugged countryside for the first time. Schools, roads, bridges, and hospitals were constructed. Unification of the country through these infrastructural improvements had the effect of neutralizing the power of the *caudillos*, that is, the local political leaders, and literally paving the way for political centralization (pp. 481ff). Instrumental in the attempt to pacify popular opposition to the United States during the occupation was the creation of the national guard. The presence of this military force also provided the means to ensure that after withdrawal of the marines, leadership of the republic would remain in the hands of those attuned to U.S. interests (Black 1986:25; Calder 1984).

In 1930, Rafael Leonidas Trujillo, having risen through the ranks of the national guard, succeeded through intrigue and intimidation in installing himself in the presidency. During the next thirty years, Trujillo pursued policies that resulted in rapid economic growth and enormous social change, touching nearly every aspect of Dominican life. His drive toward industrialization created a manufacturing sector which, using primarily indigenous raw materials, supplied the internal market and reduced exports. After demonstrating their profitability, whole industries became Trujillo monopolies. Trujillo's agricultural policies yielded manyfold increases in the production of major crops, although at the cost of unprecedented concentration of land, principally in his own hands (Cassá 1980; 1982; Crassweller 1966; Gomez 1979). Through intimidation, fraud, and frank terror, Trujillo acquired control over two-thirds of the republic's assets, including half of all agricultural land (Herman and Brodhead 1984:20).

In large part, this monumental transformation was made possible by Trujillo's total identification with, and manipulation of, the state apparatus. As the Dominican historian Roberto Cassá has noted, "the Dominican state (above all through Trujillo, Inc.) was the fundamental agent in the process of industrialization. . . . The despotic state permitted extraction of surplus from the precapitalist sector in the process of primitive accumulation fueling industrialization (1982:281; my translation). Former President Juan Bosch (1983) calculated that apart from the dictator, "Trujillo, Inc.," that is, the Dominican bourgeoisie of that period, comprised no more than some sixty to eighty close associates. The support Trujillo received from U.S. financial and political interests was also crucial to the implementation of his project (Díaz Santana and Murphy 1983:4). As Franklin D. Roosevelt is credited with having said, "Trujillo is an SOB, but he's our SOB" (Eric Williams, quoted in ibid., p. 7). Directly or indirectly, Trujillo ruled the republic from 1930 to 1961, a period that came to be known as the *Trujillato*.

During the Trujillato, emigration slowed to a trickle. Movement off the island was restricted by the policies promulgated by Trujillo. A time of rapid and often abrupt economic changes, the Trujillato witnessed an unprecedented and massive mobilization of the national labor force. Under Trujillo, the republic was transformed from an essentially agrarian economy oriented toward subsistence and the production of a few commodities to an industrializing nation firmly, if not exclusively, based on capitalist relations of production. For both economic and geopolitical reasons, Trujillo was concerned to increase the national population. The success of his pronatalist and proimmigration policies can be seen from the fact that between 1935 and 1960, the republic's population doubled from 1.5 to 3 million people (Cassá 1982:572). Trujillo's policies were motivated in part by concern over long-standing territorial disputes with Haiti, but another major goal was to gain strict control over the national labor force. Policies restricting mobility within and off the island were formulated to ensure the supply of skilled workers to the burgeoning import-substitution industries of Santo Domingo, as well as of agricultural producers on whom the cultivation of traditional export and food crops hinged. Toward the end of his dictatorship, Trujillo may have also had a political motivation for restricting population movement. The 1950s were a time of democratic reform in Latin America, a fact that threw the despotic Trujillo dictatorship into an increasingly unfavorable light. It is sometimes suggested that Trujillo continued to restrict migration off the island as late as the 1950s in an attempt to exert control over the information flowing in from such countries as Venezuela and Cuba, where authoritarian regimes were being overthrown.

By the late 1950s, too, the phenomenal, but dependent, development of Dominican industry had begun to feel the effects of worldwide recession. For despite Trujillo's drive toward industrialization, agricultural exports, most importantly of sugar, remained central to the Dominican economy. Export prices fell, the national debt grew, foreign investment ceased, and the economy stagnated (Díaz Santana and Murphy 1983:7). Internal contradictions also haunted the Trujillo regime. Trujillo's low-wage policies limited effective demand for the goods manufactured in his import-substitution industries (Cassá 1982:587 ff.), a contradiction that persists to the present. But despite increasingly high rates of underemployment and unemployment, restrictions on international population movement were preserved and emigration remained at low levels.

Increasing internal opposition in conjunction with a new U.S. disaffection led to the assassination of Trujillo in 1961. Upon his death, many of Trujillo's vast holdings passed into the hands of the state. The strong state capitalism that was Trujillo's legacy set the stage for the ensuing class struggle over control of the state apparatus. The national bourgeoisie, atrophied and weak as a consequence of the severe constraints on its expansion imposed by Trujillo, wrangled among themselves to seize control (Lozano 1985:219). These factional struggles plunged the republic into a period of political turmoil and economic instability that culminated in the second U.S. invasion and occupation in April, 1965 (Justo Duarte 1979). Overcoming a popular revolt intended to reinstate Juan Bosch to the presidency and restore the democratic constitution ratified during his brief tenure in 1963, the presence of over 40,000 U.S. marines succeeded once again in establishing the hegemony of the military and police (Herman and Brodhead 1984:33).

Elections sponsored by the United States in 1966 installed Joaquín Balaguer, a former presidential secretary to Trujillo, in the presidency. Balaguer's rule from 1966 to 1978 has been called "Trujillismo without Trujillo" and there were some important continuities between the two regimes (Black 1986:42). With the solid backing of the military forces, the Balaguer government harshly repressed political dissidence and persecuted trade unions. In 1977, Kryzanek observed that "[f]rom a purely statistical point of view the evidence of repression in the modern day Dominican Republic is shocking" (1979:98). Nonetheless, Balaguer's government benefited from very high levels of assistance from the United States. In 1966, the Dominican Republic received the highest per capita amount of aid in Latin America, second only in the world to Vietnam (Black 1986:43). The *Wall Street Journal* reported during this period that one of every four Dominicans depended on U.S. food aid (cited in NACLA 1975:11).

With the state apparatus firmly in control, the Balaguer regime pursued economic development policies designed to facilitate foreign investment in the Dominican Republic. It was in this arena that the regime broke most sharply with the past. Forging an alliance among the various factions of the industrial, commercial, and financial bourgeoisie, Balaguer reversed the protectionism of the Trujillo era (Lozano 1985:161). Laws restricting foreign ownership of land were revised. Under the Industrial Incentive Law passed in 1968, generous concessions and tax exonerations were made to foreign investors (overwhelmingly, U.S.-controlled multinational corporations) which resulted in the expansion of manufacturing, extractive industries, and a few other sectors (Gomez 1979, chapter 7; NACLA 1975). A number of exceedingly low wage, free-trade export zones were created which fell outside of the purview of legislation intended to protect labor. By the late 1970s, some 19,000 workers assembled garments, electronic equipment, and other products in these zones (Boin and Serullé 1980:22–24). Indeed, the doubling of the number of workers in manufacturing between 1968 and 1977 from 20,000 to 47,600 was in large part attributable to the creation of the new zones: some 37 percent of new jobs were located there (Bray 1987:158). As in other countries that have welcomed this route to industrialization, the great majority of the free-zone workers are women.

Balaguer also stimulated the economy and provided an important avenue of social mobility through large-scale public spending, especially in construction (Díaz Santana and Murphy 1983:21; ILO 1974). In this regard, Balaguer's policies were given a critical financial assist from massive international loans: between 1970 and 1978 the foreign debt more than tripled (World Bank 1980:183). Lavish spending benefited those members of the bourgeoisie most closely allied with Balaguer, and in turn they invested in all areas of the economy (Díaz Santana and Murphy 1983:21). A new bourgeoisie also appeared. Politics and the military were the principal routes leading from the middle class to this new group, comprised in the main of generals and high-ranking government officials who reaped the benefits of patronage and corruption (Cassá 1979:104; Díaz Santana and Murphy 1983:20).

High levels of public-sector spending also stimulated the considerable expansion of a heterogeneous middle class which ranged from petty government and private bureaucrats to well-paid managers working in finance, commerce, and administration (Lozano 1985:166). Professionals well connected with the Balaguer regime were able to secure lucrative contracts for the public works projects that proliferated during this period. Rapid expansion of universities, with many of them restructured along U.S. models, produced the young professionals and technicians who filled the growing demand for skilled labor created by the modernization process (Castro 1985:137). Indeed, the number of university graduates increased nearly 800% between 1970 and 1977 (del Castillo 1982, cited in Bray 1984:226). The rising fortune of the middle class can be seen from the fact that between 1969 and 1973, the proportion of total national income it enjoyed grew from 27.6 percent in 1969 to 30.2 percent. However, this increase was not the consequence of an improvement in the highly unequal distribution of national income. Rather, it resulted from the "trickle up" of income from the poorest 20 percent of the republic's population, whose share diminished from 2.9 percent to 1.4 percent over the same period (Lozano 1985:160).

During this period, economic growth was also greatly stimulated by the high prices received for sugar (despite the rapid changes experienced, still the republic's major export), coffee, gold, and other export commodities. With strong demand for exports, huge infusions of financial aid, and high levels of foreign investment and government spending, the "Dominican Miracle" of the first half of Joaquín Balaguer's presidency witnessed phenomenal GDP growth rates averaging over 11 percent between 1969 and 1974, among the highest in the world. However, the capital-intensive nature of most foreign investment meant a comparatively low level of job creation. In fact, the overall rate of unemployment remained virtually unchanged between 1970 and 1983 (table 1.1). In 1970 the Dominican Republic had one of the highest rates of open unemployment in Latin America (ONAPLAN 1980b). The republic's rapid growth did contribute to a decline in total unemployment in 1973, when real wages in some sectors seem to have improved. Yet in that same year, some 60 percent of Santo Domingo's labor force was estimated to be underemployed (ILO 1974:3).

In general, this burst of growth did not translate into sustained improvement in the real incomes of Dominican workers. Overall, the trend between 1968 and 1975 was one of rapidly increasing inflation coupled with stagnant wages, held in check largely through repression. The result of these factors can be seen in figure 1.1, which shows nominal and real minimum wages in the urban sector between 1965 and 1978. After 1970, real wages experienced decline, the result of wage freezes combined with inflation, particularly in the cost of food. They have since failed to return to pre-Miracle levels.

The urban bias of Balaguer's development policies penalized the rural sector, where about half the labor force was found in the early 1970s. The imposition of price controls on agricultural products, dependence on the comprador bourgeoisie for credit and marketing, and support for terms of exchange favoring urban importers and indus-

---

TABLE 1.1. Unemployment Rates in the Dominican Republic: 1969–1983

| Year | *Percentage Unemployed* | |
	Urban	*Rural*
1970	24.0	24.0
1973	20.0[a]	40.0 (underemployment)
1979	19.3[a]	—
1981	18.2	22.8
1983	21.7[a]	—

Sources: Lozano (1986) for 1970, 1981, and 1983; ILO (1974) for 1973; and Onaplan-One (1981) for 1979.
[a]Santo Domingo only.

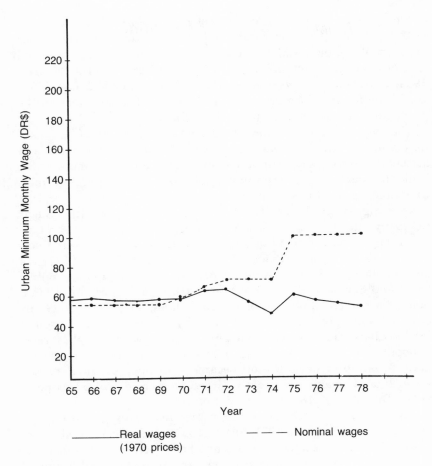

SOURCE: Adapted from Wilkie and Perkal (1984:289).

FIGURE 1.1. Real and Nominal Urban Minimal Wages in the Dominican Republic, 1965–1978

trialists all hurt farmers and helped exacerbate existing income inequalities between city and countryside (Lozano 1985:161). As a consequence, between 1965 and 1978, the proportion of GDP contributed by agriculture declined from 26 percent to 12 percent (Vicens 1982:168). Slightly over half of all agricultural land was dedicated to raising cattle, most of it in an extensive manner (Dore y Cabral 1979:19). State policies patterned after Alliance for Progress models specifically promoted beef production for export by providing cheap credit and technical assistance (Crouch 1979:192ff.). In contrast, cultivation of food staples, with the exception of rice, stagnated (Encarnación 1982:27). Productivity per rural inhabitant also declined. The resulting shortfalls of most staples necessitated increased food imports, and food prices began to climb during the 1970s (Dore y Cabral 1981:18–19). Massive food imports from the United States via Public Law 480—the "Food for Peace Program"—had a further adverse effect on the production of many staples (Crouch 1979).

The long-term trend toward increasing concentration of landholdings which began in the last decades of the nineteenth century and accelerated during the Trujillato continued and became more acute. Under favorable new laws promulgated by the Balaguer regime, multinational agribusiness corporations were able to accumulate vast tracts of agricultural land. Taking over the South Puerto Rico Sugar Company after the U.S. invasion in 1965, the Gulf and Western Corporation became the republic's largest landowner, with about 8 percent of all arable land (Black 1986:66; NACLA 1975:8). By 1971, 14 percent of all landholders owned 79 percent of all land in the republic (Boin and Serullé 1980:8). Conversely, just over 70 percent of landholders occupied 12 percent of all arable land, an average of 29 tareas, or 1.8 hectares, each (Dore y Cabral 1979:20). Fragmentation of landholdings was also exacerbated by one of the world's highest rates of population growth, averaging some 3 percent a year. Among smallholders, semiproletarianization became a strategy essential to survival. Indeed, many were really "wage workers disguised as peasants" (Duarte 1980:180; my translation).

Technical inputs into agriculture were minimal, especially on land producing food crops. In 1971, just 5 percent of all farms used mechanized production exclusively and another 5 percent combined animal and mechanical means. Only about one fifth of agricultural land was fertilized (Dore y Cabral 1979:18). To turn around declining agricultural productivity and lower the cost of basic foods, Balaguer initiated an agrarian reform in 1972 which won him the support of many of the republic's peasants. However, the slow pace of the reform, coupled with the small size of the parcels distributed, insured that the decline of the agrarian sector and pauperization of large segments of the rural population would continue.

Massive rural to urban migration was a direct consequence of the constraints experienced by the agrarian sector during this period. The flow of migrants from the countryside to the premiere city of the republic, Santo Domingo, was already significant by 1970. In that year, slightly over half of the city's population was comprised of internal migrants. In the five poorest neighborhoods studied by Isis Duarte and her colleagues toward the end of the Balaguer regime, 91 percent of the household heads interviewed were migrants, the majority from rural areas of the republic (Duarte 1980:189). Over the following decade, population movement to the cities was of such magnitude that for the first time in its history, a majority of the republic's population dwelled in urban areas. Because of the limited creation of jobs, the great majority of these migrants entered the expanding "tertiary" or informal sector of the urban economy comprising petty commercial, service, and crafts activities of generally low productivity and scant remuneration (Lozano 1985:167).

Production of the major export crops was not threatened by this large-scale rural exodus, however. Rather, reliance on the importation of extremely low wage Haitian labor, established in the early decades of this century in the sugar industry, not only persisted in filling labor needs, but intensified and spread to other major export crops, such as coffee. In 1980, an estimated 200,000 Haitians were living in the republic (Grasmuck 1982a; ONAPLAN 1980a).

In any case, the Dominican Miracle was short-lived; 1974, the year of the oil crisis and of global recession, marked the beginning of a period of sustained economic downturn. A growing dependence on the United States after 1965 made the Dominican economy especially susceptible to recession. This dependence on the United States for private investment, trade, and aid resulted in the Dominican Republic's becoming the sixth most heavily dependent of the world's twenty-three most heavily U.S.-dominated countries during the period 1950–1973 (Richardson 1978:104–5, 114–116). By 1973, the United States was the leading supplier of imports to the republic, with 58 percent of the total for that year; it was also the leading market for exports, absorbing 66 percent of the Dominican total. The Dominican Republic came to be regarded as "the best market the U.S. has in the Caribbean or Central America" (U.S. embassy report, cited in NACLA 1975:5). This desire for American consumer goods was stoked in part by the televised images of North American society to which Dominicans were now regularly exposed, as well as by movies and radio. By 1978, for example, one-quarter of the total television programming was imported from the United States (Reimers 1985:129).

With such a high level of economic dependence, the recessions of the 1970s in the United States inevitably had serious repercussions in the Dominican Republic. The drastic fall of most major export commodity prices after 1975, the sharp increase in the cost of key imports (the value of petroleum imports alone increased from DR$ 1.6 million in 1972 to DR$157.8 million in 1975; World Bank 1978:table

3.10), spiraling inflation, and the onerous debt-servicing burden all had a devastating impact on the Dominican economy in the latter part of the decade.

The defeat of Balaguer by the social democratic Dominican Revolutionary Party (PRD) candidate, Antonio Guzmán, in 1978 could do little to stanch this devastation. Indeed, Guzmán's tenure in office between 1978 and 1982 witnessed not only an increase in the national debt by 43 percent to DR$1.5 billion, but also a growing deficit in the balance of payments and exacerbated inflation (Díaz Santana and Murphy 1983:34–35). The Guzmán government did devote greater attention to the agricultural sector. Production of some foodstuffs increased, but massive imports of most staples continued to be required to feed the national population. Moreover, production of the foods comprising the worker's or agriculturalist's market basket either remained stagnant or did not increase as much as luxury items. Despite an increase in the minimum wage under Guzmán, the upward spiral of prices continued to erode real wages (Vicens 1982:170). Deterioration of the economy continued with the succeeding government of Salvador Jorge Blanco, also of the PRD. To obtain new loans, Jorge Blanco acceded to the International Monetary Fund's demands for austerity. Wage freezes, price freezes for major foodstuffs, and currency reforms that greatly increased the cost of imports were imposed. The result has been increased unemployment and severe hardship for the great bulk of the Dominican population (Murphy 1987). Reelected to the presidency in 1986, Balaguer undoubtedly will not be able to work even limited miracles amidst the present economic devastation.

The consequences of the manner in which the Dominican Republic has been incorporated into the world economy in this century and of its intensified dependence on the United States have resulted in structural changes which have fostered strong pressures on individuals to migrate to the United States, pressures that undoubtedly will continue to be felt into the forseeable future. Although the particulars are a part of its singular history, the Dominican experience as described here is best viewed as part of larger processes of penetration and incorporation which have wrought similar patterns throughout many parts of the world.

PATTERNS OF U.S.-BOUND MIGRATION FROM THE DOMINICAN REPUBLIC

It has been noted that whether local ruling classes oppose, encourage, or merely acquiesce to emigration depends upon specific historical conditions (Portes and Walton 1981:42). In the Dominican Republic, dominant classes have indeed displayed sharply different attitudes toward international migration over time. As we have seen, the Trujillista project of domestically controlled "development to the inside" required a stable and disciplined national labor force. During this period of expansion, the state and the dominant class (in the person of Trujillo and associates) adamantly opposed international migration and imposed strict restrictions on population movement.

Nonetheless, despite Trujillo's restrictive policies, during his regime some Dominicans did manage to emigrate. Between 1950 and 1960, for example, about 9,800 people emigrated to the United States as legal residents (table 1.2). These early migrants fell into roughly two categories. The first were people who were economically and socially relatively privileged. Potential migrants needed substantial economic resources to undertake the expensive migration process. In the 1950s, the cost of securing a passport alone was about DR$150, an amount exceeding per capita GNP for 1950. (The Dominican peso was until recently officially valued on a par with the U.S. dollar.) However, equally as important were political connections. The request for a passport led to a detailed investigation not only of the solicitor's own political activities, but also those of her or his kin. Carried out by Trujillo's secret police, these investigations potentially jeopardized entire extended families. Under these circumstances, few individuals could risk requesting a passport without the insurance of personal ties to Trujillo or his close associates. The other major category of migrants during this period were the political exiles who managed through one means or another to flee the island (Ameringer 1974; Georges 1984). While some settled in New York, others went to Europe, Puerto Rico, and Venezuela (Silfa 1983).

With the death of Trujillo, restrictions on population movement were eliminated, and international migration dramatically and immediately increased. From the start, the great bulk of this migration was directed to the United States and, more specifically, to New York City. The figures in table 1.2 give some indication of the magnitude of the increase. From 1960 to 1962, U.S.-bound migration increased sixfold. In nearly every year after 1962, a number equal to or greater

TABLE 1.2. Dominican Immigrants and Nonimmigrants Admitted by Year and Status

Year	Legal resident	Nonimmigrant
1950 to 1960	9,800	
1960	756	4,437
1961	3,045	9,102
1962	4,603	18,227
1963	10,683	56,236
1964	7,537	64,476
1965	9,504	52,638
1966	16,503	68,870
1967	11,514	78,791
1968	9,250	81,073
1969	10,670	101,454
1970	10,807	105,191
1971	12,624	74,252
1972	10,760	111,845
1973	13,921	124,528
1974	15,680	143,512
1975	14,066	149,386
1976[a]	15,088	207,435
1977	11,655	154,964
1978	19,458	166,519
1979	17,519	134,461
1980[b]	17,245	—
1981[b]	18,220	—

SOURCE: INS, Annual Reports and Statistical Yearbooks, 1961–1981.
[a]Figures for 1976 cover a fifteen-month period.
[b]Figures unavailable or only partially available for these years for nonimmigrant visas.

than the total for the previous decade migrated to the United States. Between 1966 and 1981, the number of legal residents admitted to the United States averaged about 14,000 per year.

In contrast to the restrictive policies of the Trujillato, the dominant classes now viewed migration in a positive light. It provided a safety valve for social and economic tensions unleashed after Trujillo's death. It was a partial solution to the growing unemployment in the cities. Indeed, in the history of Dominican migration to the United States, it is probably not accidental that the period 1962–1963 saw the largest relative increase in the number of visas issued. In his memoir, *Overtaken by Events* (1966), John Bartlow Martin, who was U.S. ambassador to the republic during this time, recounts that a leading member of the government requested of him that the United

States move to speed up the visa process. In response, the United States provided new facilities and expanded its consular staff. The result was the largest relative increase in the number of residence visas issued either before or after 1963 (Castro 1985:205).

Political factors also contributed to sharp increases in migration in 1966 and again in 1978. No doubt as a result of the social and political upheaval and consequent poor economic performance experienced during 1965, record numbers of Dominicans sought entry into the United States the following year. As table 1.2 indicates, the number of legal resident visas issued increased 74 percent, from 9,500 in 1965 to 16,500 in 1966. And many more Dominicans tried unsuccessfully to migrate. Internal records of the U.S. consulate in Santo Domingo reveal that the number of applicants for legal resident visas reached its zenith in 1965, when 25,269 applications were received. It appears that some of the migrants during this period were primarily motivated by political reasons (Baez Evertsz and D'Oleo Ramírez 1986). Ironically, to escape the repression that followed their defeat, many individuals who actively opposed the U.S. invasion found themselves seeking exile in the growing Dominican community in New York (Georges 1984). By 1970, in contrast, the number of applicants was down to 14,728, and immigrants admitted had dropped to about 10,800. Although 1970 was a presidential election year, the results were a foregone conclusion and the continuity of the Balaguer regime was never seriously in doubt.

The presidential election of 1978 was a different matter, however. The PRD victory in that election was made possible by the sliding economy, mounting political dissatisfaction, and support received from the Carter administration and the Socialist International. With a shift in the locus of patronage and jobs from the "reds" to the "whites" a distinct possibility, political and economic uncertainty mounted. The result was another peak in U.S. resident visa applications and approvals. Thus, in 1978, 23,949 Dominicans applied for visas and 19,458 were admitted as legal residents, a 60 percent increase in admissions over the preceding year.

Despite several years of exceptional growth, migration to the United States proceeded apace throughout the 1970s. In fact, over 75 percent more Dominicans were issued immigrant visas between 1971 and 1981 than in the preceding decade. It has been suggested (Bray 1984) that the types of structural constraints inherent in the model of development pursued after the late 1960s induced many of the growing number of comparatively well educated and skilled Dominicans unable to find middle-class jobs to leave the country. This "middle-class bottleneck" had a political dimension as well. Not only were desirable jobs limited with respect to qualified demand, but they did not depend on merit alone. As Kayal (1978:13) wrote during this period, "only politically cooperative high school or college graduates can find work with reasonable remuneration," adding that "[t]hose who question government policies . . . tend to come to the U.S."

The figures in the second column of table 1.2 are even more revealing of the steep and steady increase in migration in the post-Trujillo period. Many of the earliest migrants entered the United States on nonimmigrant visas (nearly all as "tourists"), and they only later managed to adjust their status to legal resident aliens (cf. Hendricks 1974; Pérez 1981). From 1960 to 1963, the number of nonimmigrant visas issued to Dominicans increased thirteen times. Once again, the steepest increase occurred in 1963, with a record 300 percent more visas issued than in the preceding year. By the mid-1970s, over 150,000 nonimmigrants were being admitted annually from the Dominican Republic. Between 1961 and 1978, approximately 1,800,000 Dominicans entered the United States on nonimmigrant visas. While the majority of these nonimmigrants fell into categories that would exclude them from the group of potential visa violators, a certain proportion remained to work after their visas expired. Of these, some would manage to regularize their status over time and become legal residents. Others would return to the republic to live.

Nonimmigrant visas have not been the only route to undocumented entry, although probably they have been the most commonly used. Very early in the 1960s, brokers appeared to provide potential migrants with false documents and forged visas (cf. Hendricks 1974). Other brokers organized undocumented entries through more indirect routes. Many Dominicans have sailed across the Mona Passage off the eastern part of the island in launches to Puerto Rico. Some have flown there in small planes chartered by the brokers. A portion have remained in Puerto Rico to live and work. As many as 60,000 Dominicans may have been residing in Puerto Rico by 1987 (Díaz 1987), and Puerto Rico remains the second most popular destination for Dominican immigrants (Bray 1987:153). For others, the island represented a way station, from which they entered the United States by "passing" as Puerto Ricans. This well-established method of entry is even the subject of a popular *merengue*, a couple dance with a limping step the lyrics of which often provide commentaries on contemporary Dominican experience. In this merengue, the singer admonishes his audience:

Puerto Rico queda cerca, pero móntate en avión
y si consigues la visa, no hay problema en Inmigración.
Pero no te vayas en yola, no te llenes de ilusiones
porque en el Canal de la Mona, te comen los tiburones.

Puerto Rico is nearby, but board an airplane
and if you get your visa, there's no problem with Immigration.
But don't go in a launch, don't be filled with illusions
because in the Mona Canal, you'll be eaten by the sharks.

(Wilfredo Vargas, Karen Records)

Another route of undocumented entry which has developed more recently is through Mexico. Brokers instruct potential migrants to obtain a tourist visa to enter Mexico; this visa is easy to obtain. In Mexico City they are met by a guide who takes them to the U.S. border, which they attempt to cross with the assistance of *coyotes,* that is, alien smugglers. By the late 1970s, many Dominicans were also stowing away on cargo ships bound for southern Florida. The reader is referred to chapter 3 for a more detailed discussion of this and other routes of undocumented migration.

The obvious fact that the Dominican Republic is an island has posed important geographical constraints on undocumented migration. It is sometimes suggested, perhaps on analogy from Mexican immigration, that the number of undocumented Dominicans may approach or exceed that of the documented (e.g., Reimers 1985:138). However, unlike Mexico, the Dominican Republic does not share a land border with the United States, and this simple fact has had significant implications for the nature and characteristics of Dominican migration. Although it is not possible to estimate with accuracy the number of undocumented Dominicans in the United States, the difficulty, danger, risk, and expense of these methods of entry undoubtedly have served to check the volume of the flow. Figure 1.2 juxtaposes the typical cost of an undocumented entry with the per capita GDP of the republic between 1960 and 1980. Costs have increased steeply and are clearly prohibitive in a country in which nearly one-third of the households earned DR$100 a month or less in 1978 (Soto and del Rosario 1978).

Indeed, one of the few studies based on a random sample of Dominicans in New York City found that the proportion of undocumented migrants did not exceed 17 percent a year (Pérez 1981:6). In Los Pinos, I found a very similar proportion: while many Pineros had

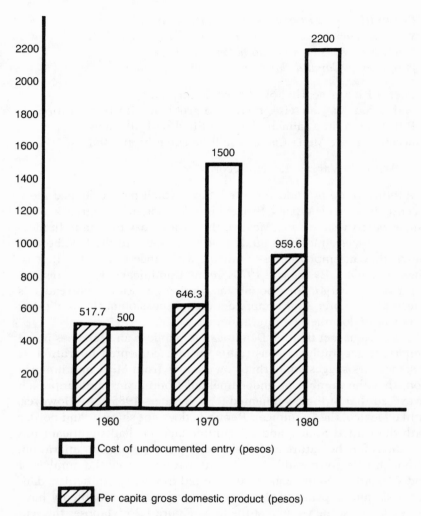

SOURCE: Per capita GDP from Wilkie and Perkal (1984:16).

FIGURE 1.2. Cost of Undocumented Entry to the United States and Per Capita Gross Domestic Product, Dominican Republic, 1960–1980

begun their sojourns in the United States as undocumented migrants, only 14 percent remained so in 1981 (see chapter 3). A recent attempt by demographers (Warren and Passel 1987) to estimate the number of undocumented immigrants in the United States based on the 1980 U.S. census and the 1980 alien registration bolsters confidence in these low proportions. This study placed a "firm lower bound" on the population of undocumented Dominicans in 1980 at around 19,000, with an unknown rate of undercount, very probably not exceeding 30–50 percent. Additional support for a downward adjustment of the undocumented population is provided by the low turnout of Dominicans for "amnesty" under the provisions of the 1986 Immigration Reform and Control Act. While there are many good reasons why undocumented migrants would be reluctant to attempt to regularize their legal status under this program, that only about 27,700 have done so suggests a relatively small pool of potential applicants (INS 1989).

Uncertainty over the number of the undocumented has made it difficult to estimate the population of Dominican immigrants in the United States. It is known that the number of legal immigrants entering between 1961 and 1981 totaled some 255,578 (Bray 1987:152). The magnitude of this flow placed Dominicans third among immigrant groups from Latin America admitted to the United States, after Mexicans and Cubans. Of course, the well-established pattern of return migration means that not all of these immigrants have remained in the United States. Given the unknown components of return and undocumented migration, estimating the total Dominican population in the United States has become the object of an ongoing "numbers game," a game with important political implications. Most estimates have tended to vary between 300,000 and 500,000 but sometimes have reached as high as 800,000 to 1,000,000. Recent demographic studies (Larson and Sullivan 1987; Larson and Opitz 1988) based on the 1981 Dominican census dispute the higher figures and suggest lower estimates around 300,000 for the continental United States.

COMPOSITION OF THE DOMINICAN MIGRANT STREAM

Until recently, very little information has been available on the composition of the Dominican migrant stream to the United States, but in the last few years, a body of research has accumulated. As the general features of the migrant stream begin to emerge, this new research has challenged commonly held conceptions of the nature of Dominican migration to the United States. However, the new studies, of which only one was conducted at the national level, do not always concur in all particulars. Thus, while a considerable body of information has accumulated over the last five years or so, some aspects of the Dominican migrant stream remain to be understood.

Because the earliest studies were conducted by anthropologists working in rural areas of the republic, it was often assumed that most migrants were peasants with small to medium-sized landholdings (Vicioso 1976) or rural proletarians (Sassen-Koob 1979). For instance, Hendricks' (1974) pioneering ethnography focused on a rural area of the northern part of the republic. His work provided a detailed portrait of a sending community and the transnational networks that sustained and directed migration. The early studies of Gonzalez (1970, 1973, 1976) also chronicled the travails as well as the "peasants' progress" of those who left the rural heartland of the Dominican Republic and settled in New York City. More recently, Bray (1983) has described and compared internal and international migratory patterns from an agricultural village in the Cibao, Pessar (1982a, b) has analyzed the role of households in international migration from a community in the eastern Sierra, and Castro (1985) has studied the causes and consequences of migration for econonomic development in a Cibao agrotown.

The work of Ugalde, Bean, and Cardenas (1979) was the first to challenge the widely held view that most Dominican migrants originated in rural areas. Their analysis of the 1974 Diagnos National Survey of 12,500 households remains the only national-level study of international migration. It revealed that although about 53 percent of the Dominican population resided in rural areas at the time of the survey, only 24 percent of all international migrants were of rural origin. That urban origins predominate among Dominican migrants has been confirmed by a number of subsequent studies (Pérez 1981; Kritz and Gurak 1983; Grasmuck 1984b; Baez Evertsz and D'Oleo Ramírez 1986).

The analysis by Ugalde et al. also challenged the view that it was the dispossessed who tended to migrate to the United States. They found that whereas 28 percent of the population of the republic belonged to the "lower urban stratum," this was true of only 17 percent of all migrants to the United States. In concluding that "migration from the Dominican Republic to the United States appears to be a predominantly urban and middle-class phenomenon," Ugalde and his colleagues (1979:240) shook conventional notions concerning the composition of Dominican migration.

Ugalde et al. also provide some indirect evidence regarding the premigration labor force characteristics of Dominicans who went to the United States. They report that among the "urban middle class," some 26 percent migrated because of unemployment; an additional 26 percent left "to make more money." Among "urban upper class migrants," the proportions giving these reasons were 13 percent and 7 percent, respectively. Only 9 percent of all rural migrants cited unemployment as the principal factor motivating migration. This finding should be interpreted with some caution. In the Dominican rural sector, as in other underdeveloped nations, open rural unemployment is rare and underemployment is widespread. However, although the Diagnos survey did not paint a precise portrait of labor force participation prior to migration, the evidence does suggest that the majority of Dominican migrants were not unemployed in the Dominican Republic and that an important motive for migration was the desire to earn higher wages.

This analysis of the Diagnos survey data inaugurated a debate over the social composition of Dominican immigration to the United States which has yet to be fully resolved. One problem is that the criteria used by Ugalde et al. to reconstruct the social class origins of migrants leave room for ambiguity. Their index of socioeconomic class, for instance, relied on literacy, education, and household type and household amenities. For migrant households, however, the use of proxies such as house size and amenities is problematic. The "Nassau houses" in northern Haitian towns with heavy migration to the Bahamas, the "London houses" in Hong Kong villages, and the "German houses" in Andulusia bespeak a widespread behavioral pattern among international migrants: the construction of modern housing well stocked with consumer goods financed by remittances and savings from abroad. The presence of upscale housing and amenities thus may often be a consequence of migration, in some cases a symbolic badge of mobility, and not a reliable indicator of class prior to migration. A second problem is the fact that the Diagnos survey obviously could not identify households that had emigrated in their entirety. It is not suggested how this omission might affect the survey findings. However, Ugalde et al. (1979:250) do report that "the lower the social class, the less likely the migrant will return." This raises the possibility that absent households may be more likely to be of presumably poorer class backgrounds. If this is indeed true, then there may be some underrepresentation of the poorest migrants.

More recent surveys have added nuance and complexity to the composite portrait of Dominican migration. Since the Diagnos study, researchers variously have characterized the Dominican migrant stream as predominantly middle class in origin (Bray 1984, 1987); lower-middle class and urban proletarian (Baez Evertsz and D'Oleo Ramírez 1986); or diverse, incorporating migrants from broad sectors of Dominican society, except perhaps the poorest (Castro 1985).

For example, in a sample of Santiago households conducted in 1980, Grasmuck (1985) found that lower-stratum origins were underrepresented among her sample of U.S. migrants from Santiago, the second largest city of the republic. In another sample of Dominican immigrants in New York City, she found that although those from urban areas of the republic were better educated than nonmigrants in the capital city, some 30 percent were unemployed prior to migration—a level higher than that of nonmigrants (pp. 158–159). Among those employed prior to migration, there was an overrepresentation of those who were lower-level professionals and technical workers when compared to the population of Santo Domingo as a whole, itself characterized by a high level of professional jobs. However, in general, the proportion of migrants with occupations characterized by lower levels of skill matched fairly closely the broader population of Santo Domingo. More recently, Baez Evertsz and D'Oleo Ramírez (1986) surveyed nearly 300 potential migrants waiting in line at the U.S. consulate in Santo Domingo to be interviewed for visas. They found that three-quarters of their sample came from the lower levels of the middle class and the urban proletariat, although they earned what in the Dominican context were "middle-level" incomes. They also found that some 26 percent were unemployed prior to migration.

Regardless of its diverse origins, in the United States, Dominican migration is heavily working-class in destination (Castro 1985:125). This is clearly reflected in a recent study based on the 1980 U.S. census. Of the eighteen numerically most important immigrant groups who entered the country between 1970 and 1980, Dominicans had the lowest median family income ($9,569 a year). They also had among the lowest levels of education. Only 3.4 percent of these recent immigrants aged 25 or older had four or more years of college education. Slightly over one-fifth had less than five years of elementary school education (Koch 1987).

Although there is some disagreement on the socioeconomic origins of Dominican immigrants to the United States, the mounting evidence concurs that they are young, predominantly urban in origin, occupationally heterogeneous, but often skilled and semi-professional, and generally better educated than nonmigrants. It also appears that although selective, the stream is also diverse, incorporating from broad sectors of Dominican society, although probably underrepresenting the least skilled and poorest. However, this evidence also suggests that, unlike many new immigrant streams from Asia and some other parts of Latin America and the Caribbean, Dominican migration to the United States cannot be considered a "brain drain" in the usual sense. Nonetheless, although the numbers of brain drain migrants are absolutely small, proportionally the Dominican Republic has lost to migration a large number of its professionals (Castro 1985:139).

This chapter has sketched a general overview of patterns of Dominican development in this century to provide an understanding of the larger social and economic forces conditioning U.S.-bound migration. I have made a case for an intimate relationship between international migration and the republic's growing penetration by U.S. interests. Perhaps it is fitting to close with a paradigmatic illustration of this relationship, the case of Dominican baseball. Prior to the first U.S. military occupation of 1916–1924, the cockfight had reigned as the national sport. The occupation introduced the cultural innovation of baseball to the Dominican Republic, and in time baseball outstripped the cockfight in popularity (Moya Pons 1980:493). Today, on a per capita basis, the Dominican Republic is the world's leading exporter of major league baseball players to the United States.

CHAPTER 2

The History and Development of Los Pinos, 1850–1961

Los Pinos has been directly affected by, and has actively participated in, many of the most important transformations characterizing Dominican society over the last century. In each stage of its historical development, the community has been marked by changes in the ways in which profit has been appropriated, in the nature of elites and their ties to nonelites, and in the influence exerted by the state and other forces of control. The specific impact of regional and national social and economic changes on Los Pinos is described and analyzed in some detail in this chapter to provide the background for an understanding of the forces that promoted large-scale migration after 1961. In the following three sections, I trace the development of the village from its earliest settlement in the last century to 1930, the watershed year in which Trujillo assumed control of the republic. During its first eighty years, Los Pinos slowly grew from a pioneer settlement into the hub of local tobacco production and later became the principal entrepôt for a thriving decentralized lumber industry. The second part of the chapter traces the consequences for Los Pinos of Trujillo's radical policies. The aim of the chapter is to illuminate in a concrete way, through a detailed narrative of the specific case of Los Pinos, the general developmental processes at work in the Dominican countryside. In the next chapter, we will examine the effect of the conjunction of these processes and its operation on the structure of rural society so as to promote massive international labor migration to the United States.

LOS PINOS: THE EARLIEST SETTLEMENT, 1850–1910

Geographically isolated, the earliest settlers lived a pioneer existence. As in most rural areas of the republic during this time, primitive communication and transportation links with a weak central government resulted in conditions of near autarky. Slash-and-burn cultivation of manioc, sweet potatoes, corn, beans, and some other less important cultivates filled basic subsistence needs. Of greater importance, both economically and culturally, was pig hunting. In 1869–1870, the North American geographer Williams Gabb visited this area and described its "cañons [which] are very deep, very narrow and rarely penetrated except by straggling pig hunters" (1881:53).[1] Semiferal pigs thrived in the dense forests, where they were hunted by mounted Serranos and their dogs. Pork and lard were major components of the diet, and salt pork, sausage, and processed pig hides were the principal commodities produced for exchange. Sporadically transported to Santiago by mule or horse, these were traded for the few items, such as salt, machetes, and cloth, not produced by the household.

By the second half of the nineteenth century, population growth and a greater reliance on agriculture led to a more settled way of life (Antonini et al. 1975:45). Population grew as a result of both natural increase and immigration. As the agricultural reserve in other parts of the republic began to shrink, its virgin lands attracted many new settlers to the Sierra. Some also came to mine the placer gold deposits in the banks and terraces of the region's many streams and rivers (p. 52). In the mid-1860s, another influx of population took place when farmers from the central Cibao Valley migrated to mountainous areas like the Sierra to escape the political turmoil caused by the War of Restoration, a guerrilla war against annexation of the republic to Spain (Hoetink 1982:174). Over the next two decades, permanent settlements were established along the trails that served as the major corridors of colonization (Antonini et al. 1975:42).

The valley of Los Pinos, formed by the Los Pinos River, was first settled in the mid-nineteenth century by two brothers, Spanish immigrants who came to the region to search for gold. Baptismal records from La Sede indicate that settlers were already in the area by 1850, a date corroborated by the genealogies of their descendants.

---

1. The way of life of these Sierran hunters was vividly described by the Dominican writer Pedro Bonó in his novel, *El Montero*, originally published as a series of articles in 1856.

The village they helped found nestled along the Camino Real—the Royal Road, actually a primitive access trail winding its way from the town of Monción in the west to Santiago in the east. In reality, as Pedro Bonó noted in 1881, "those roads denominated royal are nameless passages where absolutely no one has ever lifted a finger" (quoted in Hoetink 1982:47). Nonetheless, they served as the major corridors of colonization of the Sierra.

The new settlement was strategically located at the juncture of three distinct ecological zones. To the west lay the semiarid countryside of Monción where useful palms such as guano and cana *(Sabal umbraculifera Martius)* grew in wild abundance. Rising some 100 meters above the valley of Los Pinos to the north was La Loma, a dense pine forest *(Pinus occidentalis)* within a few minutes' walking distance from the village. To the south were the humid, more fertile uplands of Sierra Adentro, the source of coffee, and precious hardwoods, such as mahogany, oak, and ligna vitae. By the early twentieth century, the diverse resources and products of these zones had been woven into a system of regional trade, with Los Pinos at its center.

Tobacco Cultivation in Los Pinos, 1870–1910

During this period of accelerated population growth and slow but steady expansion of communication networks, pig hunting declined and the principal economic activity of Los Pinos and of the Sierra in general became the cultivation of tobacco. Nearly all of this production was destined for the Hamburg market, where German manufacturers converted the low quality tobacco into cheap imitations of Cuban cigars and cigarettes (Boin and Serullé 1979:54). Several factors encouraged smallholding agriculturalists to adopt this cash crop. First, unlike the other principal export crops of the nineteenth century, cacao and coffee, tobacco required little start-up capital; its short growing season of six months also compared favorably with these tree crops and made credit much easier to obtain; and after the harvest, land and labor could be devoted to growing subsistence crops (Hoetink 1982:66; see also Ortiz Fernández 1947).

Of perhaps greater importance to the general development of Los Pinos was the fact that tobacco, again in contrast to cacao and coffee, created important spin-offs which helped to diversify the local economy. Two closely related consequences of tobacco cultivation were the new demand for *serones,* containers with which to protect the harvested tobacco from humidity, and the demand for expanded transportation services.

Throughout the western Sierra, a handicraft industry emerged to meet the demand for serones. Serones were woven from the leaves of the guano palmetto, which flourished in the semiarid countryside immediately west of Los Pinos. Applying the traditional knowledge of weaving guano into hats, saddle-bags, and other useful items, Serrano men began to make the new serones to the specifications designated by the tobacco buyers.[2] Seron weaving, which was done right before and during the tobacco harvest, soon became an important economic activity, characterizing "entire comunes" of the Sierra (*comunes* were the subdivisions of provinces recognized during this time; Pedro Bonó quoted in Boin and Serullé 1979:81).

As was common elsewhere in the republic at this time, local intermediaries both financed production and connected the community to national and international markets. Emerging from the ranks of the largest landholders and livestock breeders, they represented the local-level link in a chain of usurer-merchants. This chain of exploitation ultimately terminated in the large tobacco export houses of the comprador bourgeoisie of Santiago and Puerto Plata, who were themselves the agents of German merchants (Boin and Serullé 1979:54; Hoetink 1982:68; Moya Pons 1980:405). With the loan capital from larger intermediaries located outside the community, these middlemen were able, on the one hand, to advance the credit that spurred local production and, on the other, to purchase the seccion's serones and tobacco at harvest time. In addition, most Pinero intermediaries owned trains of mules or burros (*recuas*), which they used to transport these goods to the cities and towns of the north. There, to complete the cycle, tobacco and serones were resold to the intermediaries who had initially advanced them the capital. Always the principal method of transport in the Sierra, mule trains grew both in number and size, with teams of up to a dozen animals carrying the bulky new products as well as the mail, messages, and money. In Hoetink's (1982:48) opinion, these muleteers "formed a separate professional group, with special abilities and group ethics." The nature of their enterprise undoubtedly allowed them to establish networks distributed widely over the northern Dominican Republic. Their control over the movement of loan capital, tobacco, and serones also enabled them to accumulate profit. As production of these commodities expanded, these muleteer-middlemen emerged as an elite linking precapitalist

2. Over the last fifty years, the price of serones has steadily declined. Accompanying this decline has been a change in the division of labor, with women and children now the principal producers; see chapter 3.

producers of the Sierra with the merchant capitalists of the north. In the 1880s and 1890s, elsewhere in the republic, mule trains were outcompeted and replaced by railroads built with Dutch, British, and North American capital (p. 52–53). But the rugged topography and geographic isolation protected the Sierra from developments in transportation for the next half a century, and the muleteers continued to flourish there.

THE DEVELOPMENT OF THE DECENTRALIZED LUMBER INDUSTRY, 1910–1930

As noted in the last chapter, the penetration of capitalist relations of production into much of the Dominican countryside in the last quarter of the nineteenth century unleashed processes of differentiation which resulted in the appearance of new social classes and the consolidation of a national bourgeoisie. As the number of capitalist farms grew, the size of the agrarian bourgeoisie increased as well, enriched too by the immigration of foreign capitalists to the republic during this period. Profits from agriculture were invested in more land, but also in other means of production and in the purchase of wage labor (Boin and Serullé 1979:269–71). Nationally, the number of small industries grew, and the occupational structure became more highly diversified (Hoetink 1982:171).

As a consequence of these developments and of concurrent improvements in communication and transportation, expansion of the government apparatus, and growth of educational institutions, the republic's cities and towns grew rapidly. In the 1880s and 1890s, over two dozen towns were either founded or promoted in administrative status to *común* (Hoetink 1982:42). Nationally, population more than tripled, from approximately 150,000 in 1871 to over 485,000 in 1897 (p. 19). The new towns, as well as the older commercial centers, attracted capitalists, merchants, and speculators (Moya Pons 1980:428). Construction boomed as a consequence, and demand for the principal building material of the time, lumber, greatly increased.

The first lumber company in the northern part of the republic was established in Santiago in 1897 (Hoetink 1982:172). Within fifteen years, with impetus from Middle Eastern merchant capital, Los Pinos was a thriving center for the lumber industry in the western Sierra. Attracted by the prosperity of the Cibao, the first Middle Eastern settlers—for the most part immigrants from Turkey and Syria but called "Arabs" by the Dominicans—arrived in Santiago in 1897. They soon established themselves as ambulant peddlers of manufactured goods in the countryside, filling the merchant niche created as a result of the agricultural transformation (Hoetink 1982:34).

Sometime between 1910 and 1915, older Pineros recall that two brothers who were called "the Turks" *(los turcos)* began visiting the village. They soon established relations with the two wealthiest intermediaries and muleteers of Los Pinos, Don Pancho Morales and Don Sixto Linares, advancing them the capital to begin purchasing logs and lumber in the sección. Don Pancho was a relatively poor young man when he first came to Los Pinos to marry. However, his new wife owned a bakery and was also a seamstress. In time, Don Pancho parlayed the profits from these businesses into land, mules, and loan capital. Don Sixto was born in Los Pinos, the son of the politically well connected mayor and owner of the cockfight pit. By the time the Turks arrived in Los Pinos, Don Pancho and Don Sixto were on their way to becoming the big men *(los grandes)* of the community.

Traveling widely throughout the north, the Turks were no doubt drawn to Los Pinos by its favorable location at the crossroads of dense pine forests to the north and rich stands of precious hardwoods to the south. Moreover, the proximity of navigable rivers to the west might also have influenced their selection: guided by raftsmen, logs could be floated downstream to their confluence with the Yaque, the most important river in the republic, and thence to the city of Santiago, located on its banks. Sometime after they began purchasing lumber, the Turks also introduced a mobile steam-operated mill into the area. Thus, Pineros could either saw their logs into boards by hand or sell their logs to the Turks to be processed at the mill.

Following the familiar chain pattern, Don Pancho and Don Sixto used the Turks' capital to make loans to others in Los Pinos for the purchase of tools to chop trees and mill the logs. At a reported interest rate of 20 percent per month, this capital was clearly expensive. But because the technological requirements were simple—an axe and a handsaw were the only tools needed—nearly every household in Los Pinos managed to finance participation in some aspect of the productive process: chopping trees, milling lumber, making turpentine, and so on. Some were able to buy a few animals to start their own small mule trains to haul lumber.

At the time of the arrival of the Turks, the virgin pines of the sección were essentially free goods. The expropriations of peasant holdings under way in the south and east since the latter part of the nineteenth century had left the Sierra untouched. Nearly every household held titles or rights to tracts of pine forest larger than could be used for agricultural purposes. Some Pineros held titles to a specific number of shares (*acciones*, pesos) of *terrenos comuneros*, technically, inherited or purchased rights of use to lands granted by the Spanish crown to the original settlers of Hispaniola (see Albuquerque 1961). Most of these title holders managed to enclose more land than they were entitled to under the original transaction. Enclosure involved staking a claim by clearing land, or more commonly by marking trees with notches or even paint, and not actual delimitation with a fence or palisade. In 1911, the partition of terrenos comuneros was made compulsory, and a national cadastral survey was undertaken in 1920 under the aegis of the U.S. occupation government. However, the survey did not reach the most mountainous areas of the republic and the entire municipio of La Sede remained unsurveyed.

Other Pineros acquired land without title, either through cash purchase or barter. Still others simply squatted on state lands, a practice sanctioned by community recognition of rights to unclaimed land through use. Such land was theoretically the property of the state but in remote areas such as Los Pinos, state lands were regarded as the communal property of the village. These lands were administered by the community, in part by a village council which distributed parcels to those in need, and in part simply through custom. State lands were an important ingredient in the resource base of Pineros. Custom, for instance, entitled Pineros to communal use of La Loma, the vast pine forest directly to the north of the village, for foraging livestock, for gathering building materials, and for collecting firewood. Most lumbering activity took place in La Loma. But whether Pineros exploited the forests found on state lands or on terrenos comuneros, access to the seemingly unlimited supply of trees was free and unobstructed.

With strong demand, sufficient capital, and abundant and free forest resources, lumbering activity grew rapidly and Los Pinos grew along with it. For example, around 1915–20, when Los Pinos comprised no more than fifty households and approximately 300 people, there were over one dozen lumber mule trains totaling more than 350 animals. That is, although capital was expensive, trade was sufficiently lucrative to enable approximately one-quarter of the heads of households to become muleteers and establish themselves as middlemen. Attracted by this bustling prosperity, migrants from other parts of the Sierra settled in the community. As a consequence, by 1935, Los Pinos' population had tripled to 945 inhabitants (Censo Nacional de Población 1935).

The local lumber industry that developed over the next two decades rested on diverse social relations of production. Wage labor was employed by the largest lumber intermediaries to harvest the pines on their own large holdings or on state lands, and to man their mule trains. The mule trains of Don Pancho, for instance, reached one hundred and fifty to two hundred animals and required crews of a dozen men or more, as well as overseers. But although wage labor was an important ingredient in the organization of lumbering, the majority of Pineros were engaged in simple commodity production. This production relied entirely upon the unpaid labor of household members and others to produce for a common subsistence fund rather than to make profits for investment to generate still more profits. As noted above, capital requirements were low and tools were simple. Since the handsaw, familiar from its use in house construction, required two people to operate, men joined in partnership *(sociedad)* to purchase their tools together on credit from the lumber intermediaries, as well as to operate the saw. Altogether, simple technological and organizational requirements and absence of exclusive control over essential resources facilitated the entry of independent partnerships into lumbering. At the same time they discouraged the development of a system of production based exclusively or predominantly on wage labor. By the same token, although Don Pancho and Don Sixto became the richest and most powerful men in Los Pinos, it was not possible for them to monopolize lumbering activity.

The Impact of the Local Lumber Industry on Pinero Social Structure

Specialization in lumbering and transportation helped diversify and enrich Pinero society and its economy in many ways. First and most important, profits from these activities were used to finance new productive ventures. Land, agriculture, and livestock were the preferred investments. But the wealthiest muleteers also explored new ways to invest their profits to generate still more profits. In 1920, for instance, Don Pancho purchased the first plow in Los Pinos—only twenty years after the first plows appeared in Santiago (Hoetink 1982:5), and much earlier than in many other rural areas of the republic (cf. Werge 1975). Using wage labor, Don Pancho not only cultivated large fields of food crops, but for the first time began commercial cultivation of sugar cane and sisal. He built a *trapiche* to process the cane and by 1930 was supplying the entire community with his coarse muscovado sugar. To fill the local need for sisal rope, which was used to secure the pine boards and logs to the pack animals, Don Pancho also introduced hand-operated decorticating devices. From the spiny leaves of the sisal grown in Don Pancho's fields, workers extracted the fibers which, dried and combed, they later twisted into rope.

A second outlet for lumbering and mule-train profits was found in commercial activity. Around 1920, the wealthiest muleteers opened the first stores in the sección. Putting to use the comparative advantage conferred by their large mule trains, they purchased bulk quantities of manufactured goods from wholesalers in Navarrete, Mao, Santiago, and other towns of the north to which they transported lumber. On their return trips, they carried these goods back to Los Pinos to sell in their stores, which were run by a son or daughter. Because of Los Pinos' favorable location at the nexus of diverse resource areas, which by this time were enmeshed in a network of trade, these stores soon helped fill the wholesale and retail needs of the entire sección. The serones of Monción, the coffee, hardwoods, and basic foodstuffs of Sierra Adentro, not to mention the pines of the entire sección—all flowed through Los Pinos, and all left a portion of their value in the hands of its intermediaries and shopkeepers.

A third spin-off of Los Pinos' specialization in lumber and transportation was an increased demand for locally crafted items used on the mule trains. Women made saddles, saddle bags, stirrups, saddle blankets, and so on, from such local materials as guano, sisal, plantain leaves, and hides. The production of these items by women represented a secondary but nonetheless important source of employment and cash for many Pinero households (Pérez 1972:224–225). The growing significance of nonagricultural activities—lumbering, crafts, transportation, and commerce—can be seen in the fact that basic foodstuffs were no longer cultivated in sufficient quantity to meet local demand. Thus, by 1930, the community's hinterlands had begun to specialize in the production of food crops, a portion of which was marketed in Los Pinos.

A final result was the spread of cultivated and improved pasture in Los Pinos. The pressing demand for fodder created by the large number of pack animals in the community stimulated the early introduction of improved high-yielding pasture grasses (e.g., yerba guinea). In addition, some households began to "rent" their fields to muleteers, a practice that provided another new source of cash.

Economic growth fueled by the lumber industry and its ramifications indisputably set in motion processes of social and economic differentiation where approximate equality had previously been the norm. Yet at the same time, other factors mitigated to a certain extent the development of extreme differentials in the way Pineros lived.

As a result of their links to Santiago-based merchants, Don Pancho and Don Sixto were in a favorable position to accumulate profit from the local development of productive forces. By 1930, they had purchased much of the land most suitable for agriculture and especially for plow cultivation. However, the agricultural frontier was still far from exhausted, particularly to the south where rainfall was more abundant and reliable. Households without land, or with insufficient land in forest to clear, petitioned the committee of villagers in charge of distributing usufruct rights to communal lands. Thus, through their access to such land, even the poorest households were able to meet the bulk of their subsistence requirements. And although the market increasingly penetrated Los Pinos, the resulting need for cash was met through a variety of means. Men worked for wages in lumber, in agriculture, in the sugar trapiche, on mule trains and on the decorticating machines. Many sold pine logs to the Turks' mills and boards to the muleteer-middlemen. Women earned cash by panning gold and by baking manioc bread. They also manufactured and sold items needed on the mule trains. A few women were specialists in weaving hats and making shoes of cloth and animal hides.

Standards of living among the socioeconomic strata of Los Pinos differed in important ways, yet these differences do not appear to have been drastic. Housing, diet, and education, to take only a few important examples, varied within narrower limits than was to be the case after 1935 or so. True, the richest muleteers had brightly painted Santiago-style houses adorned with gingerbread trim. But because building materials were abundant, locally produced, and readily available, most houses in the community were large, airy wooden structures (an indication of their roominess is that when their owners died in the 1950s and 1960s, the heirs often built two or three smaller houses with the original lumber). In the words of one Pinero, rice was "food for the rich" ("comida de los ricos"), but meat was a staple of everyone's diet. The forest and interspersed savannahs of La Loma provided abundant communal foraging areas which supported Los Pinos' large numbers of cattle, pigs, and goats. Animals were simply branded or ear-notched and left to forage unattended. Older respondents concur that Los Pinos' animal population was much larger before about 1935 and that it was common practice for households to butcher a pig every week and one cow each month (for similar reports from a community in the southern Central Mountains, see Werge 1975). Nor does the education of children appear to have varied greatly among households. By 1930, there was a school with three grades in the village. But even the richest muleteers' children helped in the fields and on the mule trains from an early age, and only a few reached the third grade.

THE TRUJILLATO, 1930–1961

In 1930, Rafael Trujillo used his power base in the national guard established during the U.S. military occupation to help install himself in the presidency. Over the next thirty years, Trujillo pursued policies that resulted in rapid economic growth and enormous social change, touching nearly every aspect of national life. As noted in chapter 1, he created a manufacturing sector which processed local raw materials to supply the internal market and reduce imports. Trujillo's concentration of landholdings and his investments in agriculture accelerated the transformation of the agrarian sector. And, following the standards of quality set by U.S. projects begun during the occupation, Trujillo's road-building program tripled mileage and led to the construction of dozens of new bridges (Bell 1981). Above all, the successful purusit of these policies was made possible by Trujillo's tight control over the state apparatus, underwritten by substantial investment in the military (Cassá 1982).

Remote areas such as Los Pinos experienced not only the shock waves of these national transformations, but frequently Trujillo's direct intervention as well. Among the many projects Trujillo introduced, the focus in the following sections is on three which had the greatest impact on the structure of Pinero life: the monopolization of the lumber industry, the development of infrastructure, and the introduction of peanut cultivation. As occurred elsewhere in the republic, these projects had profound consequences for the life of the community during the Trujillato and long after, consequences that more than anything else helped create the conditions that led many Pineros to see international labor migration as an attractive option after 1961.

The Trujillato I: Disenfranchisement and Monopoly

From the beginning, Trujillo directed considerable attention to the western Sierra. Early in his regime, he built a villa in La Sede, "La Mansión," which he visited often. Trujillo paid his first visit to Los Pinos shortly after assuming the presidency, and he maintained personal contact with prominent Pineros throughout his life. As part of his "honeycomb of power" Trujillo made it a practice to incorporate "respectable figures" into his network whenever possible (Crassweller

1966). By incorporating the traditional elite, at least in part, and granting them some concessions, he was assured of their loyalty and gained the appearance of legitimacy that he needed (Cassá 1982:449– 450). Of course, in addition to cooptation, the honeycomb of power was also supported by force and repression.

When Trujillo first arrived in Los Pinos in the early 1930s, mule-teer-middleman Don Pancho lodged and lavishly entertained him and his retinue. Don Pancho subsequently became "Trujillo's man" in Los Pinos, the only one in the sección, for example, permitted to carry a revolver, a sign of great prestige and status. A daughter of Don Pancho explained to me on one of her rare visits from the United States that Trujillo "had offered Pancho whatever he needed, because Trujillo knew he was a neutral man who was not going to betray him." Soon after this first visit, Trujillo appointed Don Pancho's son-in-law as *alcalde*, or mayor, of the entire sección. During the Trujillato, the al-calde was Trujillo's direct representative at the local level, a figure of authority, influence, and coercion. Don Pancho's son-in-law was Los Pinos' alcalde for the next thirty years. During that time, he ac-quired a reputation as a *calié*, an overbearing strongman, who used his position to seize the land and unpaid labor of others and to place his children in desirable jobs. Don Sixto was also a loyal supporter of Trujillo who duly benefited from his relationship with the dictator. Don Pancho, his son-in-law, and Don Sixto thus emerged as impor-tant mediators between the new state institutions and the local population.

Trujillo's presence in the western Sierra was felt not only directly through his visits and the relations he established with prominent Serranos, but indirectly as well, through his proxies. To deflect at least partially the popular resentment caused by his activities, Trujillo often preferred to conduct business through these trusted men, *hombres de confianza*, who represented his interests under the guise of their own (Cassá 1980:263; 1982:449). This was another tactic to achieve a degree of legitimation, and also to obfuscate the degree to which wealth was becoming concentrated in his hands. His principal rep-resentative in the western Sierra was Santos Casagrande, a Sierra-born captain in the army. In time, Casagrande forged close personal and patronage ties in Los Pinos. He became the ritual coparent (com-padre) of the richest muleteers and merchants and took Don Pancho's son's widow as his concubine. Casagrande's sister was appointed the first permanent schoolmistress in Los Pinos, a position of influence which she held for thirty years.

Through Casagrande's first-hand reports, and no doubt through his own observations, Trujillo was attracted to Los Pinos' lumber industry. Historians of this period have often noted that once Trujillo observed the economic advantages of an activity, he moved swiftly to gain control, maximizing profitability both by eliminating competitors and by establishing a monopoly over resources and technology (Crassweller 1966; cf. Cassá 1980:263). His actions in Los Pinos certainly conformed to this pattern. In order to take over lumbering effectively, Trujillo first gained complete control over forest resources. It will be recalled that because of its isolation Los Pinos, like much of the western Sierra, had escaped enforcement of the Land Act of 1920. Thus, when Trujillo came to power in 1930, its traditional systems of land tenure were still intact. In the mid-1930s, under the pretext of executing a cadastral survey of the sección, Trujillo's proxy Santos Casagrande declared all land titles invalid and all unclaimed lands property of the state. As Bell (1981) has noted, "[t]he distinction between state property and the personal property of Trujillo . . . was nothing if not blurred" (p. 348). Pineros were offered a choice: either sell the old titles now declared worthless to Casagrande, or have these revalidated and notarized by the land tribunal in Santiago. Revalidation, however, was expensive, and only the wealthiest families could afford it. Those without titles and those few who dared to refuse to sell their titles at the low prices that were offered had their land confiscated. However, although all titles were declared invalid, only those covered with forest were confiscated. Casagrande's patronage permitted Don Pancho and Don Sixto to retain their holdings practically intact, but nearly every household in Los Pinos lost some part of their land "to Santos." Once these forests passed into his control, Trujillo prohibited the unauthorized felling of trees; violators were imprisoned.

The significance of the loss of the community's pine lands and the right to cut trees cannot be overstated. In the municipio as a whole, Trujillo bought or expropriated a total of 374,431 tareas, or 58 percent of the total surface area; nearly all of this land was covered with pine forest (Instituto Agrario Dominicano 1963; cf. Gomez 1979:102). (Characteristically, all of these lands were registered in the name of a proxy). Trujillo's expropriations in Los Pinos reduced the community's land base by at least one-third, creating demographic pressure on remaining resources almost overnight. With the loss of rights to La Loma and other unclaimed lands, Los Pinos lost its immediate agricultural frontier, its principal supply of fuel and building materials, and its communal grazing site. Even more important at that time, however, was the loss of the rights—on all lands—to the trees themselves, which were the principal source of cash income for nearly all sectors of the community. By prohibiting the unauthorized cutting of trees, Trujillo had with one stroke eliminated competition from the independent partnerships and freed their labor for work for him on his newly created lumber *latifundio*.

Trujillo then turned his attention and resources to rationalizing lumber production. By the late 1930s, he had mechanized, first, milling and, soon thereafter, transportation. The diesel-powered sawmill installed in La Loma was now the center of lumbering activity in Los Pinos. To facilitate the mechanization of transportation, Trujillo undertook an ambitious road-building program. For the first time, all-weather roads linked Los Pinos with La Sede in the east and Monción to the west. Concrete bridges were built over the major rivers, eliminating delays caused by floods during the rainy season. The new roads even penetrated to some extent the dense forests of Sierra Adentro, connecting Los Pinos with this important lumber- and coffee-producing area.

These infrastructural improvements made possible the arrival of the first trucks and tractors to Los Pinos in 1939. Although trees continued to be felled by ax, now tractors as well as oxen hauled the logs to the milling site, where the diesel-powered saw processed the logs into boards. Boards were loaded onto trucks that had been driven directly to the milling sites in the forest and which then transported the boards to Santiago to be dried and sanded.

In the early 1940s, Trujillo sold the mill in Los Pinos to his administrator, a member of the emerging national industrial bourgeoisie closely tied to and dependent upon Trujillo. But although he gave up the mill, Trujillo retained ownership of the forests, collecting a fee for every pine cut. Trujillo characteristically gave his attention and, at that point in time, his not unlimited resources to those enterprises that afforded the highest return to capital. When compared to the new import-substitution industries he was beginning to establish as monopolies in the urban areas, the Sierran lumber industry did not meet this requirement. Trujillo therefore sold his mill to his trusted client, who continued the unabated exploitation of the pine forests of the region for the next two decades.

The Consequences of Trujillo's Policies on Los Pinos: The Ecological Impact. The ecological impact of mechanized lumbering was deep and pervasive. Mechanization made possible a scale of milling operation previously unknown in the region. Within five years of the sale of the mill, the largest trees in the Loma had all been cut down. The milling activity moved farther south into Sierra Adentro, carrying with it machines and some—the more privileged—Pinero workers. The damage done to the ecosystem of La Loma, however, remained with the community. With the forest canopy gone, many streams and arroyos dried up completely, while others flowed only during the rainy season. These streams had been the principal sources of potable water for Los Pinos; with their dessication, drinking water now had to be hauled from the nearest clear-running river, five kilometers from Los Pinos. A five-hour round trip by burro, this task fell to young boys, who spent and still spend the better part of each morning at this chore.

But the extension of milling activities into Sierra Adentro was to have even more profound ecological effects. Most of the principal river systems of the Sierra, and many of the nation's most important rivers, have their headwaters in that part of the Central Mountains. Mechanized lumbering also diminished the forest canopy of this region, profoundly altering the volume and regime of larger rivers. This situation was further aggravated by the agricultural activities of farmers, many of whom were attracted to the area by the building of new roads and by the extension of the lumber industry. Severe flooding in the rainy season began to alternate with the near disappearance of rivers during the driest months. The Los Pinos River, on the banks of which Los Pinos was founded, became an unreliable source of water for the community. Crops with high moisture requirements, such as onions, tomatoes, garlic, and watercress, could no longer be cultivated in the subsistence gardens. Some had to be imported into the region; others disappeared entirely from the local diet (cf. Secretaria de Agricultura 1978).

Alarmed by the adverse effects of lumbering and slash-and-burn agriculture on the nation's river regimes, Trujillo began to evict peasants from Sierra Adentro in the early 1950s and prohibited further colonization of the area. In 1956, he created the J. Bermúdez National Park, encompassing 77,972 hectares of land in Sierra Adentro, as a government-administered reserve in which all agricultural and lumbering activities were proscribed.

Trujillo's militant conservationism with regard to the region was rooted in his concern that the water supply to the fertile agricultural land of the Cibao Valley be protected. To stop further destruction of rivers and accelerated siltation of irrigation canals, Trujillo ordered the population of Sierra Adentro forcibly removed from their holdings. Some of the evicted peasants were relocated to planned colonization settlements *(colonias)* near the Haitian border, but many simply moved onto unclaimed lands on the southern fringes of the sección of Los Pinos. Thus, not only was Sierra Adentro no longer available to Pinero peasants, but an important agricultural reserve near the community was forfeited to the Serrano squatters. By 1960, with the double loss of La Loma and Sierra Adentro, Pinero agriculturalists were caught in a vise: there was no longer any significant amount of unclaimed land to be found anywhere in the sección.

The Impact of the Road Building Program on the Local Economy. The new system of roads and bridges and the changes in the technology of transportation had devastating consequences for the muleteers and a profound impact on the nature of local production and consumption in general. During the initial phase of the Trujillo lumber mills, before the roads were completed, Pinero muleteers had benefited from the increase in the size of milling operations, which generated a greater volume of lumber to transport, although they were simultaneously deprived of their right to buy pine boards. Don Sixto and Don Pancho further profited from their patronage ties with Casagrande and Trujillo by gaining permission to fell and process precious hardwoods on their extensive holdings left untouched by the survey. However, within five years, few hardwoods were left. By 1940, the first trucks had arrived and, overnight, the mule trains became obsolete. Once a major asset, pack animals now became liabilities as the new trucks replaced them in every task except hauling water for domestic purposes.

A prominent Sierran muleteer's opinion of these economic transformations was recorded by the Dominican geographer Juan B. Pérez on his trip through the region in the 1940s (Pérez 1972). In his words:

> The highways are doing us in, because, before the highways, those of us who had mule trains made money and helped others make money. Among those we helped were, first, the breeders of pack animals, when the need arose to replace animals; second, those who rented out their pastures; third, the makers of saddles; fourth, the makers of stirrups; fifth, those who weave saddlebags; sixth, the makers of sisal rope; seventh, all those on the outskirts of towns who took charge of keeping the mule-trains overnight; eighth, the muleteers themselves; ninth, the veterinarians, and so on. But today all the money goes to the pockets of the manufacturers of cars and trucks and the owners of petroleum wells, that is, to the foreigners. (pp. 224–225; my translation)

Although this muleteer's claims of helping his fellows are perhaps somewhat self-serving, his lament expresses the real, albeit gradual, downward mobility experienced by the members of his class. Unable to buy and sell lumber, their mule trains outcompeted by the new trucks, the muleteers began a long slide into social and economic decline. Trujillo's patronage offset this process to a certain extent for the two big men of Los Pinos, but ultimately they too fell nearly as far as the less well connected Pineros.

While some handicrafts, such as those enumerated by this muleteer, were rendered obsolete by the new trucks, others were eliminated by the unprecedented flow into the community of new manufactured goods. Outcompeted, many local products began to disappear. For example, within a decade or so after the first truck arrived in Los Pinos, muscovado sugar was no longer produced in the local trapiche and shoes and hats were no longer made by Pinero women. Sisal was uprooted and wheat bread began to be favored over manioc bread. Processed foods such as canned tomato paste and chocolate replaced the use of annatto *(Bija orellana)* and cacao, which were no longer cultivated in subsistence gardens. The new products were manufactured by national industries, nearly all of which were Trujillo monopolies. By facilitating the flow of manufactured goods that displaced locally produced items, Trujillo's road-building project reinforced his growing control over even remote markets such as Los Pinos.

Trujillato II: The Import-Substitution Project and Los Pinos

If the first fifteen years of Trujillo's regime were marked by the accumulation of capital through expropriation and "monopoly by decree," the next fifteen years saw the investment of that capital in the development of industry.[3] Favorable prices and increased demand for Dominican exports in the immediate postwar period helped promote Trujillo's industrialization project, but a major impetus originated in internal conditions, especially the high degree of political and economic control gained over domestic production and consumption. Using primarily indigenous materials and producing for the internal market, this type of investment was entirely new in the history of the Dominican Republic. While all of the new factories were located in

3. This is not to say, of course, that expropriations and primitive accumulation in general ceased; they did not, but rather continued to provide capital for the industrial sector (cf. Gomez 1979:99).

the urban centers, most of them in the capital, rural areas were incorporated into the industrialization process as specialized producers of cheap raw materials and consumers of the new commodities.

One of the new consumer products manufactured by Trujillo was peanut oil. Trujillo was concerned to find a substitute for the traditional edible oils: olive oil, which was imported, and pork lard. Trujillo selected as the most suitable source of oil the Valencia peanut, although it was not native to the republic. Needless to say, a national vegetable oil monopoly resulted: not only was all production of peanut oil in Trujillo's hands, but no other oil competed with it commercially. Trujillo thus had a strong interest in disseminating the new crop throughout the republic.

Peanuts were introduced to Los Pinos in 1949, and within a few years men throughout the sección had avidly adopted the new crop. Several factors led Pinero men to accept peanut cultivation rapidly and enthusiastically. In the first place, Trujillo took care with the manner of introducing the cultivate. Priests, who commanded the respect and trust of many Dominicans, were sometimes used as extension agents for his new projects; the Catholic Church was closely allied with Trujillo until the last few years of his regime (Crassweller 1966). Thus, it was a priest from La Sede who first brought the peanut to Los Pinos and encouraged its cultivation, cajoling farmers from the pulpit, planting a demonstration plot, and so on (Internal Records of the Sociedad Industrial Dominicana). Second, the introduction of peanuts coincided with several circumstances that were driving Pineros to rely increasingly on agriculture for their livelihood. By the early 1950s, local forest resources had been decimated, and milling activity had declined considerably. With diminished opportunities for employment in the mills, and with most handicraft industries destroyed, many Pinero men were turning to the land, the only resource still more or less under their control. A third factor had to do with the nature of the cultivate itself. Permitting the farmer to plant two crops a year, its sixty-day growing cycle still left enough time during the remaining six months for a brief grass fallow, or cultivation of subsistence crops. Finally, although peanuts could be sold only to Trujillo's agents at a fixed low price, producing for a market captive to his monopoly guaranteed demand and stable prices; this contrasted favorably with the volatile price fluctuations of traditional crops such as tobacco.

Production expanded rapidly in the 1950s. In 1954, a subagency of Trujillo's peanut oil company was established in Los Pinos to receive the 568,100 pounds of peanuts harvested in the sección that year. The subagency also distributed inputs, such as improved seed, fertilizer, and pesticides on credit, which was repaid at harvest time with a portion of the crop. By 1965, production increased 120 percent to 1,249,700 pounds.

In the face of low prices, high labor demands were the principal brake on peanut cultivation by cash-poor farmers. This obstacle was overcome through the elaboration and intensification of the traditional system of labor exchange. Called variously *junta, convide,* or *burricá,* labor exchanges of various kinds were an important means available to Pinero households for gaining access to additional labor without cash. These juntas occurred both between established partners and among large groups of men or women who rotated labor parties from one household to another. Juntas were used to complete a variety of agricultural and nonagricultural tasks, including among the latter house building, roof thatching, and fence raising. Women also engaged in labor exchanges, to weave serones, bake manioc bread, or perform the household chores of a sick neighbor. Although most juntas were strictly egalitarian, with like quantities of services exchanged between partners who tended to be linked by other ties as well, some were hierarchical and exploitative in nature. When Don Pancho and Don Sixto sent invitations to a junta, for instance, Pineros went not only to feast on the steer that would be butchered but also to honor the ties of patronage that bound them. In the era of Trujillo, when the alcalde organized juntas for road construction and other tasks, everyone participated out of fear of reprisals.

Beginning in the early 1950s, in response to the introduction of peanuts, the institution of the junta underwent a significant change. To meet the intensive labor requirements of this crop juntas became much larger, often bringing together fifty or more men. At the same time, they became better organized and more highly specialized. In the face of severe limitations on cash and credit, the mutual assistance provided by the juntas became critical to the production of a labor-intensive crop like peanuts. In the words of one former Pinero peanut farmer, "The peanut helped the poor, and the poor helped each other."

One task not left to the juntas was harvesting. Timing of the harvest was of crucial importance, as farmers could not afford to wait too long or the rains might rot the peanuts. In this case, labor costs were kept down by hiring women to uproot the peanuts and pack them in plastic sacks supplied by the local peanut agency. All of the women who worked in the harvest were from semiproletarian or landless households, and most were assisted by their children. Thus harvesting, the only regular large-scale use of waged labor in peanut production, became women's work. It is worth noting that, unlike the men who received a day wage, women harvesters were paid a piece-rate by the sack. The most difficult stoop labor, harvesting also became the most poorly remunerated. (And it has remained so: over the last decade men's wages have more than tripled, while the piece rates paid to women harvesters only doubled—the same rate of increase as in the cost of renting burros to haul the harvest; see table 5.4).

But it was not only the poorer Pineros who relied on the juntas. The most prominent merchants also took advantage of them to cultivate their large fields. Occupied full-time in their shops, they relegated crop cultivation to a close relative or other individual of confianza who managed their fields in exchange for a portion of the harvest. Also a professional plower, a *bueyero*, this man plowed the merchant's fields, organized the juntas, and hired the additional wage labor needed to produce and harvest the crop. The unpaid labor donated to merchants' juntas was not reciprocated, however. Patronage ties with these merchants induced Pinero men who depended on credit to cover household needs to flock to them. The following statement of one smallholder-client reveals the moral tincture with which these ties were colored: "Don Martín gave a lot of food at his juntas, but it wasn't because of the food that I went. Rather, it was because of friendship and gratitude" ("por amistad y por agradecimiento").

For a brief period lasting little more than a decade and a half, then, peanut cultivation provided an important source of cash to many peasant households. Furthermore, as Los Pinos was the site of the subagency to which all farmers had to come to get their inputs and credit and bring their harvest, merchants and shopkeepers benefited as well. One merchant compared the biannual peanut harvest to a fiesta, with trucks and people from the entire sección crowding the main street. Sales reached into the tens of thousands of pesos as farmers liquidated their debts and made purchases which they had delayed until the harvest. Other spin-offs of the peanut harvest included increased opportunities for seasonal wage labor, loading peanuts, and driving trucks to the Santo Domingo refinery. A few women took advantage of the increased circulation of people and cash to set up *fondas*, or stands, and sell prepared food to those who came to town to deliver their crop.

The new boom was short-lived, however. At the low prices received, to cultivate enough peanuts to fill the growing cash needs of their households, Pinero farmers literally "mined the soil" and in doing so, undermined their own ability to continue production. Double-cropping on the steep slopes of Los Pinos greatly accelerated the rate of erosion. Moreover, peanuts, as a pinero farmer stressed, "need the soil to move a great deal." That is, although constitutionally well suited to the crop, the sandy loams of Los Pinos had to be loosened further to permit the sprouting and filling of peanut pods. Deep plowing, weeding, and hoeing all disturbed the thin topsoil and severely damaged soil stability. This also helped to promote erosion and ultimately to destroy fields. With none of the profits extracted from peanut cultivation invested locally in measures to increase the productivity of land or labor, the intensive use of limited and fragile land resources eventually led most Pinero farmers to abandon production entirely, as will be seen in chapter 5.

The Impact of the Trujillato on Pinero Economy and Social Structure

No part of Pinero society was untouched by the profound economic and ecological transformations described in the preceding sections. In this section, I examine the effects of these changes on the principal classes and class segments which comprised Los Pinos during the Trujillato: muleteer-middlemen, merchant-usurers, wage workers in the lumber mill, and the agriculturalists with large, middle-sized, and small landholdings. It must be noted that, as in other parts of the republic and the Caribbean in general, most households, including some of the more privileged, relied (and continue to rely) on a multiplicity of income-generating activities to meet subsistence and savings needs (cf. Comitas 1973). The focus here is specifically on the impact of the Trujillato on these activities and on the household's ability to reproduce itself, that is, the ability to ensure for its progeny a similar or comparable position in the system of production and the social structure.

Indisputably the most powerful and prominent individuals before the Trujillato, the muleteer-middlemen entered a long period of social and economic decline after 1940. Clearly, the biggest blow was the annihilation of local control over lumbering and the competition from the new means of transportation. Hegemonic control over local production passed from these middlemen to the Dominican state, as mediated by proxies such as Casagrande and other agents. This shift in the locus of control all but abolished the muleteer's most important means of extracting profit from poorer Pineros. By the mid-1940s, muleteers had little choice but to turn to agriculture and livestock breeding for their livelihood. This they were well prepared to do, for by Los Pinos' standards, their landholdings were huge: Don Sixto, for example, had over 2,000 tareas of land registered with the land tribunal of Santiago and more land unregistered. The households of these muleteers were also very large and provided a supply of unpaid labor supplemented by wage workers and the occasional junta. Typically, they included a dozen children or more, often including "adopted" children *(hijos de crianza);* worker-retainers *(peones de la casa)* who lived within the household compound, ate with the family, and so on; and assorted poor relatives and neighbors who dropped by for meals and charity. Don Sixto had also established a second household in Los Pinos, a practice that occurred more or less frequently among men of some means. He supported his second spouse and granted recognition to the child produced by their union, which according to Dominican custom and law meant that he assumed responsibility for him and gave him a claim to his estate (see Walker 1972:90).

However, to meet their high household consumption expenses, muleteers were forced from time to time to sell parcels of their land. Concurrently, as alternatives to farming dwindled during the Trujillato, the children of these muleteers also turned to the family land to support their households. When sons married, fathers were obliged by tradition to provide them with subsistence plots. Moreover, at the death of a parent, equal amounts of remaining lands were distributed to all legitimate offspring. With little agricultural reserve left after Trujillo's expropriations, such practices resulted in fragmentation of holdings for all Pinero landowners. Thus, returning to the case of Don Sixto, when he died in the 1950s, his thirteen children each received about 200 tareas of land, putting them in the middle ranks of farmers. His second spouse also received the house he had built for her and a smaller share of land. Without the acquisition of new lands, Don Sixto's grandchildren faced the prospect of near-landlessness and semiproletarianization. Some muleteers were able to invest in shops which initially were managed, and later owned, by a son or by a daughter and her husband. These individuals were able to resist the spiral of downward social mobility and status deprivation which threatened their siblings. In general, however, the custom of partible inheritance, and to a lesser extent the establishment of multiple households by some men, worked as powerful leveling mechanisms in the face of a limited land frontier.

While the old muleteers were on the decline, a new elite was emerging to replace them both socially and economically. This new elite was composed of the richest merchants in Los Pinos. These merchants were able to profit from the increased commodification of the local economy and also from the continued isolation of the bulk of the population, which allowed them to fix prices at levels considerably higher than in the major cities. By the early 1950s a number of shopkeepers had migrated to the village from other parts of the Sierra. The installation of the mechanized mills, the fevered construction of roads, bridges, and housing for mill and road personnel, the influx of specialized workers from other areas of the Sierra, and the resulting increased volume and velocity of the local cash flow also increased the attractiveness of the village, which was becoming the bustling commercial center of the sección and beyond. Some of these merchant-entrepreneurs invested their commercial profits in trucks driven by their sons. At first, they hauled lumber for the mills; later they transported the peanut crop to the refineries in Santo Domingo. In each case they returned with trucks loaded with merchandise for their shops. These merchants prospered in Los Pinos, but by and large, their goal was to leave the community as soon as they were able to accumulate sufficient profit to establish themselves in Santiago or another city of the north.

Three of the largest and most prosperous shopkeepers, each prominently situated on a corner of Los Pinos' principal intersection, remained in the community. The largest shop was owned by a migrant from another Sierran town. The other two were owned by offspring of Don Pancho and Don Sixto. Replacing in time the old muleteers in wealth and connections, these three merchants, honored now with the title *Don* and *Doña*, emerged as the new local elite. Typically, they were usurers as well, using the profits from their stores as loan capital. Commercial profits were also invested in land, cash crop agriculture, and cattle. By 1961, these merchants had become the largest landowners in Los Pinos, eclipsing the old muleteers and their offspring. Besides these traditional outlets for profits, the merchants, for the first time in the community's experience, also invested in urban property and in the higher education of their children. For their oldest offspring, this meant secondary school and perhaps "business academy" for a daughter; nearly all of their younger children attended university.

Although on good terms with Trujillo's representatives in the region, these new merchants also forged close ties with the commercial-usurial bourgeoisie of Santiago. Largely because of the social, political, and economic centralization process set in motion by Trujillo's policies, Santiago became the most important city to the north. Simultaneously, links between Los Pinos and intermediate cities of the north, such as Mao, Navarrete, Puerto Plata, and Monte Cristi, once important in the days of decentralized lumbering, all but disappeared.

The new Pinero merchants were in a unique position to benefit from this shift in the focus of social and economic activity. Their business transactions with prominent importers, wholesalers, and other intermediaries in Santiago laid the foundation for forging multiplex bonds of confianza, friendship, and fictive coparenthood from which social, political, and economic advantage were derived. Known in the Dominican Republic as *enllave*, these connections with the Santiago eilite enabled Pinero merchants to glean speculative investment tips, place their university-educated younger children in prestigious and well-paying jobs, and acquire for their older children lucrative contracts for their trucking businesses and other commercial activities.

Mill employees formed the bulk of the more or less steadily employed wage-workers and represented another important class in Los Pinos. In addition to increasing the opportunities for wage labor— between 1935 and approximately 1950, no fewer than fifty Pineros were employed by the mills—mechanization of the lumber industry generated a multiplicity of tasks which greatly expanded the existing division of labor. Lumber production now encompassed four distinct work sites. Each had its own internal hierarchy of tasks and wages, as well as its own supervisor or foreman. In the pine forest *(loma)*, lumberjacks cut the pines and chopped them into pieces. Tractors and oxen hauled the pieces to a central collection area, the *batey*, where workers loaded them onto trucks. Truck drivers took the logs to the mill, where the milling cutter and his assistants operated the diesel-powered saw. In the *patio*, the area just outside the mill itself, workers sorted the boards into categories based on size and quality and loaded them onto trucks destined for the Santiago warehouses. In addition, road crews continuously cleared new trails to reach still unexploited stands of pines. At the apex of the entire milling chain of command in Los Pinos was an administrator who was closely allied to Trujillo. The administrator's office was also the site of the *bodega*, the company store which was managed by a trusted Pinero employee. Thus, where egalitarian partnerships formerly had scattered throughout the forest to fell and saw trees, there developed a hierarchy of tasks and specialized work sites. Each was overseen by a foreman, whose principal task was to speed up production, despite a workday that was already twelve hours long.

Foremen, together with the truck and tractor drivers, the bodega manager, and the office workers, were regarded as privileged individuals. Not only did they enjoy the confianza of the administrator, but they also earned superior wages. In the mid-1950s, for instance, when the average monthly salary in the Dominican Republic was DR$35.00 (Banco Central 1962), foremen earned DR$40.00. In contrast, the workers under their supervision received a daily wage of DR$.50, or approximately DR$12.00 when they could work a full month. In this regard, it is worth comparing the opinion of one former foreman, who said, "Although my salary wasn't a lot, we lived adequately on it," with the lament of a former lumberjack that "the sawmills carried off all us poor to misery." Thus, although all of these men were employed by the mill, there is evidence of what Ferguson (1987) has called a "crypto-class division" among these wage workers.

That the foremen and related workers were privileged is evident too from the fact that they were retained by the mill and moved along with it after nearby forests had been decimated and lumbering activity moved farther south. In contrast, the peones were more likely to be replaced in the new sites by local men.

As the good jobs were few, only a handful of the sons of the privileged workers also found comparable work in the mill. Others, as their labor was not essential to the household's subsistence, were able to attend school through the six or eight grades offered in Los Pinos by 1961. With the modernization taking place under Trujillo, higher educational qualifications were becoming important to the acquisition of jobs outside of agriculture. Therefore, for those who could afford it, securing an education for their children was increasingly desirable. By 1961, many of the offspring of the middle-level mill employees had become the first Pineros to find jobs as office workers, nurses, schoolteachers, and so on.

In contrast to the privileged mill employees, by the early 1950s most other Pineros were depending increasingly on agriculture for their livelihood. However, several factors undermined the ability of most farmers to maintain and reproduce their households. A few have already been noted in other contexts: expropriation of the agricultural frontier, demographic increase, partible inheritance, and erosion and soil destruction. Increasingly unequal terms of exchange between countryside and city were also of critical importance. In addition, the penetration of the market exacerbated the process of land fragmentation already underway. Beginning in the 1950s, evidence from plot histories suggests that the rate of land sales increased. Land was sold to cover a variety of expenses. Many households sold plots to pay for medical and related expenses. For example, in the mid-1950s—at a time when a cow sold for six pesos and the doctor in La Sede charged thirty pesos to visit a patient in Los Pinos—a single typhoid epidemic resulted in the sale of several hundred tareas of land in Los Pinos. The beneficiaries of these land sales were largely the ascending merchant elite, who waited to buy until necessity forced a farmer to sell at a low price. Significantly, all land purchases made by these merchants occurred between 1945 and 1961, that is, at a time when the rapid penetration of the market led to high profits for merchants and an increased need for cash on the part of peasants, while the price of land remained low and stable. Although threatening all Pineros, the progressive fragmentation of landholdings resulting from the combination of these factors posed the greatest menace to farmers with middle-sized and small holdings, since from the outset they were closer to the margin of subsistence.

The progressive fragmentation of plots in Los Pinos also obstructed the application of cultural knowledge that had helped farmers determine how best to use their fields. Because of its rugged topography, Los Pinos' agricultural land is located either on steep slopes (loma) or on plains *(llano)*. In recognition of this fact, Pinero farmers, like other Serranos (Werge 1975), dichotomously classify soils into either "hot" or "cold" categories. Hot soils are located on the slopes. They are literally hot, as rapid downslope drainage produces drier soils which absorb heat more rapidly. In addition, because the sloping hillsides erode more easily, more of the underlying rock matrix is exposed; its high quartz and feldspar content makes this matrix a good conductor of heat. As a consequence of these factors, more heat is retained by the slopes than by the less rocky plains below. With their greater soil depth and longer moisture retention, these plains are classified as cold.

Ideally, each type of land has a particular set of crops best suited to it. Crops with high moisture requirements, such as plaintains and sugar cane, should be planted in cold land. Sweet manioc and other root crops are considered suitable for hot slopes, where, if rains have been abundant, their tubers will have greater protection from rot. However, because of the increased fragmentation of plots in Los Pinos, this ideal planting protocol could not always be followed, and crops had to be sown on whatever land was available and adequately fallowed.

Another factor undermining the livelihood of all but the largest farmers was the successive elimination of a gamut of traditional ancillary economic activities which previously had helped supplement income derived from agriculture. Except for seron weaving, which by 1961 was performed exclusively by women and children, most artisanal activity had ceased. Another blow was Trujillo's devaluation of gold. Especially for women, placer mining had represented an important income supplement. Although some panning continued during the Trujillato, gold prices were kept very low, and activity was severely curtailed.

One final hardship of note was Trujillo's imposition of regressive taxation. Two taxes especially constituted a great burden for the cash-poor farmers. The first was the *cédula*, or national identification card, tax. Amounting to DR$7.50 per year, in the 1950s it was the equivalent of fifteen days of agricultural wage labor. (Better-off households usually sold livestock to meet the expense.) The second was a labor tax; under the direction of the alcalde of the sección, adult men were conscripted for two weeks of labor every year on Trujillo's infrastructural projects. Such corvée labor also helped build Trujillo's villa in La Sede and was used for many other projects in the republic (Cassá 1982:441). The largest landholders and merchants in Los Pinos inevitably managed to avoid filling this corvée, either through their enllave with the alcalde, or by sending a peon de la casa in their place. Poorer peasants, in contrast, had no choice but to donate their labor when called up by the alcalde, who, as Trujillo's direct representative at the local level, was not be refused (the resentment aroused toward the alcalde by these and other practices is reflected in the fact that immediately after Trujillo's assassination in 1961, the alcalde was forced into hiding).

For the largest landowners, the threat posed by the combination of these factors was not immediate. In general, households with the largest holdings were those that had been able to notarize the titles to their land during Casagrande's land survey. Descendants of the earliest settlers, they tended to be closely related by consanguineal bonds reinforced by intermarriage. Some also managed to obtain desirable jobs in the mills for themselves and for their sons, and their salaries helped to maintain their standard of living and retain their productive resources intact. For most of their children, on the other hand, downward mobility loomed imminent. The exception, of course, was the merchant elite; merchant's children, as noted above, were not involved in agriculture.

During this period, there were relatively few truly landless people in Los Pinos. In general, the landless had come from other rural areas to live in Los Pinos. As late as the national centenary of 1944–a date easily remembered by older Pineros because it was the hundredth anniversary of the republic's independence from Haiti—respondents claim that no more than three households were without control of at least some land. Indeed, landlessness appears to have been rare until after the mid-1950s. However, a growing number of Pineros had to rely on progressively smaller plots. To maintain their households, smallholding farmers employed two principal strategies.[4] Many became semiproletarians, combining subsistence and cash crop farming with wage labor. Important in this strategy was agricultural day labor performed for farmers with large and middle-sized holdings. The expanded junta system provided the bulk of the labor for peanut cultivation. Nevertheless, in tasks in which speed and timing were crucial, opportunities for wage labor were relatively plentiful. Those who could afford it employed men to plant and women and children to harvest crops at the optimal times. During the course of the year, poorer households met a part of their consumption needs by accumulating debts with specific shopkeepers. With the combined wages earned by all household members in the peanut fields, these debts were liquidated biannually.

The other important strategy that poorer farmers with small landholdings used to meet household subsistence needs was the securing of usufruct rights to plots on the holdings of the largest landowners. Already close to the margin of subsistence, smallholding households were cyclically launched into de facto landlessness while their land was left to fallow. To survive during the three to five years necessary to regain minimal fertility of their plots, these farmers acquired usufruct rights to land through a variety of arrangements, including sharecropping (nearly always on a one-half basis), renting, and "borrowing" land. In the last arrangement, a plot was "loaned" to a cultivator under the condition that at the end of one or two seasons the land be left sown with high-yielding pasture grass. Large tracts of land belonging to the merchant elite and other large landowners were gradually cleared and improved using this method of in-kind rent paid by poorer farmers. Once improved, however, pasture land was no longer available for cultivation by poor farmers. Eventually, land to sharecrop or "borrow" became exceedingly difficult to find.

Because the pooled labor of all household members was necessary to meet the family's subsistence needs and growing cash needs, the children of the landless and near-landless, as well as those of many farmers with middle-sized and large holdings, were productively occupied from an early age. Sons worked at agricultural tasks, while young girls helped their mothers with the peanut harvest and with

4. Roughly, smallholders are those with fewer than 80 tareas, the amount estimated by the Ministry of Agriculture (Secretaria de Estado de Agricultura 1978) to be the minimum required to provide the subsistence needs of an average household.

seron weaving. As a result, few of these children attended school beyond the third grade. As adults, they also performed agricultural wage labor, and when the informal sector of the economy began to grow in the 1960s, some became lottery venders, petty traders, and domestic servants.

The Trujillato was a period of rapid social change and economic development for the sección of Los Pinos. The economic base, if not the social status and prestige, of the largest muleteer-middlemen was irrevocably undermined. Trujillo's total control over a transformed and modernized lumber industry abruptly eliminated their role as intermediaries between the simple commodity producers of the western Sierra and the usurial-commercial capitalists of the burgeoning urban centers of the northern republic. Construction of roads and bridges dealt the death blow to this group, as trucks replaced the mule trains. After 1945, the former muleteers turned to the land, but low productivity in combination with an increased need for cash prevented them from maintaining their economic position. Economic decline eventually forced this group to disinvest in their assets to meet the consumption needs of their large households and their customary obligations to poorer neighbors and kin. With the sale of land and cattle, their economic situation deteriorated still further.

Out of the increasing commodification of the rural economy and the simultaneous destruction of traditional systems of production and exchange, a new elite emerged. The richest merchants, who were at the same time wholesalers, usurers, and large landowners, ascended as the traditional rural economy was transformed. Profits extracted from their shops and usury and from the waged and unpaid labor of poorer Pineros were invested in land, livestock, commercial agriculture, and the higher education of their children, who typically left the community to complete their studies in Santiago or the capital, Santo Domingo.

The social structure of Los Pinos was further diversified as a result of the complex division of labor introduced by the mechanization of lumbering. A comparatively privileged stratum of mill employees developed from the ranks of the better-off peasantry. This group was freed from dependence on agriculture for a livelihood, although plots were still cultivated to supply a portion of household needs. Decreased concern with agriculture and the availability of cash from salaries diminished the need for the labor of children in the fields. As a consequence, this stratum was also able to invest in the education of their children, who later became schoolteachers, practical nurses, and other skilled and semiskilled workers.

Those households with land but without steady and secure access to salaried labor turned increasingly to agriculture. The introduction of peanut cultivation occurred at a crucial moment for this segment and presented them for a brief period with a new opportunity to generate cash to meet their households' subsistence needs. Nevertheless, population growth, in conjunction with a system of partible inheritance, greatly reduced average plot size. As a result of Trujillo's expropriations of land covered with virgin forest, the agricultural frontier for most farmers throughout the western Sierra was effectively eliminated. Under these conditions, the specific requirements of peanut cultivation proved disastrous to the soil resources of these farmers. Severe erosion of topsoil and soil destruction were the result. Moreover, the long-standing system of unequal exchange between agricultural producers and the urban commercial-usurial bourgeoisie intensified with the monopolistic and monopsonistic policies of Trujillo. At the same time, little or none of the profits extracted was invested in measures aimed at increasing the productivity of land or labor. Ultimately, the extraction of profit from peanut farmers reached a degree that led many to abandon the crop altogether, as we shall see in chapter 5.

The cumulative effect of these factors was increasing impoverishment for all but the most successful merchants and salaried mill workers and some of the largest landholders. Caught in a double squeeze between diminished access to productive resources and increased need for cash, many households were forced to sell land and livestock. Consumption of meat decreased as a result, and many Pineros claimed that an absolute decline in total caloric intake also occurred. As traditional building materials became completely commodified, the quality of housing declined as well. The renowned Serrano houses not only became much smaller and more crowded; they were also more likely to have floors of dirt rather than wood. In most cases, the children of poorer households were denied education because they were required to spend their time on agricultural tasks and ancillary cash-producing activities. Educational expenses, such as books and uniforms, were also prohibitive. Thus, when opportunities for skilled employment began to appear nationally and locally, this cohort of children was effectively excluded by their lack of formal education.

The historical processes that affected the evolution of classes and segments of classes in Los Pinos have been discussed in some detail here in order to provide the background for understanding the differential ability and inclination to emigrate from the community. The structural transformations described brought prosperity and social mobility for some, but the majority found themselves pushed to a critical margin. As one Pinero explained, "by 1961, Los Pinos had become a pressure cooker ready to explode." The highly structured explosion that occurred after 1961 is the subject of chapter 3.

CHAPTER 3

International Labor Migration from
Los Pinos, 1952–1981
Evolution of a Migrant Community

In less than three decades, hundreds of Pineros have migrated to the United States to live and work. How did such a massive flow of people from a remote and economically declining community become possible in such a short time? What are the essential features of this migration? This chapter suggests quantitative and ethnographic answers to these questions. It has three goals: first, to trace the historical development and organization of the migrant stream between 1952, the year the first Pinera left for the United States, and 1981; second, to provide a profile of the basic demographic and socioeconomic characteristics of Pineros who have migrated to the United States, distinguishing documented migrants from the undocumented, and comparing these with internal migrants; and third, to introduce the reader to the community of El Guano and to examine comparatively its quite distinct migration pattern. A detailed description of Los Pinos' migrant stream and comparison with El Guano also provide the background essential to analysis of the consequences of international migration for the local economy and society—the subject of the remaining chapters of the book.

THE EARLIEST MIGRATIONS: 1952–1961

Only a handful of women and men left Los Pinos for the United States during the 1950s. These early migrants were a socioeconomically selective group characterized by social networks that linked them to Trujillo. Their ties were either direct ones with the dictator and his proxies or indirect, through participation in Trujillo's own party, the Dominican Party (Partido Dominicano). With a few exceptions, they belonged to the economically privileged sectors of the community. Indeed, most were children and grandchildren of Don Pancho and Don Sixto.

For the descendants of the old muleteers, the prospect of migration provided an alternative to imminent downward mobility and status deprivation. As described chapter 2, the large landholdings of their parents and grandparents had been gradually reduced through division among offspring and through land sales. Moreover, although some of the muleteer's sons helped manage and farm these lands, few were strongly oriented toward the kind of own-account or "peasant" agriculture they would have been forced to undertake on the middle-sized parcels they received. At the same time, alternatives to agriculture that would have permitted them a standard of living and social status similar to that of their parents were few in the 1950s. These factors operated to a greater or lesser extent on all Pineros, but only the offspring of the muleteers were able during this period to rally the economic and social resources necessary for emigration.

Despite a decade of decline between 1940 and 1950, the most prominent muleteers still enjoyed the wide personal networks created during prosperous times. Their networks provided access to information, as well as to channels of social and economic patronage. Equally as important were their links with Trujillo's proxies and, in some cases, with Trujillo himself. Don Pancho's children, for example, were urged to migrate to New York by their godmother, a well-connected woman whom they frequently visited in Santiago and who had been a migrant herself. As a reference on their passport application, they were able to cite Trujillo, who had stayed in their father's house during his visits to the western Sierra. Their passports were issued without delay.

A few other early migrants foreshadowed what was to become a small but significant component of the stream after 1961. These migrants were from a household that, although also headed by a former muleteer, was neither rich nor socially prominent. Migration from this household was initiated by one of the first Pineras to move to Santiago and find work as a domestic. In Santiago, this energetic woman, criticized by some Pineros for being what they considered "mannish," became an active member of the Dominican Party. Through her enllave with the party she was able to obtain a passport in 1952 and became the first person from Los Pinos to migrate to New York.

Lacking social, political, and economic resources, the bulk of the Pinero population could not circumvent Trujillo's antimigration policy. But however small in number, the earliest migrants, all of whom settled in New York City, were nonetheless important for the immediate example they provided to future migrants. They demonstrated that migration was feasible. Once the next wave of Pineros began to arrive in New York, these pioneers provided many with a place to stay, with orientation, and with other forms of assistance. For example, Don Sixto's grandson, one of the first men to migrate from Los Pinos, found union jobs for over a dozen later arrivals in the large New York hotel in which he worked for fifteen years. Similarly, for many of her kin who migrated after her, the roomy upper Manhattan apartment of one of Don Pancho's daughters was the first place of residence.

ORGANIZING MIGRATION: 1961–1981

Historically, active recruitment by core employers and their agents played a critical role in initiating labor migration of the "old immigrants" from Europe, Mexican migration in the early decades of this century, and more recently migration from Puerto Rico (Piore 1979:19–24). In contrast, the new wave of immigration to the United States has been largely self-initiated and self-financed. The integration of peripheral nations such as the Dominican Republic into the world capitalist system has promoted the flow of information into even remote regions and has facilitated the movement of people across long distances. In general, this movement has taken place at no cost to core employers (Portes and Walton 1981:49).

From the start, migration from Los Pinos has followed this pattern. This self-organized migration has been made possible in part by the development of an extralegal system that is heavily underwrittten by the social ties of kinship, patronage, and friendship among villagers. This is a system in continuous adaptation to the ever-changing feasibilities of different means of entering the United States. This section explores how this self-organized migration from Los Pinos was made possible on a large scale and how the migration system as it has evolved has helped condition the specific composition of the international migrant stream.

After Trujillo's assassination in 1961, restrictions on population movement were revoked and the rate of international migration from Los Pinos rapidly accelerated (table 3.1). Despite the large numbers of people who left Los Pinos, not all who wanted to migrate to the United States were able to do so. Although restrictions by the Dominican government were lifted, other factors operated to con-

TABLE 3.1. International Migration from Los Pinos by Sex, 1952–1981

| | Sex | | | | | |
| | Male | | Female | | Total | |
Years	N	%	N	%	N	%
1952–1960	6	3.1	9	4.4	15	3.8
1961–1970	70	36.7	93	45.8	163	41.4
1971–1981[a]	115	60.2	101	49.8	216	54.8
Total	191	48.5	203	51.5	394	100.0

[a]To September 1981.

strain the outflow of Pineros and select among aspiring migrants. One significant factor has been the absence of a temporary worker program, such as the bracero program in place for Mexicans between 1943 and 1964 or the offshore labor program for selected commonwealth Caribbean islands. Such programs have facilitated the temporary migration of workers who, because of economic and social disadvantages, might not otherwise have been able to find the means to enter the United States. Geography, as noted earlier, is another important constraint which has had significant implications for the socioeconomic characteristics of the Dominican migrant stream. Because the U.S. border is distant and difficult to penetrate by sea, the potential migrant generally had to obtain some form of permit to enter the country. For these reasons, U.S. immigration and consular policies became critical determinants of the composition of the post-Trujillo wave.

Most of the Pineros who migrated during the early and mid-1960s entered the United States on tourist visas. To approve the request for such a visa, the U.S. consulate required proof of sufficient resources to attract the tourist home again. Acceptable documents included titles to land, tax registers to stores, deeds to vehicles, and savings passbooks. Of course, not all Pineros could fill these requisites. Thus, consular policies clearly favored the wealthier sectors of Los Pinos society. Among the first to migrate during the early 1960s were the middle-level mill employees and their offspring, large landholders and their offspring, and storekeepers with middle-sized shops who were not of the merchant elite.

The first two groups shared some essential features which prompted their migration. Like those who left in the 1950s, both were more or less privileged groupings experiencing actual or threatened economic decline. By the early 1960s, mill employees faced the imminent prospect of joblessness. The volume of milling activity had been diminishing steadily, and the lumber industry was in its last days. In 1967 the enactment of conservationist legislation by President Balaguer prohibiting logging throughout the republic dealt the coup de grace to an already moribund industry. While all mill workers were threatened, it was only those with the middle-level jobs who had access to the resources to finance a move to the United States. This differential ability to migrate underscores the practical significance of the crypto-class division among mill workers noted in the previous chapter. In some instances the wives of these mill employees, in anticipation of their husbands' loss of employment, migrated first. Their husbands clung to their jobs until the end, and then they too left to join their wives in New York. The problems that all farmers in Los Pinos faced by the late 1950s were discussed at length in the preceding chapter. Like the mill employees, the farmers also left to avoid the downward spiral of dwindling resources and loss of status.

The shopkeepers present a somewhat different case, however. The expansion of commerce was one of the principal consequences of the many transformations that Trujillo's policies wrought in Los Pinos and this trend was deepened during the Balaguer regime. By and large, the owners of middle-sized stores went to the United States to accumulate the capital to enable them to participate more fully in this expansion. Their goal was to return to Los Pinos after a brief stint of hard work and self-denial, move their shops to more favorable locations near the center of the village, and expand their stock.

The following story of one such migrant typifies the determination of some small merchants to use migration as a means to accumulate the capital to improve and maintain their economic and social standing in the community. Juanito Sánchez, 53, owns 400 tareas of land and over a dozen head of cattle. In the mid-1960s, he opened a small shop on the outskirts of the village, which, despite its size and location, was quite profitable. On the basis of his land titles and store registration, Sánchez was granted a tourist visa in 1967. He put his wife in charge of the shop in Los Pinos and left for New York. He lived frugally in Manhattan with his sister, who had migrated six years earlier. Working as much overtime as he could, Sánchez loaded boxes in a clothing factory in New Jersey during the week and washed dishes in a friend's restaurant on weekends. After a year and seven months, Sánchez returned to Los Pinos with US $7,000 in savings.

He used the money to open a new store in a choice site in the center of the village and to buy a truck to haul his merchandise.

Juanito Sánchez prospered during the early 1970s, but the steady deterioration of the economy after 1975, as well as the growing competition from the many new stores opened in Los Pinos with migrant capital, caused him to accumulate debts which he was unable to repay. Now in his fifties, Sánchez reemigrated in 1980. He returned to his sister's apartment in New York and for the next two and a half years worked in a factory in the daytime and in a nephew's bodega in the evenings. When I visited him in Los Pinos in 1987, he had been doing quite well since his return in early 1983: he had built a new house, his stock was considerably expanded, and his business was much improved.

Many of those who failed in their attempt to obtain a tourist visa through the consulate resorted to the services of urban visa brokers who supplied them with forged visas or false documents. The latter included false titles to landholdings, forged savings passbooks and so on, with which legitimate visas could be obtained. In the course of arranging for their sons' illegal migration, two Pinero men, both large landholders, established relations of confianza with brokers in Santo Domingo and Santiago. For the next decade, they themselves acted as intermediaries between these urban visa brokers and the local population.

Thus, by the late 1960s, a complex migration system had begun to take shape in Los Pinos. Local visa brokers, called *buscones*—literally, "searchers," both of people and of profits—played a critical role in recruiting and channeling migrants from the village. Their professional networks facilitated the migration of many Pineros who lacked the social contacts and economic resources of the largest landholders and old muleteers. Equally crucial were the *prestamistas*, usurers who specialized in making loans specifically to cover the huge cost of false documents. Those who could not obtain what Pineros called a "free" visa from the consulate simultaneously enlisted the services of a buscón and a prestamista. Varying between DR$500 and $800 in 1965 and $1,000—1,500 in 1970, and reaching $2,200—3,000 in 1980, buscón fees were obviously steep (cf. figure 1.1). One of the great ironies of Dominican migration to the United States as it took shape in the 1960s and 1970s was that those with the most wealth were able to get free and legitimate visas whereas others with fewer assets were forced to pay large fees.

To secure the loans to meet these fees, potential migrants had to provide the prestamistas with collateral in the form of land and cattle up to two times the value of the loan. At first, the merchant elite and some of the largest landholders provided these loans. Soon, however, Pinero migrants in the United States were attracted by the favorable terms: interest rates ranged between 5 percent and 10 percent a month, and loans of Dominican pesos were made to be repaid in an equal amount of U.S. dollars. In 1981, for instance, these terms added another 23–29 percent to the value of the loan, in addition to interest. Thus, the savings accumulated by some U.S. migrants were invested in financing the migration of yet more Pineros to the United States, albeit at a steep price.

Over the years, methods of undocumented entry changed several times in response to national and international conditions. By the late 1960s, the U.S. consulate in Santo Domingo had begun to exercise greater skepticism in the evaluation of requests for tourist as well as resident visas and had become increasingly demanding with respect to proof of intent to return, that is, with respect to proof of assets in the republic. As it became more difficult to secure tourist visas in the 1970s, visa brokers sought other channels of entry. It was during this period that urban brokers began to route potential Pinero migrants through Puerto Rico. This route had apparently been used earlier in other parts of the Dominican Republic, but only after 1968 in Los Pinos. An elaborate and expensive system developed whereby individuals were flown in small planes to isolated landing strips outside of San Juan. There they were met by a guide and taken to a hotel for a day or two. The guide then took them to the airport, where, posing as Puerto Ricans, they purchased their airline tickets and flew to New York. The total cost of this means of entry in 1970 was around DR$1,500. By the time I began fieldwork, the contact for this route had disappeared and Pineros were no longer using it.

In the mid-1970s, buscones developed two new routes of undocumented entry into the United States. In the first, migrants flew to Mexico City and, assisted by guides, took a bus to the U.S.-Mexico border. Crossing into the United States at night with the help of a coyote, or alien smuggler, they then flew on to New York. In 1978, this method cost DR$2,000 or more. The second route, considered the most desperate and dangerous, involved smuggling the migrant to south Florida as a stowaway on a cargo ship ("ir en barco," to go in a ship) and then flying him (nearly all stowaways are men) to New York. Most Pineros strongly disapprove of this means of entering the United States, and in fact only one has ever used it. However, for many in neighboring hamlets who were late in joining the migrant stream, it was often the only method available. Since 1975, a new group of buscones (none from Los Pinos) has emerged to promote and channel the stowaway traffic. In 1981, the costs of stowing away to south Florida and flying from there to New York ranged between DR$2,200 and $3,000.

Underscoring the great risks as well as the popularity of this method of entry among many in the sección was the "Regina Express" tragedy which occurred while I was in the field. A cargo ship, the Regina Express also regularly carried stowaways to south Florida. On September 5, 1980, harbor police in Santo Domingo boarded the vessel to investigate reports of alien smuggling. To evade detection, the stowaways were hidden in the ship's ballast tank. While the investigation on board dragged on, the thirty-four men crammed into the sealed tank began to asphyxiate and cry out for help. By the time the police discovered the stowaways, twenty-two had died (*Listín Diario*, September 6–9, 1980). Many of the stowaways on board were from the hamlets neighboring Los Pinos and from a nearby sección. For days after the incident, ambulances sped through Los Pinos, taking the victims back to their villages for convalescence or burial. One of the survivors I spoke with from a neighboring village continued to be wracked by nightmares months after his rescue. When police arrived to question villagers about the buscones who operated in the sección, however, they received little cooperation. It is revealing of villagers' mixed attitudes toward buscones that, although they were generally considered to be avaricious and not entirely trustworthy, they were not denounced to the authorities. After a few weeks in hiding, the local buscones were once again traveling the countryside on their motorcycles, recruiting potential migrants and helping them arrange loans.

Pineros had a single term that encompassed all of these various methods of undocumented migration—"viajes por la izquierda," literally, "trips on the left." This term did not necessarily imply immorality or wrongdoing, but rather something indirect. Indeed, there was little or no stigma attached to undocumented migration by Pineros. "Trips on the left" were contrasted with the less frequently heard "viajes por la derecha" ("trips on the right"), which referred to straightforward, documented entry. But Pineros also had developed a taxonomy that distinguished among three classes of undocumented migrants. Furthermore, these classes were ranged along a continuum of increasing desirability and approval. At the bottom were the completely undocumented ("sin papeles," without papers), composed of those who had entered the United States through Puerto Rico or Mexico, or as stowaways. Next were those who entered the United

States legally as tourists but overstayed the terms of their visa; at least initially, these migrants had papers. The best, that is, the least hazardous, undocumented entry was that made with a purchased or borrowed residence visa ("con papeles de otro," with the papers of someone else). This last type of entry could offer the migrant some protection from detection. In their study of an extended family of migrants from Santo Domingo to New York, Garrison and Weiss (1979:279) also found a hierarchical ranking of the various modes of entry. Although differing in some points from Pineros' order of preferences, their study suggests that some sort of ranking of entry modes in terms of their advantages and desirability generally characterized Dominican migrants and potential migrants.

Clearly, by 1980 undocumented migration had become an exceedingly expensive enterprise. Rising land values and the growing network of migrants in the United States willing to assist their poor kin in Los Pinos financially compensated to some extent for the high cost of illegal entry. For most aspiring undocumented migrants, however, soaring buscón fees had to be pieced together with loans from several migration prestamistas. Always selective, undocumented entry became an option open to fewer and fewer Pineros. Thus, as we shall see in greater detail below, in contrast to the popular stereotype of undocumented migrants as desperate, in Los Pinos for the most part they came from the relatively more privileged segments of the population.

With time, the growing community of Pineros in the United States became a valuable resource for those desiring to migrate. Migrants in the United States not only provided loan capital to finance undocumented entries, but perhaps more importantly they were a pool of highly desirable potential mates. As migrants managed to regularize their status and become U.S. residents, they were able to use the family reunification provisions of U.S. immigration law to sponsor the migration of the appropriate categories of kin. A legitimate marriage to a legal migrant ("matrimonio por amor") became a common means of gaining documented entry to the United States, as spouses could sponsor each other's migration.

Some Pineros also used the family reunification provisions to expand the system of extralegal migration. A counterpart to the marriage "for love" emerged: the business marriage ("matrimonio de negocio"). This is a popular method of entering the United States. Pineros hoping to migrate paid legal migrants to marry them and then used the family reunification provisions to acquire a legal resident visa. Costing about US$500 in 1970 and reaching US$2,000 by 1980, business marriages are meant to be undone: they are sealed by civil ceremony only, rarely consecrated by a church wedding, and sexual relations between "business spouses" are proscribed. Only those with at least middle-sized landholdings (over 80 tareas) were able to meet the high cost of the business marriage, as well of most other methods of undocumented entry.

Despite the selective pressures that militated in favor of those from households with middle-sized and large landholdings, about one-quarter of the migrant stream from Los Pinos was composed of members of semiproletarian households who at the time of migration had only sub-subsistence plots (under 80 tareas) or were landless (table 3.2). From the onset of international migration, bonds of kinship, patronage and friendship helped poor Pineros to migrate in a variety of ways. Some, such as a loyal sharecropper or a trusted store clerk, managed to secure collateral-free loans from patrons with whom they shared a relationship of confianza. Out of a sense of moral obligation, ("prestando una ayuda," or "lending a helping hand"), some migrants helped needy members of their kindred and to a lesser extent other members of their networks to travel to the United States. In some instances, this was accomplished by loaning one's U.S. residence documentation—the coveted "green card"—to a relative resembling the identification photograph on the card. One U.S. migrant in his sixties, for instance, loaned his residence card to his younger brother, a smallholder who was barely able to keep his wife and seven children fed by farming and occasional wage labor. To prepare him for a convincing performance with customs officials at John F. Kennedy

TABLE 3.2. Size of Family Landholding Prior to Migration

Size of family landholding (tareas)	Number of individual migrants	Percentage of individual migrants
0	19	4.8
1–79	71	18.0
80–159	90	22.9
160–399	98	24.1
400–799	52	13.2
800–1599	40	10.2
1600+	24	6.1
Total	394	100.1[a]

[a]Due to rounding.

airport, his migrant nephews coached him on how to dress, how to walk like an older man, and how to respond to the officials' questions. Other migrants "lent a helping hand" by marrying their poor cousins or other kin without charge in order to sponsor their migration. In such cases, as with business marriages for money, sexual relations between "marriage partners" were proscribed. Still other migrants included the child of a poor relative or neighbor as their own on a legitimate visa application. This was accomplished by using the birth certificate of a deceased son or daughter as the documentation for the child being claimed as one's own. High rates of infant death in the past and the fact that such deaths often went unreported meant that many households potentially could use this means of entry. Through these methods, the priority assigned by U.S. immigration law to family reunification was imaginatively articulated with the moral obligation to help needy kin.

The game of cat and mouse played by aspiring migrants was one in which the U.S. consulate in Santo Domingo was an active and wily participant. Well aware of the practices just described, the consulate's special staff frequently scoured the countryside in their distinctive blue vans to investigate applicants' claims. Neighbors and other villagers were interviewed about a child's biological relationship to the applicant, a spouse's degree of relatedness, and so on. In some cases, village solidarity came to the rescue of some potential migrants, and answers favorable to the applicant's request were provided. In other cases, a villager might cooperate with the consular investigators, sinking the applicant's chance of obtaining a visa in order to settle a grievance. One Pinero, for example, cooperated fully when consular employees came to Los Pinos to investigate the relationship between a man and the spouse whose immigration he was sponsoring. Anticipating the investigation, this Pinero had hinted broadly to the aspiring migrant that he should be "tipped" in advance in case he was asked any questions. Rebuffed, he retaliated by cooperating fully with the consular investigators. Some Pineros have since tipped this man generously.

Others from poor households, particularly daughters, took part in a process of step migration: young women who were at a relative disadvantage in the rural labor market were attracted to Santiago where they had greater employment opportunities. In the city, some accumulated the material resources, acquired patrons, or established other social ties which enabled them to migrate. Because this component of the stream had its own unique features closely associated with gender roles and the division of labor by gender, it is taken up in greater detail below in the discussion of the gender composition of the Pinero migration.

Before concluding this section, I must also note who had not migrated from Los Pinos to the United States over the last twenty years. Overwhelmingly, nonmigrants were found at the two extremes of Pinero society. At one end of the socioeconomic spectrum were the landless poor. Unable to garner the resources necessary to secure a tourist visa or pay buscón fees, they stayed in the community and became increasingly dependent on occasional wage labor and handicrafts for their livelihood. Some migrated to other rural areas of the republic in search of wage labor; others ultimately settled in the cities. At the other end of the spectrum was the merchant elite. On the ascent since the 1950s, they had little cause to leave the republic. Members of elite households did travel to the United States, but not as labor migrants. Rather, like many other better-off Dominicans, they went as tourists to visit relatives and to shop. For example, two daughters from one merchant household visited New York for a year to perfect their English. As cultural and economic ties with the United States became stronger than ever during the 1970s, knowledge of English became an increasingly marketable skill in the cities of the republic. These women went to live in a Dominican neighborhood with kin who were labor migrants, but they themselves did not work. On their return, they were able to find administrative jobs in the Santiago branch of a multinational bank.

BECOMING LEGAL: STATUS REGULARIZATION

Although a great many Pineros began their sojourn in the United States without proper documentation, only fifty-three individuals, or 13.5 percent of the total international migrant stream, were undocumented in 1981. Regularization of status was a priority, and most Pineros managed to become legal residents within three to five years of arrival, often at considerable expense.

Regularization was a complicated process, frequently requiring the services of an immigration lawyer. The most commonly used manner of changing legal status was through marriage to a legal resident alien or a U.S. citizen. That most migrants tended to be young, and often single, when they first came to the United States increased the likelihood that they would marry there, and this in turn facilitated the regularization process. Indeed, a recent study (Gurak 1987) found that Dominicans were more likely to have formed their current marriages in the United States than in the Dominican Republic. Most of these marriages were with other Dominicans, but the relatively high rate of interaction with Puerto Ricans, who, of course, are U.S. citizens, helped some Dominicans obtain their legal resident status. In 1975, for example, some 20 percent of Dominican marriages in New York were with Puerto Ricans (Fitzpatrick and Gurak 1979). After a visa was requested by the spouse, the applicant often must travel outside the United States to petition the change in visa status. Most Pineros went to Canada, but some, on their lawyers' advice that it would improve their chances of getting a residence visa, had traveled as far as Austria and Brazil.

Undocumented migrants might contract a business marriage in an attempt to regularize their status. Bonds of kinship, friendship, and common residence in the Dominican Republic, as well as the significant amount of money involved, helped many undocumented migrants find a willing partner among Pineros in New York. The following history of one Pinero's undocumented entry and subsequent regularization typifies this complicated process and illustrates the high costs involved. Cano Pérez, 36, supported his spouse and twelve children by raising peanuts on his 40 tareas of land in Los Pinos, panning gold, and working as a day laborer, lottery vendor, and lumberjack. In 1975, with loans from five of his siblings, two of whom were in the United States, Pérez made an undocumented entry to New York via Puerto Rico.

For the next two years, Cano worked a forty-hour week as a janitor at a university during the day and forty-four hours each week cleaning office buildings at night. Because regularization was his goal and he wanted "to do everything correctly," Cano took no deductions for the dependents he supported in Los Pinos. Although only earning a little above minimum wage at his daytime job, and the legal minimum at the evening one, after two years Cano had saved enough to repay his loans and arrange a business marriage with his cousin, a legal U.S. resident for many years. Cano hired an immigration lawyer to help his "wife" request a resident visa for him. After a year of paperwork and waiting, he went to Canada, accompanied by a friend who spoke English to serve as his guide, to be interviewed in the U.S. consulate. His request was approved. A year later, he divorced his cousin and married his "real" wife, with whom he had lived in consensual union for nearly twenty years, in order to request a resident visa for her and their oldest children.

As table 3.3 indicates, the costs of status regularization might well exceed the fees paid to buscones for illegal entry. In this case, they were twice as high. This example also illustrates how the prevalence of consensual unions in the Dominican Republic, especially in the countryside, helps a potential migrant to regularize her or his status. In Los Pinos, many long and stable unions were consensual, especially among older couples. When a spouse in such a union made an undocumented entry to the United States, that migrant was free to make a business marriage in order to obtain a resident visa. Of course, some Pineros attempting to regularize their status had already been married in a civil or church ceremony; if they were to effect a business marriage, they first had to obtain a divorce from their legitimate spouse. In a few cases, wives in Los Pinos adamantly refused to agree to a divorce, suspecting that status regularization was not the husband's primary motive. In many more cases, a migrant's status regularization resulted in the formalization of a long-standing consensual union with a marriage ceremony so that the appropriate documentation would be available then to bring family members legally to the United States.

After obtaining legal resident status, these migrants typically requested additional visas for family members still in the republic. In other words, they became the anchors to which chains of future migrants attached themselves.

As the Pinero migration system evolved and matured over time, kinship became the principal mechanism of recruitment. Dominicans call the process of successive displacement of family members to the United States the *cadena*—the chain of migrant kin linking the sending community in the Dominican Republic to the migrant community in the United States. As migrant chains began to proliferate in the late 1960s, more and more Pineros were able to enter the United States as legal residents.

TABLE 3.3. Costs of Cano Pérez' Undocumented Migration and Regularization (US$)

Buscón fees for entry via Puerto Rico	$2,000.00
Fee to cousin for business marriage	1,500.00[a]
Lawyer's fees	1,426.00
Trip to Canada (includes expenses of friend who spoke English)	500.00
Divorce from cousin through laywer	700.00
Total cost	$6,126.00

[a]Because they were cousins, the woman Pérez married discounted $500 from the going rate for a business marriage.

CHAIN MIGRATION AND THE U.S. MIGRANT HOUSEHOLD

The decision to migrate most often was embedded in the needs of the household, the fundamental social and economic unit in Los Pinos. Migratory moves were discussed by spouses and parents, and strategies to raise the relatively large amount of capital needed to finance a move were jointly planned, often with the assistance of the larger extended family. Especially if the migration was undocumented, as was the case for Cano Pérez, the larger circle of kindred might have to be mobilized to meet the high cost involved.

A critical note about the role of the household in U.S.-bound migration is in order at this point. In recent years, considerable attention has been devoted to the household as the central social unit mediating between larger social forces and the individual and constraining choice in response to these forces (e.g., Wood 1981, 1982; Wallerstein, Martin, and Dickinson 1979). While the household undoubtedly does play a significant role in organizing migration, its a priori selection as the primary unit of analysis nonetheless may sometimes obfuscate other important processes. On the one hand, it may obscure the semi-autonomous operation of household segments in some circumstances. On the other, it may exclude an analysis of the relations and transfers that occur between and among households linked in a larger network of exchange (Guyer 1981).[1] For a full understanding of migration from Los Pinos, in addition to the household unit itself, both intrahousehold segments and extrahousehold networks must be included in analysis.

If a migratory attempt was successful, physical separation of family members often would result. For this reason, in migrant communities such as Los Pinos, the definition of the household must depart from usual usage (e.g., Yanigasako 1979). Obviously, migrant households were not coresidential groups. Some members resided in the United States and others in Los Pinos, while all might contribute to the maintenance of the household unit. As Murray has noted:

---

1. Ironically, although a focus on the household has been proposed as a solution to the theoretical impasse between equilibrium and structural-historical approaches to the study of migration, it suffers some of the shortcomings of both. Such an approach often assumes the functionalist cost–benefit analysis that characterizes equilibrium studies; instead of occurring at the individual level, these rational calculations now take place at the level of the household. It also often assumes that the form and behavior of households can be deduced from the imperatives of the world system, another form of the functionalism that characterizes the structural-historical approach (see Bach and Schraml 1982).

> One problem is to distinguish clearly between its [the household's] tangible manifestation as a partially co-residential group—the unit of observation in the village—and its overall functional manifestation in terms of income-generating activities. It is helpful to retain the term household when referring to both these aspects of its identity, because the household remains the unit of economic viability whether or not its members are physically dispersed at any one time. (1981:45)

The term, *household* is used herein to refer both to the coresidential unit of observation in Los Pinos and to the basic economic unit of analysis. I have restricted the use of the term *U.S. migrant household* to those households in which at least one nuclear family member (husband, wife, or child) was residing in the United States (and the few who were living in Canada) at the time of fieldwork. Obviously, with migration kindreds and social networks also become transnational.

Depending upon who becomes the anchor, the cadena in Los Pinos followed one of a few typical patterns. The first occurred when either spouse of a household migrated. Gender ideology emphasized the role of the husband-father as the breadwinner and decision maker within the household, and, indeed, in most cases it was he who migrated first. Nonetheless, who went first depended also on the networks of each spouse. For example, if a wife had an appropriate category of kin to sponsor her visa application and the husband did not, she might be the first to leave. In some instances, the impetus for her migration might derive from her migrant kin and not necessarily from the specific needs and decisions of her household. For example, after learning that her father in the Dominican Republic had taken a mistress, one migrant Pinera (who was a U.S. citizen) became very upset and made the decision to sponsor the migration of her mother to remove her from a painful situation. In other instances, as the example below of Rita Morales illustrates, migrants might grow weary of supporting kin in the republic and decide to sponsor their migration, often becoming U.S. citizens expressly in order to do so. Siblings or parents in such situations of dependency frequently were not in a position to refuse to migrate.

Once established in a job, the migrant typically requested a residence visa for his or her spouse and their children of, or near, working age. Less frequently, visas would be requested for young children. One migrant Pinero, Polo Rodríguez, explained how he decided whom to request: "In New York, my head was split in two. I had expenses here and expenses there and I couldn't save anything. So I brought my wife and two oldest girls over. The youngest children stayed behind with their grandmother, because a woman with two or three small children in New York can't work."

Polo Rodríguez' statement succinctly captures some of the major considerations involved in the migration of married women. Recently, the predominance of women immigrants to the United States has been explained as primarily the consequence of women joining migrant husbands in their new communities (Houstoun, Kramer, and Barrett 1984). Polo's wife Lucinda did in fact migrate to New York to join her husband, but as his statement suggests, an important consideration was the availability of work for her there. Indeed, since emigrating seven years ago, Lucinda de Rodríguez had worked in a curtain factory along with one of her daughters—when not laid off. The "feminization" of a significant portion of low-wage jobs in core countries like the United States (Fernandez-Kelly 1985:219–220) had expanded opportunities for immigrant women like Lucinda to enter the labor force and contribute their wages to the income fund of migrant households.

Visas generally were requested for the rest of the children as they approached working age. In the meantime, they were most often left in the care of their grandparents or parents' siblings. In some cases, nonkin were hired as live-in caretakers of the children left behind. Poorer nonmigrants welcomed as a significant supplement to household income the remittances received from migrants for child-care services. However, for others, especially aged grandmothers, assuming the caretaker role could be a heavy burden which remittances did little to relieve. The hardships this strategy could create can be seen in the following story of Gladys Pérez and her mother, Nina Morales.

Gladys' husband, Luis, migrated to New Jersey in 1975. His sister, who had lived in the United States since 1960, had become a U.S. citizen in order to sponsor the migration of her four brothers in Los Pinos, who made a meager living by performing day labor and other occasional jobs. After two years in the United States, Luis requested visas for Gladys and their eldest son, age 17. Their other six children remained in Los Pinos with their grandmother, Nina. Nina complained to me, "When my daughter is in New York, I am a prisoner. I don't see my other daughters until she returns and takes back her children." Of course, the burden of separation for Gladys and Luis was also great. Gladys traveled to Los Pinos twice a year to visit her children. On her last visit, she stayed for six weeks to put the finishing touches on the modest new house that she and Luis had built just outside the village, which remained empty most of the year. When the time came for her to take her children to her mother's and return to New Jersey, she was extremely distressed. The doctor she consulted at the local clinic gave her some diazepam (Valium), after aspirin, the second most frequently dispensed drug in Los Pinos. When I went to say goodbye to her, she was already in a dazed state from the several diazepam she had taken to prepare herself for the impending separation.

Sometimes separation, despite a family's best efforts, became permanent. There were a few chains in Los Pinos in which all family members had migrated to the United States except for physically or mentally disabled offspring. In all cases, parents had repeatedly requested visas for these children. Time and again, the children had been screened out by the rigorous medical and psychological examinations required by the consulate prior to the visa interview. Parents nonetheless continued to spend a great deal of time and money in renewed efforts to obtain visas for these children.

Another common migratory pattern occurred when a son or daughter left the parental household in Los Pinos to travel to the United States. There they married and formed new households. As the wife began to bear children, the couple was faced with the possibility of her temporary or permanent withdrawal from the labor force. One alternative to this or to costly and often inadequate day care, was to bring over either spouse's mother to take care of the children and the household in general. Until 1976, another reason to bring parents to the United States was that they themselves might be able to request visas for their children still in the republic. After 1976, a new preference system for the Western Hemisphere narrowed the categories of kin who could be sponsored by legal resident aliens to spouses and unmarried children only (Garrison and Weiss 1979:277). U.S. citizens, however, might sponsor both parents and siblings. In this manner, new migratory chains continued to be forged.

In itself, the initiation of new chains of siblings was often a secondary but nonetheless significant consideration on the part of migrants who requested visas for their parents. Whether directly sponsored by U.S. citizens, or, prior to 1976, indirectly by legal residents through their parents, sibling chains were one means by which migrants fulfilled the obligation to help out family members. At the same time, their remittance burden was eased, since there were now more family members in the United States to send money to fewer dependents in the Dominican Republic. Migrants were often very explicit about these considerations. Rita Morales, a migrant who had been a schoolteacher in Los Pinos, explained why she decided to request a visa for her divorced sister, a woman highly respected in the community:

> I became a U.S. citizen to improve my chances of bringing Mamá and Papá over. But I also wanted to bring over my sister, Rosita. We [Rita and her nine siblings] have been supporting Rosita and her children for ten years now and that is enough, more than anyone else would have done. I know in her heart she doesn't really want to come—a woman like Rosita working in a factory! But I must think of returning to the republic soon and Rosita must be able to defend herself and bring her children to the U.S. And now she can help us [financially] take care of Mamá and Papá.

This example also illustrates how, as the international migrant kindred was constituted over time, responsibility for decisions that affected family members' lives often came to fall in the hands of migrants in the United States. Here, Rita, who initiated her family's large chain in 1961, decided it was time for her parents, her sister, and her sister's children to leave Los Pinos.

Of course, residence visas were not requested for all parents. About 7 percent of Los Pinos's 1981 population was of age 65 and older. This relatively large proportion reflected the high levels of migration of the young and the relative immobility of the elderly.

DURATION OF MIGRATION

Anthropological studies of migration often classify entire sending communities according to the "typical" or modal length of sojourn in the receiving society. Communities are said to be characterized by patterns of "circular," "temporary," or "permanent" migration. Migration from Los Pinos is not so easily classifiable, however. Although nearly all migrants with whom I spoke regarded their sojourn as temporary, some were, so to speak, more temporary than others. The duration of residence abroad consequently varied within a wide range. The first person to leave the village thirty years ago was still residing in the United States (and still planning to return to Los Pinos), whereas one or two legal migrants had returned to Los Pinos permanently after only a few unhappy months abroad.

A few migrants did participate in a pattern of circular migration. They worked in jobs—in hotels, in some kinds of factories—that have defined "dead" or slow seasons. Taking a few months' leave of absence without pay, these migrants return to Los Pinos and live from the savings accumulated at their U.S. job.

Most Pinero migrants, however, worked year-round at jobs in the United States. They managed to return to the Dominican Republic once every year or two for two to three weeks. During these vacations, they might behave much like tourists, renting cars, touring the beaches, and patronizing restaurants that cater to foreigners. One Pinero told me he had seen more of the republic since he moved to New York than when he lived on the island. "Dominican Yorkers," as U.S. migrants were often called, had become an important element of the island's tourist industry.

A few migrants, such as the shopkeepers mentioned earlier, enjoyed considerable access to productive resources in Los Pinos and undertook relatively short sojourns to the United States solely to augment their assets. Arrighi (1973), who also found this pattern in Africa, has called those who are not motivated strictly out of absolute necessity, "discretionary migrants." The discretionary migrants of Los Pinos made trips lasting from a few months to two or three years to accumulate the cash to meet specific goals. While many Pinero migrants spoke of cutting their consumption to minimal levels in the United States (for instance, going to only one movie in five years), extremes of self-denial were seen among discretionary migrants, as the following example illustrates.

Don Fonso Rodríguez, 50, was one of Los Pinos' largest landowners. Some of his land was in commercial agriculture, but most was devoted to cattle raising. In 1965, a severe drought destroyed his crops and fields and made it impossible for him to repay a loan to the Agricultural Bank without selling some of his assets. Unwilling to do this, Rodríguez rescheduled his debt, obtained a tourist visa on the basis of his land titles, and went to New York. There he worked as a dishwasher for an average of one hundred hours a week. After seven months of doing little else but work and sleep, he had saved enough to return to Los Pinos, pay off his debt, and hire the labor to improve his pasture lands.

Thirteen years later, in 1978, another drought caused similar problems. By this time, however, tourist visas had become more difficult to obtain. With documents borrowed from a relative, Rodríguez returned to New York, where he washed dishes for from eighteen to twenty-one hours a day for ten months. When he returned to Los Pinos, he not only paid off his debt to the bank but also invested in the improvement of his land. In addition, he purchased a small diesel-powered saw and established a workshop for making wooden chairs which employed six men.

In 1981, he emigrated once again, this time to accumulate the DR$10,000 he needed to buy a share in his nephews' wholesale business in Santiago.

Arrighi's distinction helps refine our understanding of the complexities of Dominican migration. However, often it is only after the fact that migrants can be classified as discretionary. This is because, like Don Fonso Rodríguez and Juanito Sánchez, almost everyone migrated to solve a problem—to build a house, repay a debt, send children to the university, recover from a divorce, learn English, escape low wages—and return as quickly as possible to continue life in the republic. The reality, however, was that only a few were able to realize their initial intentions. All but a fraction of Pinero migrants were still in the United States.

Also problematic in the Dominican context is the concept of permanent return. Only about 12 percent (47 people) of the total number of Pinero migrants had returned to live in the republic. But even among these returnees, very few were willing to relinquish their U.S. residence visas. A fundamental sense of political and economic insecurity was reflected in the adage many Pinero migrants adduced to explain this unwillingness: "One knows what happens today, but not what happens tomorrow" ("se sabe el día de hoy, pero no el día de mañana"). To keep their visas from being revoked, migrants had to return to the United States at least once every year. Once in the United States, they commonly worked for two or three months to recover their travel expenses. Thus, even return migrants continued to participate in the U.S. labor market long after their ostensibly permanent return to the Dominican Republic (see chapter 6). Ironically, to avoid these annual visits, some became U.S. citizens immediately before returning to resettle in the Dominican Republic.

GENDER AND THE INTERNATIONAL MIGRANT STREAM

The first three migrants from Los Pinos in the early 1950s were women, and women migrants continued slightly to outnumber men. Such a high level was not unusual but paralleled that of Dominican women nationally. Nevertheless, given a strong patriarchal ideology which attempted to proscribe women's activities within narrow domestic limits, the high rate of Dominican women's participation in international migration was striking. Several factors were responsible for

this high level. First, there was the availability of employment opportunities for women in the "secondary sector" of the U.S. economy,
that is, the sector composed of unskilled, low-wage, non-unionized,
dead-end jobs of insecure tenure (see Edwards, Reich, and Gordon
1975). This sector had grown rapidly in recent times and, as noted
earlier, had become increasingly feminized. Its expansion undoubtedly encouraged many women throughout Latin America and the
Caribbean to migrate to the industrial centers of the northeastern
United States. Dominican women were no exception to this pattern
(see, for example, Gurak and Kritz 1982).

Another factor promoting the international migration of women
was found in the dynamics of the migratory chain discussed above.
Given a division of labor in which women were assigned to housework and child care, there was an explicitly recognized preference
for bringing over mothers, rather than fathers, to help out working
women in migrant households. Thus, like U.S. immigration law itself,
many migrant households had their own hierarchy of kin preferences
which, in this case, helped contribute to the preponderance of women
in the international migrant stream.[2]

The high level of participation of Dominican women in documented migration to the United States is evident from table 3.4. The
predominance of women over men is especially intriguing since in
interviews at the U.S. consulate in Santo Domingo, the consul general
and a panel of vice-consuls, who made the day-to-day decisions concerning visas, indicated that they were totally unaware of a bias toward women. Consular officials stressed that the most important criterion in deciding a visa request was whether the applicant seemed
likely to become a public charge once in the United States. Since
women were eligible for more forms of public assistance than men,
and most public assistance recipients in the United States were women
and children, some vice-consuls explicitly stated a preference for ap-
proving "unencumbered males" for this reason. Yet in only one year
between 1965 and 1979 were more visas issued to men than to women,
and the overall ratio of women's to men's visa approvals was 1.16.
(Of course, it simply may be that a much larger number of women
applied for visas in the first place, so that even if vice-consuls did in
fact give preferential treatment to male applicants, the number of

---

2. Kim (1981:42) reports identical reasons for the preference for requesting visas for mothers among South Korean immigrants to the United States; see also Houstoun, Kramer, and
Barrett (1984:924) for a notion of how widespread this preference is among new immigrants
in general.

TABLE 3.4. Residence Visas Issued to Dominicans by Sex and Year, 1965–1979

	Sex		Ratio
Year	Men	Women	Women:Men
1965	4,290	5,214	1.22
1966	7,150	9,353	1.31
1967	4,709	6,805	1.45
1968	4,083	5,167	1.27
1969	4,845	5,825	1.20
1970	5,072	5,735	1.13
1971	5,963	6,661	1.12
1972	5,087	5,673	1.12
1973	6,570	7,351	1.12
1974	7,567	8,113	1.07
1975	6,639	7,427	1.19
1976	5,714	6,812	1.19
1977	5,191	6,464	1.25
1978	9,355	10,103	1.08
1979	8,868	8,651	.98

SOURCE: INS annual reports and statistical yearbooks, 1966–1980.

women applying was great enough to result in a larger number of approvals for women.)

Women's differential participation in internal migration might also ultimately, if indirectly, contribute to the high rate of women's international migration. In the Dominican Republic, as in almost all countries in Latin America (Orlansky and Dubrovsky 1978), the market factors promoting expulsion from the countryside and attraction to the cities were stronger for women than for men.[3] On the one hand, women had few opportunities for wage labor in their own communities. In Los Pinos, agricultural labor, with the exception of the harvesting of some crops, was men's work. As we shall see in chapter 4, in recent years the Pinero economy diversified considerably, yet most of the better-paying work opportunities that were created also fell under the rubric of men's work.

In the cities, in contrast, women had favorable access to jobs as domestic servants and factory operatives. Exceedingly low paid, do-

3. A 1978 survey of migrants to Santo Domingo and Santiago found that some 56 percent were women (Ramírez 1980, cited in Larson 1987b:257).

mestic service was women's work of the most characteristic sort. But many of the new factory jobs had also been filled by women. Particularly important to Pineras was the large industrial export processing zone, the *zona franca*, or free zone, located in the heart of Santiago. One free zone administrator I spoke with was explicit about the categories of people preferred as assembly workers in these complexes. In descending order of preference they were divorced or separated women with small children to support, single women, and lastly, married women. As a consequence of preferences such as these, the free zone labor force, which numbered 6,275 in 1980, was composed almost entirely of women (*El Sol*, December 9, 1980). Obviously the factory lay outside the domestic environment, yet several features made it suitable for women to accept such work: it did not require their free movement, it was closely supervised, and the work place contained very few men. Women who worked in the free zone received what might be called a "divorcée wage," comparable to the "bachelor wage" paid to male migrants who work in the mines of southern Africa. In both cases, income from additional family members is necessary to complement the wages earned. Women's internal migration thus resulted from the intersection of several factors: the income needs of the woman's household, the division of labor by gender, the comparative lack of income-generating opportunities in Los Pinos, and the expanded opportunities for low-wage employment in the city.

Although labor market forces were arguably the most important, other factors also promoted the differential internal migration of women which might ultimately lead them to the United States. Many girls from poor households, whose parents were unable to afford to continue their support and education, were sent to live with better-off Pineros who had moved to Santiago. In exchange for child care and domestic work, these girls were given room, board, and often educational expenses. This arrangement was far more frequent for girls than boys because in the urban context boys' work (fetching water, collecting firewood, milking cows) was less valuable to the household than that of girls, whose domestic labor might help free other adult women for wage labor. In addition, young women from wealthier households were also sent to Santiago to live with their kin. Some went to continue their education, often at an *academia*, or secretarial school; there was no equivalent to the academia for men, since women were overwhelmingly preferred for secretarial work in the Dominican Republic. Still others were sent to the city merely to be on display in the hope of making a good match. One matron from a well-to-do household explained that she sent her daughters to Santiago to live with her sister after they finished primary school because, as she put it, "Whom were they going to meet in Los Pinos?" One of her daughters married a U.S. migrant and subsequently migrated.

As table 3.5 indicates, Pinera women were far more likely than men to have migrated to a major city in the Dominican Republic prior to their move to the United States. While over three-quarters of the men migrated directly from Los Pinos to the United States, this was true of only a little more than half of the women. Three times more women than men had experienced a move to Santiago prior to migration abroad, and women were more than twice as likely as men to have lived in Santo Domingo before emigrating.

For many women, particularly for women from poorer households, internal migration appeared to be a critical step toward U.S. migration. This was less so for the access to economic resources that urban waged employment made possible, for most jobs were low-paying. More important were the social ties that women were able to establish once in a major city, ties that could aid them in making their international move. Through their greater participation in step migration by way of Santiago and Santo Domingo, women thus had more opportunities to build networks and form ties that could provide them with access to the material and social resources necessary for migration. The following examples illustrate two different strategies employed by women internal migrants to enable them to migrate to the United States.

TABLE 3.5. Residence of Pinero Migrants Prior to U.S. Migration by Sex

| | Sex | | | | | |
| | Men | | Women | | Total | |
Residence	N	%	N	%	N	%
Los Pinos	148	77.5	111	54.7	259	65.7
Santiago	25	13.1	74	36.5	99	25.1
Santo Domingo	4	2.1	10	4.9	14	3.6
Other Urban DR	7	3.7	5	2.5	12	3.1
Rural DR	5	2.6	1	0.5	6	1.5
Venezuela	2	1.1	0	0	2	0.5
Puerto Rico	0	0	2	1.0	2	0.5
Total	191	48.5	203	51.5	394	100.0

Silvia Pérez, 26, worked for six years as a domestic in Santiago and Santo Domingo. With migration to the United States as her goal, she always sought to work for foreigners, who paid slightly higher wages—in 1980, DR$80-90 per month—compared to the going rate of DR$60 to $70. During her last three years of service, she accumulated DR$1800. She did this by deferring almost all consumption, saving her wages and using them to make loans at 10 percent interest per month. She also organized rotating credit clubs for a fee.[4] In 1981, she was able to meet buscón fees and emigrate.

Laura Rodríguez, 32, went to Santiago to work as a laundress in 1975. In 1977, she entered a consensual union with Tomás Andújar, a national guardsman who had an important patron in the Balaguer government. After the PRD electoral victory over Balaguer in 1978, his patron helped Tomás migrate to the United States on a tourist visa. Tomás subsequently sent Laura part of the money to pay a buscón; the remainder she raised herself, obtaining collateral-free loans from usurers who had a relationship of confianza with Tomás and who felt sure he would repay them if anything went wrong. After her first attempt to leave failed and she was briefly imprisoned in the Dominican Republic, Tomás sent her more money for another try. She successfully entered the United States in 1979.

Silvia Pérez was especially single-minded in the pursuit of her goal. Her entry into the waged labor force, in conjunction with other entrepreneurial activities, enabled her ultimately to purchase her entry into the United States. In the second case, which represents a much more common route of U.S. migration for women, it was the social ties established by living and working in the city that afforded Laura Rodríguez the wherewithal to migrate.

Disaggregating the migrant stream according to gender thus sheds some light on the unresolved issue of the relationship of step migration to international migration. Gonzalez (1970), Hendricks (1974), and Pessar (1982a) imply that the typical Dominican rural migrant moves directly from her or his village to the urban industrial centers of the northeastern United States. Others, such as Bray (1983), Kayal (1978), and Ugalde et al. (1979), describe a pattern of step migration in which migrants spend some time in a Dominican city prior to going to the United States. By examining the different migratory routes taken by men and women, additional light is shed on the relationship be-

---

4. Organizing a rotating credit club, or *san*, is a common occasional income-generating activity engaged in by women from poor households.

tween internal and international migration. The case of Los Pinos suggests that international migration from the Dominican Republic might be characterized by a "split stream" composed of two tracks in which women and men participated differentially. To a considerably greater extent for women than for men, living in a major urban center of the republic could provide a significant indirect means of entry into the international migrant stream.

DEMOGRAPHIC FEATURES OF THE PINERO MIGRANT STREAM

Women's propensity to migrate had important repercussions for the demographic makeup of Los Pinos. Women comprised some 52 percent of the international migrant stream, and another 55 percent of the internal stream. This fact had significant effects on the age and sex distribution of the population residing in Los Pinos. Figures 3.1 and 3.2 respectively depict the age and sex distribution of the population residing in Los Pinos in 1981 and of the national population in 1960 and 1970. When Los Pinos' population structure is compared to the nation's, some striking differences are apparent. In comparison with the national population, Los Pinos had a considerably smaller proportion of population in the 0-9 years age groups. This difference was especially pronounced for the 0-4 cohort. Again in contrast to the national distribution, the Los Pinos population pyramid bulged for the 10-19 years groups, was cinched for the productive years of 20-59, and flared out once again for those age 65 and older. The latter category comprised 7.1 percent of Los Pinos' population, but only 3.1 percent of the nation's (de los Santos et al. 1981).

In certain respects, then, Los Pinos' population deviated surprisingly from what we commonly expect for migrant communities. Typically, such communities have hourglass-shaped distributions, the result of higher proportions of the young and the old than of those in their prime productive and reproductive years. For this reason, they are characterized by what demographers call high dependency ratios. This ratio is defined as the proportion of individuals between the ages of 0 and 14 and 60 and older (dependents) to those of age 15–59 (economically active population), multiplied by 100. In contrast to other areas of the world with large-scale migration (see, e.g., Murray 1981 for Africa), Los Pinos had a dependency ratio of 98.65. This near-parity of dependents and producers is especially striking when we note

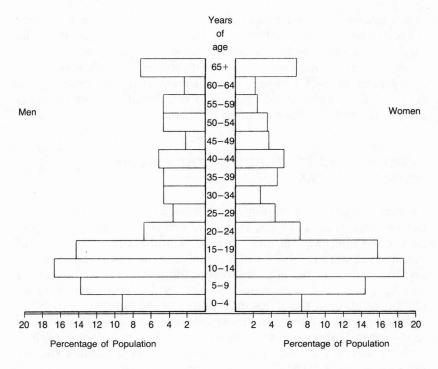

FIGURE 3.1. Distribution of Population by Sex and Age Group, Los Pinos, 1981

that, in addition to the large flow of international migrants, internal migration was also substantial. As figures 3.3 and 3.4 indicate, both internal and international migrants were overwhelmingly concentrated in the productive years of 15 to 59.

What factors account for this unusual demographic profile? Most important is the small proportion of individuals in the 0–4 years group. Directly responsible for the low numbers of infants was the age-specific gender composition of the Pinero migrant stream. Not only were women well represented among migrants; as a glance at figures 3.3 and 3.4 confirms, they overwhelmingly tended to be in their prime childbearing years. Nearly three-quarters (73.7 percent) of women international migrants were between the ages of 20 and 39 years; among internal women migrants, 63.6 percent fell into this cohort. Conversely, among the population remaining in Los Pinos, only 19.4 per-

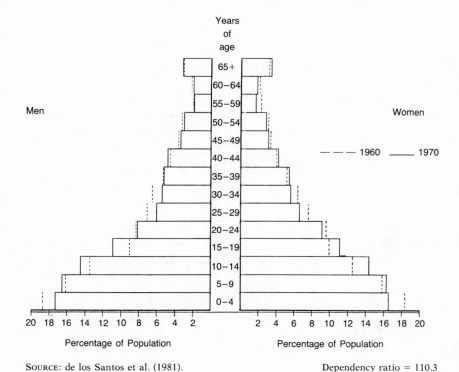

SOURCE: de los Santos et al. (1981).

Dependency ratio = 110.3

FIGURE 3.2. Distribution of Population by Sex and Age Group, Dominican Republic, 1960–1970

cent of all women fell between the ages of 20 and 39.[5] The high levels of migration among women of prime childbearing age thus had resulted in the abnormally small population of young children and was one of the primary determinants of the favorable dependency ratio found in Los Pinos.

OCCUPATIONAL SELECTIVITY

A grasp of the occupational characteristics of international labor migrants is central to any evaluation of the socioeconomic impact of

5. That the factors promoting the migration of women in their prime childbearing years from Los Pinos are operating throughout the nation is seen in the differences between the national distribution in 1960 and in 1970 (figure 3.2). These shifts, especially the notably smaller number of children aged 0–4, have been attributed in part to the effects of international migration (de los Santos et al. 1981).

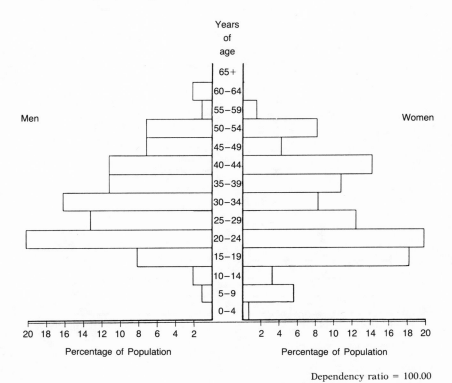

FIGURE 3.3. Distribution of Internal Migrants by Sex and Age Group, Los Pinos, 1981

migration on the sending community, the subject of chapters 4 and 5. Whether migrants were employed prior to migration and in which sectors of the economy they were employed have implications for evaluating the distribution of the effects of migration among members of the sending community. In this section, the occupations of Pinero men and women migrants are examined and compared.

Table 3.6 shows the distribution of the primary occupations of Pinero international migrants prior to migration. Several features of this distribution help place the Pinero stream in theoretical perspective. First, only 2 percent of the men and no women were reported to be completely unemployed prior to migration. Without doubt, a certain amount of underemployment characterized many of these Pineros. For some 30 percent of women migrants, housework was the primary occupation prior to migration. Yet this category may be deceptive, concealing underemployment or unemployment. Many of the

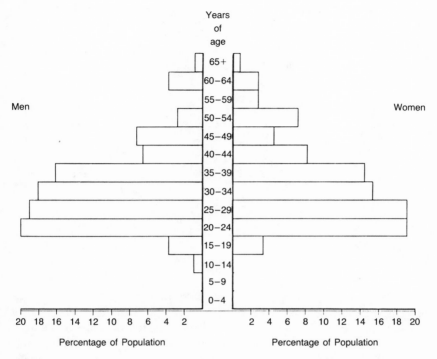

FIGURE 3.4. Distribution of International Migrants by Sex and Age Group, Los Pinos, 1981

men engaged in agriculture and, especially, unskilled activities also undoubtedly experienced underemployment before going to the United States. Nonetheless, open unemployment appears to have been rare for migrants, at least among men.

Second, the largest proportion of Pineros were students at the time of their migration. That students accounted for 22.8 percent of the migrant stream reflects the dynamics of Dominican chain migration discussed earlier. Sponsored by their migrant parents, nearly all students entered the stream as documented migrants. Pineros had come to place a high value on their children's education, even if the schooling of some had to be interrupted out of economic necessity. Secure income from remittances enabled many children in migrant households to remain in school longer than those of nonmigrants (see chapter 6). They therefore were less likely to be in the work force at the time of their own migration.

Third, as might be expected for a small rural community such as

TABLE 3.6. Primary Employment Prior to Migration by Sex

Sector	Men		Women		Total	
	N	%	N	%	N	%
Agriculture[a]	62	32.5	1	0.5	63	16.0
Skilled/Semiskilled	31	16.2	16	7.9	47	11.9
Unskilled	11	5.8	33	16.3	44	11.2
Commerce[a]	19	10.0	9	4.4	28	7.1
Artisanal production	18	9.4	24	11.8	42	10.7
Urban industrial	10	5.2	7	3.5	17	4.3
Housework	0	0	59	29.1	59	15.0
Student	36	18.9	54	26.6	90	22.8
Unemployed	4	2.1	0	0	4	1.0
Total	191	48.5	203	51.5	394	100.0

[a]Own-account.

Los Pinos, the largest proportion of male migrants (32.5 percent) was engaged in agriculture. This reflects both the former importance of agriculture to the local economy and the division of labor by gender.

Less expected, however, was the large proportion of men (16.2 percent) who were engaged in what, in the Dominican context, can be considered skilled and semiskilled activities prior to their migration. A mixed category, this included school teacher, office worker, technical assistant to professionals, and professionals such as doctor, engineer, architect, and agronomist. The most highly skilled of these Pinero migrants resided in the major Dominican cities prior to their migration to the United States, but others, such as the teachers and some technicians, lived in Los Pinos. In the context of a community like Los Pinos, the loss of these men, as well as of skilled women and many of the students, could be viewed as a veritable "rural brain drain."

There were significant gender differences with respect to skill levels. A salient feature of the Pinero migrant stream was the decreased selectivity for skill among women. Among women, those engaged in unskilled occupations prior to migration outnumbered those in skilled and semiskilled occupations two to one. In contrast, men were three times more likely to be skilled and semiskilled than unskilled workers. Put otherwise, twice as many men worked at skilled and semiskilled jobs before migrating as women. The lower skill level found among women migrants was closely related to the differential internal migration patterns of men and women discussed above. That is, women's greater participation in internal migration gave them entrée into the lower levels of the waged labor force; at the same time, it afforded them social advantages which in some cases outweighed their occupational and income handicaps vis-à-vis male migrants.

Despite their relative concentration in unskilled jobs, the labor force participation of Pinera women migrants prior to migration was considerably higher than that of women in the republic as a whole. In 1979, only 15.7 percent of adult Dominican women worked outside the home, as opposed to 32.5 percent of Pinera migrant women (Wilkie and Perkal 1984:260, table 1300). Pineras' higher rates of labor force participation underscore once again the point that work outside the home and, more specifically, outside the village, could be a significant route to international migration for some women.

Other important components of the migrant stream included shopkeepers (7.1 percent) and artisans (10.7 percent). Among the latter were many, such as tailors and chair makers, who also owned their own businesses. Factory workers, nearly all of whom lived in Santiago or Santo Domingo prior to migration, accounted for only 4.3 percent of all migrants (nationally, in 1980, 8.1 percent of the work force was employed in manufacturing; Wilkie and Perkal 1984:260, table 1301).

It is evident from table 3.6 that the composition of the Pinero migrant stream was quite diverse and that no occupational category accounted for a majority of U.S. migrates. This diversity was a reflection of the variegated occupational structure of Los Pinos, its privileged access, as the site of the sección's high school, to formal education, and its pattern of internal migration. It also suggests that strong pressures to migrate had been experienced by broad sectors of Pinero society.

The portrait that emerges from this and the preceding descriptions of Pinero's premigration characteristics is not one of a disadvantaged "surplus" rural population, pushed off the land and into the cities by absolute poverty. On the contrary, migrants tended to be members of landholding households with large and medium-sized parcels at the time of migration. Their average educational level (5.6 years) was higher than that of those who remained in Los Pinos (4.0 years), although not as high as those who migrated to Santiago and Santo Domingo (6.7 and 6.5 years, respectively; many of the latter were university students). And the majority were either students, relatively skilled workers, or self-employed merchants and artisans. In brief, migrants to the United States, as well as many of those who migrated to the major cities of the republic, were characterized by preferential access to material resources, human capital, and social connections not equally distributed among the population.

COMPARISON OF DOCUMENTED AND UNDOCUMENTED MIGRANTS

Interestingly, the occupational characteristics of undocumented men and women exaggerate the selective tendencies just described. In fact, the portrait of the undocumented Pinero population that emerges is quite the contrary to popular conceptions of the economically desperate "illegal alien."

At the time I finished compiling the roster of Pinero migrants, 53 Pineros, 19 women and 34 men, were residing in the United States as undocumented migrants. In contrast to documented migrants, only one man and two women were students at the time of their migration. Undocumented men were only half as likely as documented men to have been engaged in any kind of agriculture prior to migration. Over two-fifths (41.2 percent) of the undocumented men worked at skilled and semiskilled jobs, and nearly one-fifth (17.7 percent) owned their own shops. These proportions are approximately double those for documented men. In contrast, undocumented women were three times as likely as the documented women to have worked in unskilled jobs. The great majority of these women had migrated to Santiago where they worked as domestics before going to the United States.

Two factors were largely responsible for these particular features. The first was the high and rising cost of undocumented entry, which intensified selection for socially and economically advantaged Pineros. The second was the recency of the undocumented stream. Over 80 percent (43 migrants) of the currently undocumented had been in the United States five years or less. In other words, most left the republic in the mid-to late 1970s. This was a time when agriculture was in severe decline (see chapter 5). In Los Pinos, as in many rural communities throughout Latin America during the 1970s, access to land became less important to survival than access to wage labor and other sources of cash income. It was also a time when rising educational levels among younger Pineros made it possible for some to acquire skilled and semiskilled technical and service jobs created during the Balaguer regime, even if most often, this required migrating to a large city.

Thus, even less than the documented population, the undocumented did not form part of the republic's labor surplus prior to migration. Rather, their relatively more privileged incorporation into the national economy appears to have provided them with the springboard from which to launch a costly international move.

INTERNAL AND INTERNATIONAL MIGRATION COMPARED: A VIEW FROM THE SECCIÓN

In the western Sierra, as in other regions of the republic characterized by intensive U.S.-bound migration, not all communities participate equally in the international migrant stream. In the Sierran case, it is inaccurate to view migration as diffusing in a linear fashion from the major cities to village after village as information on the process becomes available (e.g., Piore 1979:137-138). True, close ties with Santiago, the original site of enllave, patronage, information, documentation, and visa brokers, provided much of the initial impetus for Pinero migration. But if the idea diffused from Santiago, it did so in a leapfrog fashion, skipping many communities along the way. Nonetheless, those villages not contributing to the international migrant stream did exhibit high levels of internal migration. Every community in the sección was characterized by one of two migratory patterns. In about one-third of the sección's fewer than twenty villages, migration was predominantly international, whereas in the remaining two-thirds, it was internal. In communities in which international migration prevailed, internal migration was also significant but proportionally less so. On the other hand, the communities with high levels of internal migration had very low levels of international migration.

To examine this inverse relationship between levels of international and internal migration, it is essential to leave the village-bound analysis we have pursued up to now in this chapter and place Los Pinos in the context of its sección. In the following sections, Los Pinos' migrant flow is compared with that of El Guano, a neighboring hamlet typical of other internal migrant communities of the sección. Such a comparison will help clarify the essential features of the two streams, as well as the dynamic relationship between them. Before turning to this comparison, the economy and social structure of El Guano, to which I will return often in the following chapters, are briefly described.

Non-U.S.-Bound Migrant Communities: The Example of El Guano

With a 1981 population of some 170 inhabitants, El Guano was a small village not far from Los Pinos. Poor agricultural resources and dependence on artisanal production made El Guano much like the sección's other small and impoverished communities which sent few migrants to the United States. Situated on a high, narrow ridge, El Guano was an area with thinner topsoils and more limited agricultural land than international migrant communities, all of which were favorably nestled in river valleys. Bitter manioc, rarely grown in Los Pinos, was the principal crop, and processing it into casave, or manioc bread, was an economically important activity.

Surpassing subsistence agriculture and cash crop production in importance was the handicraft production of esteras. Estera weaving illustrated well the conditions characterizing much of the production of other artisanal goods in these communities. All were highly labor-intensive processes which relied entirely on household labor. Within the household, the multiple tasks involved in production fell predominantly to women and children. To make esteras, some women, with occasional help from their husbands, went into the fields and forests to gather the guano leaves, which were cut from the tall palms with serrated blades made of tin cans secured to long poles. The leaves had to be torn into strips and decorticated. The women boiled the strips with a bit of detergent to whiten them and, after further blanching in the sun, wove the now supple fibers into long coiled bands. Using thick wooden needles, they sewed these bands into sheaths with twine thread which they also laboriously made from guano. Commenting on the intensive labor demands and low returns of estera production, a woman from El Guano ruefully observed, "If you stop to think about all the work that goes into making an estera, you wouldn't do it. That's why I try not to think about it."

Despite the exclusive use of unpaid household labor, estera production was marked by very low economic returns. Low returns had been exacerbated by the growing need to purchase guano leaves. Until the recent past, guano palms were a free good which grew abundantly in forests and pastures. But as a result of population increase, land fragmentation, and the deterioration of agricultural resources, more communities had come to rely on palm–weaving for their livelihood. This had led to greater demand for all kinds of leaves, which had become increasingly commodified. This was less true in Los Pinos, where few depended on weaving to any great extent. But in the poorer villages which relied heavily on this type of activity, more palm leaves now had to be purchased. Increased demand for guano leaves also meant that women had to travel farther to find them. Always meager, the returns from palm–weaving thus became minimal, as can be seen from table 3.7. To place these returns in context, table 3.8 lists the costs of a typical noonday meal, the largest of the day, for an El Guano family of six which derived almost all of its cash income from a combination of estera weaving by the wife-mother of the household, and occasional day labor by the father-husband.

Terms of exchange for esteras were not always so dismal (table 3.9). As travelers' reports and respondents' recollections agree, in the past men wove serones and esteras. It appears that, as the terms of exchange deteriorated, the task of palm-weaving was relegated to women, with the help of children.

To meet consumption expenses in the face of such meager returns to labor, many households in the noninternational migrant communities engaged in a system of lien-barter with local shopkeepers. In El Guano, one shopkeeper dominated most economic transactions. This shopkeeper was also the largest landowner and therefore the largest supplier of guano leaves, as well as the most important employer of wage labor in El Guano. He was also the local link in the chain of estera intermediaries. This man advanced most poor households the credit to buy food in his store. Credit was repaid with esteras, which he purchased at DR\$.40 a pair, that is, DR\$ .10 below the standard "market" price. As can be deduced from a comparison of tables 3.8 and 3.9, if a household was forced to subsist primarily by weaving esteras, it could remain perpetually in debt to the shopkeeper. This resulted in a relationship of dependency that had implications for other aspects of the local economy and social structure as well. The

TABLE 3.7. Inputs and Yields of Estera Production, 1981

Cost of 1 salta (standard bundle) of guano	DR\$.50
Number of esteras/salta	4 pairs[a]
Number of esteras woven in a "full" day[b]	4 pairs
Price paid by intermediary	.50/pair
Net earnings for a full day	\$1.50

[a]Esteras are always spoken of and sold in pairs.
[b]One woman with the help of two small children devoting eight hours to estera production. Because of the demands of other household activities, few women could produce this number of esteras every day. Most women did not weave on Sunday.

TABLE 3.8. Minimum Cost of One Noonday Meal for a Poor Family of Six, 1981

Item	Quantity	Cost	Cost/Meal
Rice	2$\frac{1}{2}$ lbs	DR$.30/lb.	DR$.75
Beans	$\frac{1}{2}$ lb	.60/lb	.30
Oil	$\frac{1}{3}$ bottle	.90/bottle	.30
Recao[a]			.15
Sugar	$\frac{1}{2}$ lb	.26/lb	.13
Total			DR$1.63

[a]Recao is the seasoning consisting of garlic, onion, and tomato paste used to flavor and color rice and beans.

TABLE 3.9. Approximate Cost of Selected Basic Foods and Estera/ Seron Prices, 1930–1981

	Year		
Item	1930–1940	1960	1981
Estera/Seron	DR$.10/pr	DR$.20/pr	DR$ .50/pr
Meat	.04/lb	.20/lb	1.50/lb
Casave	.02/cake	.30/cake	.60/cake
Corn	.03/cajon[a]	.40/cajon	1.40/cajon
Percentage of 3 items purchasable with 1 pair of esteras:	111%	22%	14%

[a]One cajon = 12 lbs.

most notable instance of this dependency was the obligation binding the adult male members of these debtor households to work for the day-wage the shopkeeper dictated. At around DR$2.50, the day wage for agricultural labor in El Guano was considerably lower than in Los Pinos, where a man with a reputation as a good worker might receive twice as much. Yet because workers were tied to their shopkeeper-patron by debt obligations imbued with quasi-moral overtones, few were able to work for the higher wages offered down the road in Los Pinos.

Nevertheless, the people of El Guano and Los Pinos maintained frequent and close contact. El Guano and the other villages of the sección depended on Los Pinos for basic services such as education beyond the third grade, mail, dollar exchange, private and public health care, and direct transportation to Santiago and Santo Domingo. Los Pinos was also the wholesale and retail hub of the sección, as well as the site of its church and cockfight pit. But just as a situation of unequal exchange had existed historically between Los Pinos and the urban centers of the republic, a similar situation was maintained between Los Pinos and the smaller villages of the sección. Los Pinos was the center of a variety of intermediaries who lived by extracting profits from the surrounding countryside. Pinero intermediaries were the principal buyers of the esteras, serones, logs, manioc bread and gold produced in El Guano and other poor communities. Also from these the intermediaries purchased agricultural produce, cana leaves, and cattle. Their considerable rates of profit are evident from table 3.10.

The economic disadvantages experienced by neighboring villages vis-à-vis Los Pinos were translated into social handicaps as well. Long-standing ties such as those that linked Los Pinos with Santiago were few between poor villages and major urban centers. The contact that did exist was often mediated by Pinero middlemen. As a consequence, many poor individuals from El Guano and other small villages tried to establish patron–client relations with better-off Pineros. This pattern of economic and social dependence, in turn, had implications for the patterns of migration from these villages, as discussed in the next section.

TABLE 3.10. Estimated Gross Rates of Profit on Principal Artisanal Products Produced in Los Pinos Sección, 1980

Item	Purchase price (in sección)	Resale price (in Santiago and Santo Domingo)	Gross profits
Esteras	DR$.50/pr	DR$.75	50%
Lumber	100/100 boards	300	approx. 200%[a]
Cana	2.50/50 leaves	5.00	100%
Gold	17.00/gram[b]	27–28[b]	59–65%

[a]Because this activity was completely illegal, bribes had to be made to police at checkpoints in several towns and villages. Lumber therefore undoubtedly involved the highest costs to the intermediary.
[b]November 1980.

Migration from El Guano and Los Pinos

A pattern distinct from that of Los Pinos characterized migration from El Guano. Of the 83 individuals who had left El Guano, only 6 had migrated to the United States, three after marrying legal residents from Los Pinos and another migrant town in the municipio and another three as undocumented stowaways, a method of entry shunned by Pineros. The other 77 settled within the republic. Thus, like the sección's other small, poor communities, El Guano had a high rate of internal migration. Whereas internal migrants composed only 35.8 percent of the total migrant stream from Los Pinos, they composed 92.8 percent of that of El Guano. Moreover, the destinations of internal migrants from El Guano and Los Pinos were notably different. Especially striking was the large proportion from El Guano who migrated to other rural areas of the republic. In fact, with regard to the destinations of internal migrants, El Guano and Los Pinos were mirror images of each other: a total of 71.8 percent of the Pinero internal migrant stream was directed to urban areas of the republic, in contrast to 37.7 percent of that from El Guano, whereas rural areas of the republic received 28.2 percent of Pinero internal migrants and 62.3 percent of those from El Guano (table 3.11). Santiago and Santo Domingo alone received 60.5 percent of all Pinero internal migrants, but only 35.1 percent of those from El Guano. Thus, the orientation of Pinero internal migrants was overwhelmingly urban, whereas that of El Guano's migrants was just as strongly rural.

At the time I censused Los Pinos and El Guano, people from landless and semiproletarian households predominated among nonmi-

TABLE 3.11. Rates of Internal and International Migration from Los Pinos and El Guano (Percentages)

| | Total migrant stream | | Internal migration | |
Destination	Los Pinos	El Guano	Los Pinos	El Guano
International	64.2	7.2	—	—
Internal	35.8	92.8	—	—
Santiago	14.3	16.9	40.0	18.2
Santo Domingo	7.3	15.6	20.4	16.9
Other urban DR	4.1	2.4	11.4	2.6
Rural DR[a]	10.1	57.8	28.2	62.3

[a]A community is classified as rural if its 1981 population is under 2000.

grants and migrants to rural areas of the republic (table 3.12). In contrast, migration to urban areas was more selective for size of family landholding. Thus, while 23 percent of the national population had access to 80 tareas of land or more, this was true of 34.5 percent and 32.3 percent of urban-bound migrants from El Guano and Los Pinos. These findings also support the point made earlier with respect to international migration, a point contrary to the belief of many neoclassical as well as Marxist economists, that is, that migrants are drawn from a "surplus" rural population, which dispossessed of its land, is made "free" to move to the cities to work for wages. Instead, as I have argued, migrants were more likely to come from households with more privileged access to resources strategic in the rural context.

The wider applicability of these findings is suggested by a recent study by the Dominican sociologists Duarte and Pou of working-class and informal sectors of Santo Domingo. On the basis of their survey of these sectors, they conclude that "[i]n terms of land tenure and relations of production it is not the most pauperized nor the dispossessed—those who are in the worst working conditions—who migrate. Rather, it is the children of families with access to the means of production" (i.e., those households with more than 80 tareas of land; 1983:11, my translation). In short, people who had been "freed" from their land often found that their opportunities for migration out of the rural sector were limited.

In both El Guano and Los Pinos, members of landless and semiproletarian households were less likely to migrate out of the countryside. However, selectivity for size of landholding had been less

TABLE 3.12. Size of Family Landholdings of International Migrants, Internal Migrants, and Nonmigrants, Los Pinos and El Guano (percentages)

Destination	Landless and semiproletarian <80 tas.		Subsistence and commercial ≥80 tas.	
	El Guano	Los Pinos	El Guano	Los Pinos
Nonmigrants	65.0	76.0	35.0	24.0
International	0	57.7	100.0	42.3
Urban DR	65.6	67.7	34.5	32.3
Rural	83.3	88.7	16.7	11.3
Total DR[a]	77.0		23.0	

[a]SOURCE: Duarte and Pou (1983, table 2).

severe for international migrants from Los Pinos. How are we to account for the marked differences between Los Pinos and El Guano with respect to international migration? Part of the explanation for the weaker relationship between size of landholding and international migration found in Los Pinos lay in its diversified economy, where salaried state-sector employment and productive resources other than land were also significant. But perhaps more important still were the social resources available to many Pineros as a result of the long history of unequal exchange with, and economic dominance over, surrounding villages. In Los Pinos, the historically nodal position that some of its members occupied in the larger "web of exploitation" (Soares 1977) had enabled them to concentrate profits and contacts in their own hands. Privileged Pineros thus could establish and maintain wide social networks which encompassed important cities like Santiago. As we have seen, these links were of critical importance to the earliest migrants. After 1961, better-off Pineros followed the example set by these pioneers; they used their superior resources to obtain legitimate or purchased visas. Intense trafficking with urban visa brokers quickly led to the establishment of local recruiters in Los Pinos who facilitated the migration of many Pineros during the 1970s. With the establishment of the merchant elite, the largest landowners, and later the migrants themselves as the usurious backers of migrants, the self-organized system of migration was complete. And once the system was in place, multiplex ties among its members proved a resource valuable enough to help many compensate for a disadvantage in terms of access to productive resources. Such a system did not and could not develop in smaller, poorer communities such as El Guano, caught less favorably in the larger web of exploitation. In these, therefore, only the wealthiest were able to migrate.

Internal Migration from El Guano and Los Pinos Compared: Basic Selective Features

Inequalities between Los Pinos and El Guano were manifested in several other ways as well. Not surprisingly, migrants from El Guano had considerably lower levels of education than Pinero migrants. Whereas 76 percent of Pinero migrants had completed more than four grades of school, this was the case for only 35 percent of El Guano's population. And, except for one or two shopkeepers, the people of El Guano rarely experienced the social advantages enjoyed by many Pineros. These differences translated into distinct occupational patterns in the area of destination. Table 3.13 shows the occupational

TABLE 3.13. Primary Occupations of Urban Migrants from El Guano and Los Pinos

Occupation	Los Pinos		El Guano	
	N	%	N	%
Agriculture	3	2.0	0	0
Skilled and semi-skilled	44	29.1	2	7.4
Unskilled	25	16.6	16	59.3
Commerce (own-account)	18	11.9	0	0
Urban industrial	5	3.3	1	3.7
Housework	25	16.6	1	3.7
Day labor	12	8.0	3	11.1
Student	19	12.6	4	14.8
Total	151	100.1[a]	27	100.0

[a]Due to rounding.

distribution of urban internal migrants from El Guano and Los Pinos. Table 3.14 shows this distribution for rural internal migrants from the two communities. Not surprisingly, Pinero migrants—whether destined for rural or urban areas, were more likely to work in skilled and semiskilled occupations and less likely to work in agriculture and

TABLE 3.14. Primary Occupations of Rural Migrants from El Guano and Los Pinos

Occupation	Los Pinos		El Guano	
	N	%	N	%
Agriculture	6	9.8	7	15.2
Skilled and semiskilled	9	14.8	3	6.6
Unskilled	2	3.3	2	4.4
Commerce (own-account)	8	13.1	2	4.4
Day labor	2	3.3	7	15.2
Housework	19	31.2	5	10.9
Artisanal	10	16.4	16	34.8
Student	5	8.2	4	8.7
Total	61	100.1[a]	46	100.2[a]

[a]Due to rounding.

day labor. Moreover, Pinero migrants were ten times more likely to be in business for themselves. Thus the inequalities characterizing Los Pinos and El Guano in the countryside were carried with the migrants and replicated in their areas of destination, whether rural or urban.

MIGRANT STREAM PROFILES: THEORETICAL IMPLICATIONS

In this chapter, I have described the evolution of a locally initiated system of migrant recruitment and analyzed how the interplay between this system and U.S. immigration policy led to the induction of some segments of Pinero society into the international migrant stream while excluding others. This interplay, of course, occurred within the context of social and economic reorganization in both the Dominican Republic and the United States. In villages like Los Pinos, the agrarian base of the economy had been undermined drastically, and the means to social and economic stability and improvement were now generally located outside the community. In cities like New York, Pineros, together with other new immigrants, helped meet the demand for low-wage labor in declining industries as well as in expanding sectors, such as services and light manufacturing. Moreover, the feminization of a significant proportion of these jobs incorporated record numbers of women, both native and immigrant, into the labor force. All the while that these changes were taking place, the Dominican Republic was experiencing ever greater integration into the world system and, in particular, a growing articulation with United States interests.

Against this background, it becomes evident that Pinero migration to the United States was a dynamic process which did not entirely conform to prevailing models as discussed in the introduction to this volume. The functional division of labor between sending and receiving societies posited by Meillassoux and others, although initially applicable, did not remain in effect for long. Over time, given the migration of women in numbers comparable to men, new migrant households were formed in the United States. Or, households divided by migration were reconstituted as migrants used the family reunification provisions of U.S. immigration law to displace household members from the sending community to the United States. As the migratory process gained momentum, many of the offspring of migrant households were not born and reared in the sending community. Contrary to predictions, this process, as it evolved in Los Pinos and other sending communities in the Dominican Republic, had not resulted in a population bottom-heavy with young dependents who were reared by the unpaid labor of women for future migration. Although this might have been the case in the earliest period of migration and grandmothers and aunts might temporarily replace some mothers, the migration of women in their prime reproductive years had led to the transferral of part of the "nursery function" to the receiving society.

All this is not to say that it was not cheaper to rear a worker in the rural Dominican Republic than in the urban United States. Nor is it to say that important costs—for instance, education and maintenance of the aged and the disabled who were denied visas—were not borne in part by the sending society. It is only to argue against a teleological and static view of the international division of labor and the implicit passivity of those in the periphery. In the absence of repressive constraints on family reunification, migrants seized the opportunities available and deployed their cultural resources to create new ones in order to maximize the economic benefits of migration and minimize its emotional cost. Through their networks, Pineros thus were able to fashion a transnational undercurrent, "running counter to dominant structures of exploitation" (Portes and Walton 1981:60). And by doing so, they transformed some of the conditions initially so favorable to capitalist employers in the core.

CHAPTER 4

The Impact of International Migration on the Local Economy Modernization and Informalization

During the Trujillato Los Pinos witnessed profound economic, social, and political transformations, the effects of which continued with equal force after Trujillo's death. After a brief anarchic hiatus in the early 1960s, the Balaguerato of 1966–1978 reestablished authoritarian patterns of control reminiscent of Trujillo's long regime. It also pursued profoundly new development policies which redounded with special force in rural areas like Los Pinos. The previous chapters examined the development of a migration system in response to these changes and other transformations resulting from national and international capitalism and its policies.

This chapter resumes the narrative begun in chapter 2: it describes the development of Los Pinos in the post-Trujillo years, with special focus on the consequences of the migration system for the local economy and society. Discussion of the consequences of migration for Pinero agriculture is reserved for chapter 5.

LOS PINOS IN THE POST-TRUJILLO PERIOD

A watershed in recent Dominican history, the demise of the Trujillo regime had an immediate and profound impact on Los Pinos. As seen in chapter 3, international labor migration took off as individuals who lacked the enllave to migrate during the Trujillato began to secure visas and leave the community.

For those who remained, the period of political anarchy following the assassination opened new possibilities in several sectors of the economy. During this period, Pineros ran the Trujillista mayor into hiding and once again wrested control of local affairs into their own hands. Relaxed control over rural communities throughout the Sierra resulted in the reactivation of a decentralized lumber industry, a rash of squatters' claims to state lands, and innovative extralegal activities in various spheres of the local economy (Antonini et al. 1975:56).

Known in Los Pinos as *La Libertad*, a time of freedom, the years between 1962 and 1966 witnessed a succession of political regimes at the national level, culminating in civil war and the invasion of the republic by U.S. troops. One of the first local responses to La Libertad was *La Zafra*—the harvest—which involved the widespread clear-cutting of state and privately owned forest latifundia. Once again, pines were harvested on a large scale for sale in Santiago. In addition, pressures created by demographic growth, the parcelization of holdings, and state expropriations of vast tracts of land during the Trujillato led many during La Libertad to claim plots in La Loma. Pinero smallholders established their claims by clear-cutting parcels of land and planting them in subsistence crops. But shallow soils and steep gradients ensured that, once deforested, the Loma slopes would erode swiftly and drastically. After one or two harvests, the land became useless for agriculture, and plots were put permanently into pasture.

Local intermediaries purchased the lumber from these claims and transported it to Santiago in their trucks. Most of these intermediaries were sons of the largest local merchants; some were in-migrant merchants attracted to Los Pinos during the heyday of the sawmills. When the opportunity presented itself after 1961, they moved swiftly into the lumber intermediary role. Later, with capital accumulated from lumber, they financed their moves to Santiago and Santo Domingo. Thus, during La Libertad Pineros were able to revive their decentralized lumber trade and expand their agricultural base somewhat. In other words, the years 1961–1966 presented Los Pinos with a brief respite from the economic deterioration of the 1950s.

The election of Reformist Party leader Joaquin Balaguer as president of the republic in 1966 once again reversed the community's fortunes. Balaguer's declaration of the conservationist Forestry Law in 1967 prohibited unauthorized cutting of trees on all lands, private as well as state-owned. Control over forests was transferred to the military, and open lumbering activity and squatters' claims to state lands abruptly ceased. During the Balaguerato, heavy vigilance and stiff penalties prevented significant circumvention of the new law. Nonetheless, limited contraband logging continued circumspectly at night.

With the 1978 electoral victory of the Partido Revolucionario

Dominicano (PRD), control over the forests became simultaneously more relaxed and more politicized. Regarded as spoils of the election, forests were placed in the hands of *forestales* (forest rangers), all loyal PRD supporters, who ensured that clandestine exploitation of forest resources was carried out by other loyal PRD supporters and members of their networks. Nestled in the more remote parts of the forest, small diesel-powered sawmills began to proliferate in Los Pinos. With the establishment of the sawmills—also largely under the control of PRD supporters—Los Pinos cast a faint shadow of its former prominence as the center of lumber production and distribution in the sección.

At the time of my fieldwork, lumbering formed part of a flourishing underground economy. Trees were cut in La Loma at night. Logs were then hauled by oxen over covert trails to the sawmills, where they were milled into boards. Approaching the sawmill through supposedly secret entrances, intermediaries loaded the boards, hidden under a blanket of cana leaves, onto their trucks. The new sawmills were strategically located on side roads which could be entered without passing police checkpoints. Bribes were usually required at the other checkpoints passed en route to Santiago, where the lumber was sold to the large construction companies. Actually, this contraband logging was an open secret; by observing the way a truck's tires sagged under the weight of the wood, even children could tell when it was carrying lumber rather than lightweight cana leaves.

Related to clandestine logging and the sawmills, another new feature in the Pinero economy emerged by the early 1970s. Home workshops for the production of Sierran straight-backed chairs and rockers began to proliferate in the community. Attracted by the more abundant supply of labor and raw materials (lumber and royal palm fronds), a wealthy workshop owner from another Sierran village established the first workshop in Los Pinos in 1972. His village is renowned in the republic for its furniture craftsmanship, and it has filled the national demand for finely crafted mahogany and oak furniture since the early twentieth century. The workshop established by this entrepreneur in Los Pinos, however, produced inexpensive, rough-hewn pine chairs for a different market: the urban and rural poor of the republic. Soon, Pineros began to set up their own workshops. Although during the conservationist Balaguer years lumbering was curtailed, the nocturnal contraband trade generally was able to provide an adequate supply of pine for the new workshops; after the PRD gained control of the central government the number of workshops sharply increased. Like the sawmills, these were located on the outskirts of the village, beyond the police checkpoint.

At a time of near collapse of local agriculture and reclamation of La Loma from squatters, the workshops represented an opportunity for independent artisanal activity that was avidly seized by Pinero women and men alike. Chair workshops became associated with semiproletarian households which relied almost entirely on the labor of members to produce the chairs. Artisanal production of chairs became organized by a fairly strict division of labor: the men cut and hewed small pines into chair frames, and the women and children gathered, processed, and wove royal palm fronds into backs and seats. Not only did chair production generate a greater income than agriculture, but it also promised increased security. For the men, too, chair making was considered less arduous and "cleaner" than agriculture and day labor. By the 1970s, low returns from agriculture and the growing availability and prestige of nonagricultural work led many, especially younger, Pineros to distinguish between "trabajo sucio," dirty work in the fields, and "trabajo limpio y sin sol," clean work outside the fields, without the hardship of exposure to the sun and other elements. Preferring the clean, shady work of chair making, the men of these smallholder households increasingly turned away from agriculture. The women abandoned serron and estera weaving in favor of the slightly more lucrative chair weaving.

Relaxation of central authority and abolition of extreme repression after 1961 also created conditions for the emergence of another new occupation: the illegal lottery vendor. Under the control of the state since its appearance, the national lottery was distributed by authorized, licensed vendors during the Trujillato. After the mid-1960s, unauthorized vendors, *riferos cimarrones*, began to proliferate. Recognized by the small notebook in their front pockets in which they keep track of the numbers, vendors scour the countryside on foot and muleback to sell their "pieces" (*pedazos*) of the weekly lottery prize. As the economy of Los Pinos became increasingly monetized, the number of vendors and the volume of lottery transactions had steadily grown.

Some thirty vendors operated on a full-time or part-time basis in the community. In Los Pinos, as elsewhere in the republic, most lottery vendors were men. Some supported their households solely by selling numbers; others merely earned enough cash to supplement the weekly budget. The size of a vendor's business was not limited simply by demand. Rather, limits were commonly set by the size of the capital fund from which winners had to be paid. Some vendors were able to back themselves; others worked on a commission basis (10–20 percent of weekly sales) with the backing (*respaldo*) of a wealthier individual.

Pineros, like many Dominicans, had a strong and abiding interest in the national lottery. It was a rare person, man or woman, who did not play the lottery. Dreams were discussed and interpreted for clues as to which numbers to play, and commonplace events were viewed as signs indicating lucky numbers. In fact, the lottery had become a central image in Pinero life: love, marriage, and the outcome of U.S. visa petitions were all compared to it, underscoring the elements of uncertainty and chance common to all three.

U.S. migration helped underwrite the expansion of the illegal lottery in two ways. First, as a result of the increased cash flow from remittances, migration boosted aggregate community demand for lottery pieces. Second, backing illegal lottery vendors was a popular form of investing U.S. savings. Thus, migrants' investments helped support the ever-increasing number of riferos in the community.

It is interesting to note, too, that Pineros replicated this institution in the United States. Winning numbers there were pegged to the national lottery in Santo Domingo. In New York, migrant riferos sold their pieces to townmates, neighbors, and friends, in some cases the same clientele they had in Los Pinos, as well as to Hispanic coworkers on the job. Some spent their weekends riding the subways to the boroughs of New York to visit their regular customers, as they once rode their mules to the hamlets of the sección. Thus, the lottery formed yet another cultural link that migrants had forged between Los Pinos and New York.

The migration system as it evolved in Los Pinos created an entirely new set of exploitative intermediary roles. Buscones, always men, frequently roamed the countryside attempting to find new clients. *Tributarios*, individuals who, for a generally steep fee, filled out the appropriate forms for a legitimate visa application also emerged. From the mid-1960s, postmasters automatically became the semiofficial changers for the thousands of dollars that entered the sección each week. Individuals from all the hamlets of the sección collected their mail in Los Pinos. Those who received money orders or cash from the United States often converted their dollars to pesos in the post office where they opened their mail. Most owners of middle-sized and large-sized shops also changed dollars. These dollar changers always paid a lower rate of exchange than those located in Santiago.

Both directly and indirectly, migrants' remittances and savings also enlarged a variety of traditional employment opportunities in Los Pinos. Like migrants in many other parts of the world (Baucic 1972; Marshall 1985a, Rhoades 1978; Watson 1975, inter alia), Pinero migrants gave priority to upgrading their housing. Dozens of new houses had been built in Los Pinos over the past two decades, and repairs and improvements were an ongoing process. Migrant-sponsored construction projects boosted local demand for carpenters, masons, housepainters, and electricians. One individual in Los Pinos made a career of purchasing migrants' old houses throughout the sección, tearing them down, and selling the lumber in Santiago. Santiago itself experienced a boom in the construction of moderate-income housing as a result of strong migrant demand (Grasmuck 1985:167), as did certain neighborhoods in the capital.

Since shortly after migration from Los Pinos began, migrants also repatriated earnings to the republic to purchase land, livestock, públicos, trucks, and stores. In addition to the illegal lottery, they invested liquid capital in savings banks and in usurious loans, often to other migrants. A few invested in nonagricultural productive resources. For example, two return migrants in Los Pinos purchased sawmills and established chair workshops; these two employed between six and eight men each. A third constructed a manioc bread factory which employed three workers. In Santiago, a woman return migrant opened a garment factory which created jobs for fifteen employees, including several Pineros. Another return migrant started a cement block factory in the capital which employed six full-time workers, three of whom were the owner's cousins who migrated from Los Pinos to work for him. (When this return migrant needed wooden molds to make the cement blocks, he commissioned them from his cousin, a sawmill owner and carpenter in Los Pinos.) Many other migrants had invested in small grocery stores, bars, or billiard halls in the community, sometimes managed by a parent or sibling. One migrant had four stores, each under the management of a poor Pinero who kept half the profits, the usual arrangement for managing a migrant's business. Because of migrants' investments, then, the number of públicos, minibuses, and grocery stores grew and so too did the number of men employed as drivers, shopkeepers, and clerks.

GENDER IDEOLOGY AND MEN'S AND WOMEN'S DIFFERENTIAL ACCESS TO NEW EMPLOYMENT OPPORTUNITIES

To understand the differential distribution of new employment opportunities between women and men in Los Pinos, it is necessary to examine in greater detail women's subordination, the division of labor by gender, and the ideology that supports these.

Although practice varied considerably according to class, ideally Pinera women were socially defined as housewives and men as breadwinners. In the cultural construction of gender in Los Pinos, as in the rural Dominican Republic generally (Rosado, Fernández, and Hernández 1987), the arena of women's activities was confined largely to house and patio (the cleared area behind the house) and nearby streams for washing, with occasional visits to the center of the village to make purchases, attend mass, or take a público to town to see a doctor, arrange documents, or visit a son or daughter. Within this circumscribed sphere of activity, women were responsible for tasks revolving around the reproduction of the household: cooking, cleaning and other household chores, and care of children and of the small animals that roam the patio. This close identification of women with the house and household was reflected, for example, in the common practice of designating a household solely by the name of the wife-mother. Pineros said they were going to visit "the house of Ramona," not the house of "Antonio and Ramona" or "of Antonio." Similarly, a man commonly referred to his residence as "the house of my wife" ("la casa de mi mujer"). Thus, when a man left a woman, it was customary for him to take only his clothes; the woman remained with the house and all its belongings.

"Esa no sale de su casa"—"that one never leaves her house"—was high praise for a woman who conformed to cultural expectations. The opposite of a "serious woman" (*mujer seria*) was a woman "of the street" (*de la calle*), the spatial domain of men and boys. The latter term had a sexual connotation as well. The sexual behavior of the domesticated serious woman who remained closely confined to house and patio was presumed to be under greater control than that of the woman who symbolically was associated with the domain of men, whose sexual behavior was normatively allowed much greater berth. Thus, serious women in general belonged to stable nuclear families. In contrast, the extreme poverty of some nonmigrant women who headed their own households led to a greater degree of role flexibility and spatial mobility (see Brown 1975). As a consequence of this flexibility and of their tendency to form serial relationships and have children with more than one man, these women might carry the stigma of being "of the street," and become the object of rumors, gossip, and even a degree of shunning.

Tasks closely associated with the domestic sphere, yet requiring frequent excursions into the street, such as hauling water from the river and making the daily food purchases, fell to young boys. Young girls stayed at home to help their mothers with the household chores. Until the age of about eight, girls might also go to the store for their mothers, but after puberty, their sphere of activity became considerably narrowed. After a girl became a señorita (reached menarche), her sexuality had be controlled in order to preserve her virginity, the highest value attributable to a woman (see Rosado et al. 1987). This was accomplished by the vigilance of other household members and by the restriction of the girl to the household compound.

Public spaces such as shops and bars where men gathered to chat and drink were rarely frequented by women and girls, although the wives of shopkeepers might work behind the counter with their husbands. The cockfight pit, the center of Pinero social action on weekends, was almost entirely the domain of men. One woman sold fried chicken from an enclosed stand on one side of the ring, but foods prepared by other Pineras in their homes were hawked to the crowd by young boys. An exception to the strict gender segregation of the cockfight was one old widow, an aficionada from a nearby hamlet who never missed a fight; her age, knowledge, and seriousness about the sport appeared to exempt her from disapprobation.

It must be mentioned that although women's spatial mobility was circumscribed, they did not live in social isolation. All households in Los Pinos, with the possible exception of the richest merchants and a few of the wealthiest landowners whose networks tended to be oriented more extralocally, were enmeshed in dense exchanges with neighbors, kin, and friends—frequently overlapping categories given patterns of land inheritance and a tendency toward village endogamy. Women often visited each other and together washed clothes in the stream, gathered coffee in their backyard plantations, toasted it in their kitchens, and watched television in each other's company at night. Moreover, women were kept abreast of much of the village's news through their children. Children, especially boys, were frequently sent on errands to public places or to other people's houses. Dawdling to chat and observe, they brought a wealth of secondhand information to their mothers. The proscriptions on women's habitual movements within the village appeared to fall heaviest on teenage girls who were caught in the contradictions of social change. New roles and work aspirations, fasionable clothes sent by kin in the United States and intended for display, and frequent parties and dances in the local bars and social club all enticed girls to be more visible in the community; yet they were criticized if they appeared "in the street" too often.

Given the gender ideology outlined above, it may appear paradoxical that the first three Pineros to migrate to New York were women and that women were well represented from the beginning of international migration. Many of the earliest women migrants were in proper unions at the time of their migration. Others were single women from the most respectable households in the community. But regardless of their marital status, these women did not travel alone. In nearly all cases they were accompanied by other, older women or couples who already had experience in living in New York. The presence of these chaperons may have blunted criticism and gossip to a certain extent, but it did not necessarily provide total immunization. It was sometimes said of these early women migrants that they were going to New York to become prostitutes, to cuckold their husbands, and so on. After U.S.-bound migration became more routine after 1961, these criticisms apparently died down.

The subordination of Pinera women had both ideological and material foundations. Most married women had limited opportunities to earn cash outside the home, and in any case the husband was expected to be the principal provider for the family. Nonetheless, women in stable unions with single mates often did contribute cash earnings to the household's income. They worked alongside their husbands in the shops or engaged in a variety of artisanal activities in the home. But their social definition as housewives first and foremost—the "housewife ideology" (Mies 1982; cf. Pessar 1982b)—led many women to answer in the negative when asked if they worked. When pressed, women would discuss the productive activities they engaged in, but they tended to regard these as supplementary, a way to help out their husbands who were the principal income providers. (Indeed, one of the reasons why I adopted the use of a checklist of women's economic activities in the community census was to probe the many cash-generating activities in which women did engage but which were not recognized.) In combination with the limited possibilities to work outside the home, the devaluation of their own contribution reinforced women's dependence on their husbands and hence their subordination.

This apparent digression is essential to an understanding of how most of the new work opportunities that began to appear in the late 1960s were patterned according to gender—in other words, how jobs and skills came to be "gendered" (Benería and Roldán 1987). Whether created by migrants' investments or by general trends in the Dominican economy, the great majority of income-generating opportunities were filled by men. This was especially true of those that were the most highly remunerative. Different kinds of work opportunities were created for women. Most derived from the fact that the migration process had contributed to the commodification of previously nonwaged work performed within the domestic economy. When a woman migrated and children were left behind, her labor in the household had to be replaced. Many women, often close kin, were employed as caretakers for the children of migrants; they were sent remittances for their services and also for household expenses. In the past, only the wealthiest merchants employed servants. Now many migrant households, as well as several of the households headed by teachers, employed women from poor households to clean house, wash clothes, and care for children. The number of women thus employed increased considerably over the 1970s. Domestic service, however, was low-status work characterized by extremely low pay and poor working conditions. Servants, for the most part young unmarried women, worked for ten or eleven hours each day, six days a week, and earned only DR$30 to $40 a month, plus three meals a day. Some women from the poorer hamlets who came to work as domestics in Los Pinos received lodging as well. In contrast, a man who worked full time as a lottery vendor made between DR$120 and $160 a month, and did not have to suffer the close supervision that characterized domestic service.

In Los Pinos' division of labor by gender, men generally controlled the tasks that required the use of tools, while women were excluded (see Deere and Leon de Leal 1981; Mones et al. 1987). In agriculture, men worked the fields with plows, hoes, and the broad machetes called *colines* (after the Collins Steel Company that manufactured them). Women from poor households might harvest certain crops such as peanuts—with their hands. Similarly, men wandered the Loma in search of pines to fell by axe. Thus, the reemergence of a significant amount of logging created supplementary income-generating activities principally for men. Lumbering was triply men's work: it required lonely excursions into isolated stands of forest; it was regarded as heavy work (*trabajo pesado*) in contrast to the "weak" work (*trabajo débil*) reserved for women because of their assumed weakness; and lastly, it demanded the use of tools. Similarly, when chair making was introduced in the early 1970s, men used axes, saws, and hammers to fashion the chair frames; the less remunerative work of hand-weaving palm fibers into seats and backs fell to women and children.

As a rule, the agricultural labor male migrants performed for the domestic unit was not fully replaced with waged workers. Rather, crop production was often reduced or, in some cases, simply abandoned (see chapter 5). However, many migrant households with large landholdings employed men to manage their land and herds in their absence. Typically, these overseers (*encargados*) received some cash remuneration for their services (between U.S $25 and $50 per month), as well as use of part of the migrant's land to sharecrop, graze their own cattle, and collect firewood, cana, and palma.

Related to the restrictions on women's free movement inside and outside the village, the illegal lottery, too, was almost exclusively a man's occupation. A few women sold a limited number of pieces from their kitchens, mainly to other women and to neighbors; for the most part, their clients had to come to them. The men, on the other hand, ranged widely through the village and the sección to hawk their pieces. They visited their regular clients in their homes to secure their weekly business, struck deals with the police, and gathered in the center of the village with other riferos each Sunday after all bets were made and before winning numbers were announced for great shouting matches called *peleas* ("fights"). In these matches, the vendors attempted to trade lottery pieces with each other to reduce risk should they have had too many customers betting on the same number.

The transportation boom that resulted from migrants' investments in públicos and minibuses also created jobs exclusively for men. Five of the community's nine publicos, for the most part Japanese compacts which could be coaxed into carrying up to six passengers, were migrant-owned. These vehicles provided the only service between hamlets of the sección and Santiago and Santo Domingo. Depending on the agreement struck with migrant owners, drivers kept a varying portion of the profits (generally one-half) and were responsible for all the expenses, including repairs. Drivers supplemented the income they earned from fares by performing a variety of services for a tip: changing dollars in the city, carrying messages, filling prescriptions, and making other special purchases of goods not locally available.

Migration simultaneously stimulated demand for transportation services. Members of migrant households were more likely to make trips to Santiago to go to the doctor, to shop, and to visit. Visa arrangements required them to travel frequently. Potential migrants might total a dozen or more trips to the municipal seat, where birth certificates were obtained; to Santiago, where documents were certified; and to Santo Domingo, where medical examinations were made and consular appointments were met. During holidays such as Christmas, Holy Week, and Mother's Day, público drivers might earn the bulk of their total annual income. Pouring in from New York at these times, migrants commissioned drivers to meet them at the airports of Santo Domingo or Puerto Plata and drive them to Los Pinos. The one-way trip cost as much as DR$100. Other migrants hired driver and car to take them to the beaches and other resorts. Drivers thus benefited from increased demand for their services generated by visiting migrants and by potential migrants. At the same time, this demand stimulated migrants to invest in more cars, públicos, and minibuses. Most of the men who worked as drivers were able to support their households on the DR$125–200 they cleared each month from fares and tips.

A Pinero man gave the following response to my inquiry as to why men, and not women, worked as drivers and lottery vendors:

> The man is dedicated to searching for the maintenance of the house, the household needs. Work at the level of the street is more for a man than a woman. A woman lottery vendor? That would look very bad. In her house, that's another thing. . . . There is a woman driver in Santiago who takes children to school in her car. That looks good. But not a woman [público] driver. Because of her nervousness [*nerviosismo*], people would be afraid of accidents.

This response exemplifies the ideology which assigned to women tasks closely associated with the domestic sphere. In this man's opinion, a woman's nerviosismo, a manifestation of her putative weakness, precluded her driving adults in a público; nonetheless, it was not regarded as affecting her ability to chauffeur small children to school. This ideology appeared to hold sway beyond Los Pinos as well: for the nation as a whole, the occupational group with the lowest rate of absorption of women between 1970 and 1981 was transportation equipment operators (Larson 1987a:76).

MODERNIZATION, MIDDLE-CLASS JOBS, AND CHANGING WORK ASPIRATIONS

A policy of modernization and integration of rural areas through public education, infrastructural improvements, and expanded social services began under Trujillo, faltered during La Libertad, but burgeoned after Balaguer took office. This policy helped to increase greatly the number of state-funded service jobs, particularly in education. Between 1966 and 1974, Los Pinos' school grew from eight to twelve grades and enrollment more than doubled. This expansion in educational facilities created a demand not only for primary and secondary teachers but also for ancillary personnel, such as school secretaries, concierges, nightwatchmen, and gardeners. In addition, the establishment or expansion of the police station, post office, and rural clinic and of agricultural extension and forestry services also opened new occupational opportunities for Pineros, especially for those with some formal education. All of these jobs were highly prized for the secure income they provided in the form of monthly government paychecks. Those who "live from the check" ("viven del cheque") comprised a privileged, often envied group in Los Pinos. Education had become a requisite credential for obtaining many of these new jobs, but political patronage was also crucial.

Beginning in the mid-1970s, the educational qualifications of teachers rose sharply. Whereas older Pinero teachers had between four and six years of schooling, all of the younger cohort (mainly in their late twenties and thirties) had some secondary education, many were *bachilleres* (high school graduates), and a few had a year or two of college as well. In contrast to most of the other income-generating opportunities which opened up in the 1970s, women with the appropriate credentials—generally, some secondary schooling—filled many of these new positions, especially in education. Women were able to fill these jobs because in recent years Pinero households have valued the credential of education roughly equally for girls and boys. It is noteworthy that in their excellent study of rural women throughout the Dominican Republic, Rosado et al. (1987) encountered two contradictory positions vis-à-vis the education of girls. While some households preferred to concentrate resources on the education of sons, others focused on daughters. This was precisely because women were perceived to be at a disadvantage in the labor market and therefore in need of an education to expand their employment opportunities. As one of their respondents explained:

Men can defend themselves more easily than women. Ultimately, a man can work as a day laborer anywhere, but a woman
is more defenseless, and, because agriculture is not work for her,
she has to learn other skills that will permit her to defend herself. [p. 199, my translation]

As a result of such changes in attitude, education became a new source
of status for some young women. Nonetheless, in Los Pinos, women
tended to become the primary school teachers, while most of the better-paying secondary teachers' jobs were filled by men (see table 4.1
below).

Given the clientelistic and paternalistic climate of the Dominican
political system, the tenure of state jobs was often insecure. Especially after elections, these positions were redistributed as spoils to
loyal supporters of the victorious party. A large number of Dominicans
are affected when jobs are shuffled during election years. Threatened
with the imminent loss of their jobs, many state employees in Los
Pinos, as elsewhere throughout the republic, applied for visas in years
preceding and following presidential elections (see also Bray 1984:230).
Despite this insecurity, state sector jobs were still highly coveted.

Among those who lived from a check it was the teachers who received the highest salaries. Young and well-educated by Los Pinos'
standards, the teachers formed the backbone of what might be called
the community's new middle class. Although rooted in the countryside, from which they derived their livelihood and prestige, these
teachers aspired to an urban middle-class style of life. Their houses
rivaled those of many long-time migrants in the number and array
of appliances with which they were stocked. Of the two noncommer-
cial cars in Los Pinos, one was owned by the richest merchant, the
other by a schoolteacher (the merchant's car was paid off, however;
the school teacher's was not). Most of the teachers owned motorcycles, on which they traveled each weekend to the universities of
Santiago and La Vega to continue their studies. As noted earlier, many
employed women from poor households to do the housework and care
for their children.

In many cases, however, aspirations to increased consumption and
to rising status through additional education led to severe strains on
budgets. Despite the fact that many teachers were married to other
teachers and thus received two paychecks (for a combined salary of
over DR$400 per month—handsome by community standards), they
had to live beyond their means to maintain their costly life-styles.
Many were perpetually in debt to local shopkeepers, as well as to

TABLE 4.1. Primary Occupation of Household Head by Sex, Los Pinos, 1981

Occupation	Men		Women		Total	
	N	%	N	%	N	%
Agrarian Sector						
Own-account agriculture	36	22.6	1	1.3	37	15.9
Cattle raiser	2	1.3	0	0	2	.9
Cana, palma vendor	1	.6	0	0	1	.4
Day laborer	7	4.4	0	0	7	3.0
Housework	0	0	41	54.7	41	17.5
State Sector						
Primary teacher	0		5	6.7	5	2.1
Secondary teacher	6	3.8	0	0	6	2.6
High school secretary	0	0	1	1.3	1	.4
High school director	1	.6	0	0	1	.4
Tractor driver	1	.6	0	0	1	.4
Watchman	4	2.5	0	0	4	1.7
Forest ranger	2	1.3	0	0	2	.9
Mayor, *síndico*[a]	2	1.3	0	0	2	.9
Post office clerk	2	1.3	0	0	2	.9
National guard	2	1.3	0	0	2	.9
Public works employee	1	.6	0	0	1	.4
Informal Sector						
Transportation						
Público driver	6	3.8	0	0	6	2.6
Commerce						
Shopkeeper, vendor	20	12.6	5	6.7	25	10.7
Truck owner-intermediary	2	1.3	0	0	2	.9
Estera intermediary	0	0	1	1.3	1	.4
Service						
Lottery vendor	11	6.9	0	0	11	4.7
Laundress	0	0	2	2.7	2	.9

[a]A *síndico* was an elected official who was in charge of public works and other community affairs.

furniture and appliance store owners in Santiago. The cachets of education and comparatively high salaries nonetheless made the teachers among the most highly respected members of the community. As will be discussed in chapter 6, both male and female teachers took an active leadership role in Los Pinos and were the prime movers behind the social club, the savings and consumer cooperatives, and other community organizations. They were at the forefront of introducing new and "modern" ideas and behavior into the community;

TABLE 4.1. (Continued)

Occupation	Men		Women		Total	
	N	%	N	%	N	%
Waged child caregiver	0	0	2	2.7	2	.9
Domestic servant	0	0	3	4.4	3	1.3
Overseer	2	1.3	0	0	2	.9
Prepared food stand operator	0	0	1	1.3	1	.4
Firewood gatherer	1	.6	0	0	1	.4
Dentist[b]	2	1.3	0	0	2	.9
Artisanal						
Chair workshop owner	7	4.4	0	0	7	3.0
Barber	3	1.9	0	0	3	1.3
Seamstress	0	0	7	9.3	7	3.0
Chair weaver	0	0	4	5.3	4	1.7
Sawmill owner	3	1.9	0	0	3	1.3
Carpenter	3	1.9	0	0	3	1.3
Tailor	2	1.3	0	0	2	.9
Sawmill operative	2	1.3	0	0	2	.9
Estera weaver	0	0	1	3.1	1	.4
Mason	1	.6	0	0	1	.4
Butcher	1	.6	0	0	1	.4
Baker	1	.6	0	0	1	.4
Cobbler	1	.6	0	0	1	.4
Lumberjack	1	.6	0	0	1	.4
Other						
Cockpit owner	2	1.3	0	0	2	.9
Gold placer miner	1	.6	1	1.3	2	.9
Fighting cock trainer	4	2.5	0	0	4	1.7
U.S. hotel worker	1	.6	0	0	1	.4
No occupation	15	9.4	0	0	15	6.4
Total	159	68.0	75	32.0	234	100.4[c]

[b]The "dentists" in Los Pinos were self-taught practitioners who specialized in pulling teeth.
[c]Due to rounding.

along with U.S. migrants, they were the cultural emissaries of urban life-styles and tastes to Los Pinos.

The desirability of these salaried jobs in terms of income and status had led to a tendency on the part of many parents to ignore agriculture to help their children obtain the newly valued credential of education. Young people also aspired to middle-class professional jobs and often held very negative attitudes toward work in the fields. They cited the risk and uncertainty involved, the difficulty of the work and its "dirtiness." The comments of Ramón Morales, a nineteen-year-old

Pinero who had just become a schoolteacher, illustrated the increased aspirations of many young people and their rejection of farming: "I like agriculture. But the earnings are low and you get very tired. You die tired and poor. . . . Before I became a schoolteacher, I wanted to be an agricultural engineer." Many parents shared this negative view of agriculture and made every attempt to keep their children in school as long as they could. Hearing his son's comments, Ramón's father, a smallholder who had spent much of his life sharecropping, said, "I didn't want my children to work in agriculture. I saw that it didn't give results. Because of this I sacrificed myself, so that my children could go to school."

Monguita Rodríguez was another example of the way many Pinero parents viewed education. The wife of José, a farmer with over 200 tareas and several head of cattle, Monguita took in laundry for two schoolteachers and also wove chair seats in order to buy her four children's uniforms, shoes, texts, and supplies. Although rich in land, José had many *vicios*, literally, vices. In the countryside, as Gudeman (1978:40) has pointed out, this is a concept with a "fundamental economic resonance." José's vices were the usual ones in which some Pinero men indulged and which depleted household incomes: drinking, smoking, and betting on cockfights. In 1980–81, Monguita earned a total of DR$240 washing and ironing clothes and another DR$288 weaving chairs. Monguita insisted that the money she made from laundry and chair weaving was hers to keep and spend as she saw fit. However, a strong ideology of "maternal altruism" guided the way most of this money was used (see Benería and Roldán 1987). Her expressed desire was to see her children all graduate from high school. Besides taking on this additional work to pay for the children's school costs, Monguita also assumed some of her daughters' household chores to free time for their studies. José, one of the few remaining dedicated farmers in Los Pinos, was unusual in expecting his young son to help him in the fields. More commonly, both parents would take over some of their children's chores to free their time to attend school and do homework. In short, the strong desire parents expressed to see their children progress and improve themselves (*progresar, mejorarse*) had resulted in much decanting of Pinero sons out of the fields and Pinera daughters out of the kitchens and into the schools (cf. Nevadomsky 1983:73). In both cases, parents absorbed the time costs resulting from the reduction in children's household labor.

OCCUPATIONAL STRUCTURE IN 1981: THE RISE OF THE INFORMAL ECONOMY

The recent changes in Pinero economy described above had profound implications for the occupational structure of the community. The strong drift away from agriculture can be seen from a comparison of the primary occupation of Pinero men with that of their fathers. Slightly over 80 percent of male household heads said that their fathers had worked primarily as agriculturalists—*agricultor* is the term always used to refer to a man who works the land (see Geffroy 1975). By 1981, the forces undermining both commercial and subsistence agriculture had become so severe that only 23 percent of male household heads listed agriculture as their primary occupation; another 21 percent listed it as an ancillary activity.

This decline in agricultural employment closely paralleled national trends. In the intercensal period between 1970 and 1981, agricultural employment throughout the republic dropped from about 46 percent of the labor force to about 24 percent, and the agrarian sector was among those absorbing the fewest new workers (Larson 1987a). In contrast, the informal sector in Los Pinos grew in importance as a source of employment, again mirroring national trends (Duarte 1980; Lozano 1987).

In practice, the informal sector was composed of a congeries of disparate economic activities including both the production and circulation of goods and services. But informal sector activities did share certain basic characteristics. They were labor-intensive and small-scale, required little capital or technology, and, typically, avoided formal state supervision (Long and Roberts 1984; Geertz 1963; Moser 1978; Hart 1973; see also Portes and Walton 1981). To date, the informal sector has been described principally as a development of peripheral cities, the cumulative result of the options of rural migrants with scant employment alternatives. Perlman (1976), Mangin (1967), and others have demonstrated that the informal sector of Latin American cities is not a marginal, vestigial phenomenon, but a dynamic, expanding, and integral component of the city's capitalist development. The case of Los Pinos suggests that, in a context of peripheral capitalist development, the informal sector may be an important element of some rural economies as well, particularly in those areas where agriculture has been severely undermined with no concomitant appearance of a wage labor market.

By 1981, Los Pinos, like the Caribbean communities on which

Rubin (1962:449 cited in Nevadomsky 1983:78) commented over two decades ago, appeared "more semi-urban than rural." But whereas Rubin was referring to inroads of urban culture such as schools, movies, radio, and so on, in Los Pinos the economy itself had come to have commonalities with the cities of the republic. Nor was the community unique in this regard. Commenting generally on the Dominican countryside, the rural sociologist Bendezú Alvarado (1982) recently observed, "Land has ceased to be the only factor of survival. . . . The new form of organization in the villages and secciones tends toward an urban type, especially in those villages in which there is a certain concentration of population, such as sección and municipal seats" (pp. 110–111; my translation).

When compared to the usual image of a rural community, the wide array and heterogeneity of economic activity—entrepreneurial, professional, service, wage, and artisanal—found in Los Pinos was especially striking. As noted earlier, some of these employment opportunities were directly created by migrants' investments. Others had been encouraged by remittance subsidies that migrants sent to their households in the community. Still others were generated by trends in the Dominican economy and expansion of government bureaucracy resulting from state policies pursued after 1966. Altogether, the informal sector employed some 40 percent of Pinero household heads and many additional household members as well. Always significant in Los Pinos, artisanal production became an expanding component of this sector. Especially for poorer households, its contribution to family income surpassed that of agriculture.

Finally, informal commercial activities grew as well. A consequence of the demise of primary production in Los Pinos, the increasing commercialization of subsistence needs also was accelerated and intensified by migration. The progressive displacement of family members to the United States meant that much of the food and other items formerly produced by household members now had to be purchased. At the same time, the massive inflow of remittances from abroad, to be examined shortly, also encouraged commercialization. That is, as subsistence crops became increasingly difficult to produce, the ability to purchase these commodities simultaneously became both necessary and possible. Moreover, with the deterioration of land resources and the deleterious impact of state policies, even nonmigrant households with ample labor could not fill as much as half of their annual food needs through subsistence agriculture (chapter 5). As a consequence of these factors, Los Pinos experienced an expansion in many aspects of its commercial life.

Indicative of this expansion was the fact that after housework and agriculture, the largest primary occupational category in Los Pinos was shopkeeper or vendor (table 4.1). One out of every thirteen household heads owned, co-owned, or operated a shop. Shops ranged in size from small *ventorillos*, or stands from which fruit and vegetables were peddled, to large wholesale and retail enterprises which sold food, clothing, hardware, and many other items to local customers as well as to smaller stores in the surrounding hamlets. There was roughly one grocery store for every fifteen households. Over half were migrant-owned, and all relied heavily on migrant household patronage.

The recent changes in Los Pinos' economy are further highlighted when that community is compared to El Guano. Table 4.2 lists the primary occupations of men and women household heads in El Guano. Small and poor, El Guano had less than one fourth the number of primary occupations as Los Pinos. Conspicuously absent were the state sector jobs and the broad array of informal activities that distinguished Los Pinos. Clearly, economic options in El Guano were restricted. Despite the poor soils and steep gradients of its fields, agriculture was the primary occupation of the majority (65 percent) of

TABLE 4.2. Primary Occupation of Household Head by Sex, El Guano, 1981

	Men		Women		Total	
Primary occupation	*N*	*%*	*N*	*%*	*N*	*%*
Agriculture						
Own-account agriculture	15	65.2	0		15	50.0
Plower	1	4.4	0		1	3.3
Informal Sector						
Tailor	1	4.4	0		1	3.3
Shopkeeper	1	4.4	0		1	3.3
Estera weaver	0		4	57.1	4	13.3
Casave baker	0		1	14.3	1	3.3
Mason	1	4.4	0		1	3.3
Carpenter	1	4.4	0		1	3.3
Basket weaver	1	4.4	0		1	3.3
Other						
Placer gold miner	0		1	14.3	1	3.3
No occupation	2	8.7	1	14.3	3	10.0
Total	23	76.7	7	23.3	30	99.7[a]

[a]Due to rounding.

its male household heads. As will be discussed in the following chapter, El Guano's distribution of land was more equitable than that in Los Pinos. Combined with the paucity of alternative employment opportunities, El Guano retains the appearance of a peasant community, an appearance that has vanished almost entirely from Los Pinos.

OCCUPATIONAL MULTIPLICITY, MIGRATION, AND REMITTANCES

Based as it is on the distribution of primary occupations, table 4.1 does not capture the wide range of combinations of occupations in which Pineros engaged. Nor does it indicate the degree of underemployment that was concealed in many of these occupational categories. It is important to emphasize that an activity regarded as primary was not necessarily performed full time. Indeed, the majority of income-generating activities in Los Pinos were engaged in only part of the time. Throughout the Dominican Republic, occupations such as mason, carpenter, electrician, and many others often presented only fortuitous and irregular opportunities to earn cash. Such irregular activities frequently were not conceptualized as occupations but fell under the folk category of *chiripa*: lucky windfalls (Bosch 1983; Bray 1983:226). Just as women who engaged in part-time income-generating activities frequently said that they did not work, so too Pinero men sometimes tended not to consider chiripas as occupations.[1]

Pineros, then, like rural dwellers in many other areas of the Caribbean, had to combine activities in their attempt to meet subsistence expenses. The result was a high incidence of "occupational multiplicity," a strategy which, as Comitas (1973:171) has noted, "offers maximum security with minimum risk, in a basically limited environment." Of course, the need to interweave multiple income-generating activities into a coherent economic strategy had characterized most segments of Pinero society for much of this century. But the nature of the activities had changed markedly over time. In the past, agriculture, day labor, and lumbering were combined by all but the richest Pinero men, while their wives interspersed seron weaving, manoic bread baking, and gold panning among their household chores. Even the old elite supported their wealth and social standing on the several pillars of transportation, commerce, agriculture, and the pro-

1. For these reasons, it was useful to probe ancillary activities by including in the community census comprehensive checklists of income-generating occupations relevant to both Pinero men and women.

cessing of agricultural products. By the early 1980s, agriculture and day labor in the fields constituted fairly insignificant components of men's multiple income-producing strategies. On the other hand, handicraft production and other informal activities, which could be flexibly integrated into daily schedules, became increasingly important to both men and women. Nor did the new merchant elite depend solely on commercial activities; they were able to maintain their position in the community through their combination of extensive cattle raising, loansharking and other investments.

The degree to which occupational multiplicity characterized most Pineros was revealed clearly by the community census. Pinero male heads of household reported an average of 2.8 income-generating occupations throughout the year. Female household heads engaged in an average of 1.3 occupations. Except for the most highly educated who lived from the check, occupational multiplicity characterized heads of households for all of Los Pinos' major groupings. Male heads of migrant households showed a somewhat stronger tendency to have no occupation at all (due in part to their greater average age: 64 years as opposed to 47 for nonmigrants), or just a single occupation; however, for those who did work, the differences between migrant and nonmigrant households with respect to occupational multiplicity were not striking. Nor were there notable differences among landholding groupings. In short, occupational multiplicity characterized all but the most highly educated Pineros.

The investment strategies of U.S. migrants helped reinforce this occupational pattern. With a few exceptions, such as the managers of the largest grocery stores and the público drivers, jobs created by migrants' investments were not full time. Rather, they tended to be part time and supplementary and became woven into the preexisting pattern of occupational multiplicity. Despite their ancillary nature, migrant-created jobs nonetheless might provide an important boost to the total income of nonmigrant households. The following examples illustrate some of the ways in which the derivatives of migrant investments can spread across existing social networks to benefit nonmigrant households.

1. Blanca Rodríguez, 66, was the sole supporter of four grandchildren, ages 14 to 7. Blanca had a small plot of land next to her house which she planted in high-quality feed grass and rented to cattlemen in the community for DR$60 a year. Her principal source of steady income, however, was from her daily sales of milk and gasoline. Blanca obtained the milk she sold from her nephew, Bolo Rodríguez, a prominent cattleman who managed his migrant sib-

lings' herds (see below). Her eldest grandchild was married to Bolo and lived on his cattle ranch. Blanca's grandsons helped Bolo around the farm. In exchange for this assistance and because of the multiple kinship bonds between them, Bolo gave his milk exclusively to Blanca to retail in Los Pinos. She earned a commission of DR$.10 on each of the approximately 20 liter bottles she sold daily when the cows gave milk. Blanca's principal source of income, however, was the sale of gasoline. The nearest gas station was located in the municipal seat and Blanca was one of two Pineros who sold gas locally. Prior to 1979, she could afford to buy only ten gallons a week to resell. In 1979, a nephew (her father's brother's daughter's son) returned from the United States and bought a gasoline station in Santiago. As a favor to his aunt, and to increase his own sales, he advanced her the money to expand her gasoline purchase to 62 gallons a week. The DR$4.50 a week it cost her to have the gas hauled to Los Pinos she paid to her son, who drove a público belonging to another U.S. migrant. Making a net profit of approximately DR$.50 per gallon, Blanca enjoyed a substantial increase in income as a result of this collaboration.

2. Gordo Morales, 22, was a full-time lottery vendor in Los Pinos. He was single and lived with his mother and five siblings on the edge of the village, adjacent to his family's middle-sized holding of about 180 tareas. His older brother, also unmarried, helped support this household by fattening calves on this land and by buying cattle in the sección and reselling them to the slaughterhouse in Santiago. Gordo contributed to the household's income fund by selling pieces of the lottery on commission for a successful U.S. migrant who invested some of his savings in backing vendors like Gordo. Young, hard-working, and well-liked, Gordo earned approximately DR$140 to $160 a month selling his lottery numbers until mid-1980. At that time, his cousin, who was also a close friend, was apprehended while attempting to enter the United States on forged documents. To help him pay the heavy debt to the prestamista, Gordo gave his cousin half his weekly pieces to sell.

3. The household of Luis and Mechi Sánchez was one of the poorest in Los Pinos. Practically landless, Luis relied on a number of activities to provide the subsistence needs of his family. In 1980–81, he earned a total of DR$90 for fifteen days of wage labor conditioning the fences and pasture on two landholdings, one of which belonged to a U.S. migrant. He also purchased young turkeys and guinea hens and fattened them with corn for resale. Especially during holidays such as Christmas, better-off households in Los Pinos bought these birds for festive family dinners. Migrant households comprised most

of Luis' customers. Luis and Mechi had three children who migrated to Santo Domingo and Santiago, but because of their own family obligations and low earnings the children were able to remit a total of only DR$160 to their parents over the year. The rest of the household in Los Pinos consisted of their son, Guillo, 21, and Mechi's brother, Samuel, a widower in his late sixties. Samuel contributed to the household's income by traveling to Santiago to buy fruits and vegetables, which were very difficult to find locally, and reselling them in Los Pinos. As in the case of Luis, most of his clients belonged to migrant households. His earnings were very meager, however. Samuel was also the "favorite uncle" of two of his nephews in New York, who sent him a total of DR $45 in 1980–1981, which he also contributed to the household income pool. In the past, Samuel, like other Pineros, has written to his migrant nephews to make specific requests, generally related to his medical expenses, which they seldom refused.

All of the Sánchez' activities combined, however, would not have generated enough cash to purchase half of their minimal annual income needs of about DR$1,100. The household was able to survive because of Guillo. When a U.S. migrant neighbor invested in a small grocery store just outside of the village, he asked Guillo, with whom he had a relationship of confianza, to manage it for him. Guillo's half of the annual profits totaled DR$700. Most of this profit was deducted from the food purchases his family made at the store to make up for the family's income shortfall.

Hinging as it did on informal ties between a U.S. migrant and local Pineros, access to many of these income-generating opportunities sometimes entailed a degree of insecurity. One migrant might sell a shop to another, who would replace the manager with a new one from among his own network. The following story illustrates the adverse effects that this type of turnover can have for poor households. Martín Pérez, 49, was the overseer for his U.S. migrant neighbor's moderate-sized landholding (about 120 tareas) for seven years. During that time Martín was able to devote his own 80 tareas to food and cash crops and use part of his neighbor's land to graze his own cattle, along with his neighbor's herd. He also gathered and sold the cana from this land and kept the profits; his wife collected the guano and wove it into esteras. By combining these activities, Martín and his wife were able to support themselves and their five children. When his migrant neighbor died in the United States in 1978, his heirs sold the land to another migrant. Martín was replaced by a new overseer and now had to rely solely on his own resources. After two years, he had fallen heavily into debt and was forced to sell all but one cow and 40 tareas of his land. When I left Los Pinos, he was once again heavily in debt to local shopkeepers for food and was planning to sell another parcel to cover expenses.

These examples illustrate some of the intricate, although sometimes precarious, ways in which nonmigrants might be boosted economically by migrant investments and their collateral effects. Thus, while migrants' investments created just a few full-time employment opportunities, they increased the possibilities for ancillary income-generating activities which nonetheless represented important supplements to the budgets of many households. Furthermore, the multiplex bonds linking villager to villager caused some of the income benefits of migration to spread across diverse segments of the community along the lines of kinship and friendship.

MIGRANT SELECTIVITY AND JOB CREATION IN LOS PINOS

In addition to migrants' investments, the occupational vacancies created by migration also opened new possibilities for those who remained in the community. Central to an understanding of the impact of international labor migration on the creation of jobs at the local level is the issue of migrant selectivity. To a great extent, the effects of migration depend on the position migrants occupied in the economy and social structure prior to migration. In chapter 3, it was noted that international migrants from Los Pinos did not belong to the supply of surplus labor prior to migration. On the contrary, U.S.-bound migration was occupationally selective. Nearly all migrants were employed at the time of migration; many worked at skilled and semi-skilled jobs. And rather than landless laborers or smallholders with sub-subsistence plots which would not permit full-time agriculture, those engaged in agriculture tended to belong to households with middle- and large-size landholdings. The exodus of these individuals from the community opened a range of opportunities and resources for those left behind. The following stories were selected to exemplify the three primary ways in which jobs were created through migration.

1. Nancy Rodríguez graduated from ninth grade in Los Pinos in 1976. After graduation, she tried unsuccessfully to find work in an office in Santiago. While in Santiago, she heard that the high school secretary in Los Pinos had married a migrant who was requesting a visa for her. Promised the job by her cousin Augusto, who was the director of the high school, Nancy decided to work as an operative

in an assembly plant in the Santiago industrial free zone until the secretary was issued her visa. After two years of factory work, she returned to Los Pinos in 1978 to take over the job of secretary.

2. Julio Pérez was the baker in Los Pinos until 1969, the year he migrated to the United States. He left his bakery and all its profits to Roberto Reyes, his brother-in-law, a smallholding farmer. When Roberto migrated too in 1977, he in turn left the bakery to his assistant, a landless young Pinero who continues to operate it and keep the profits.

3. Bolo Rodríguez, 39, was a national guard for twenty years in Santo Domingo. Over the last fifteen years, all of his nine brothers and sisters have migrated to the United States. His aged parents moved to Santiago to live in a house owned by one of their migrant daughters and take care of the young children she had left behind. They also wanted to be near medical facilities, as Bolo's father had a heart condition. After retiring from the military in 1978, Bolo returned to Los Pinos to live on the family land. With 400 tareas of pasture, he was able to obtain a loan from the Agricultural Bank and start his own herd of cattle. His brothers, sisters, and parents also have cattle, which he tends along with his own. Bolo has since become one of the most important and innovative cattlemen of the community, raising high-quality meat and milk breeds, selling milk locally, and buying and selling cattle throughout the sección.

The first case illustrates the situation in which desirable salaried jobs (office worker, teacher, nurse) were opened through migration to qualified nonmigrants who had to compete in a tight market but who had a competitive edge in their home community through networks of kinship and patronage. In a context of dependent development, the combination of expanded educational facilities, devaluation of agriculture, and aspirations to middle-class employment resulted in more qualified young people than desirable jobs. Therefore, like the republic in general (Bray 1984), Los Pinos experienced rapid growth in the numbers of its educated but unemployed young people. While the sending society had to bear the social costs of educating the young people who later leave for the United States, a reserve of the educated unemployed waited in the wings to replace them.

The second case illustrates the spreading of nonagricultural resources (bakery, butcher shop, tailor shop, público). Thus, although many artisans and other individuals holding skilled and semiskilled jobs had migrated to the United States, there was no evidence that this considerable "rural brain drain" left jobs unfilled for a lack of qualified personnel. The third case illustrates how the improved person–land ratio resulting from migration benefited those who stayed behind and filled the overseer role for migrant households.

REMITTANCES

Another way through which migration profoundly affected Los Pinos' economy and occupational structure had to do with the massive flow of migrants' remittances into the community. The volume of remittances and the uses to which they are put are central points in the ongoing debate over the consequences of international labor migration for sending societies. Sanguine conclusions derived from the principles of neoclassical economics have been challenged in recent years by an array of empirical studies. The majority of these studies suggest that instead of being invested productively and increasing efficiency and output in rural areas, migrants' remittances have been used primarily for consumption. When remittances are saved, they tend to be invested unproductively in housing and land. These studies also imply that, from a national perspective, the balance of payments may have failed to benefit fully from the foreign exchange remittances provide. Part of this much-needed foreign exchange may be spent to satisfy new tastes for imported consumer goods stimulated by migrants' displays (see, for example, Bohning 1975; Castles and Kosack 1973; Lipton 1980; Swanson 1979; Weist 1979; and for a recent overview, Russell 1986). By examining the social and cultural context into which remittances flow and within which they circulate, the following discussion specifically addresses these issues.

This flow of dollars into Los Pinos partook of a larger remittance system that operated similarly throughout the republic. This was an informal system that bypassed official channels almost entirely, making any accounting exceedingly difficult. Remittances were sent as a rule by postal money order, but often cash would accompany letters or would be hand-delivered by visiting migrants. On their trips to the village, migrants might carry thousands of dollars in cash, the accumulated savings of several friends and relatives. They distributed this cash according to instructions jotted down on a scrap of paper.

This system had led to a good deal of secrecy about migrants' plans to visit the community. In most cases, only the driver who met the migrant at the airport and the closest relatives who commissioned him to make the trip knew of the migrant's arrival. Such secrecy was a wise precaution; in addition to large amounts of cash, migrants came laden with gifts of new and used "American" clothing, shoes, towels and linen, soap and cosmetics, watches, small appliances, and a multitude of knicknacks. Thieves in New York were known to take advantage of the dense exchange of information between villagers and migrants and use it to track potential victims. Migrants had been stalked and mugged in their hallways as they left their apartment buildings in New York for the holidays, laden with cash and gifts. Muggings and theft were common enough occurrences in New York to have led to the introduction of a new loan word into the local vocabulary: *el joló*, the holdup, a crime committed by *joloperos* (*j* is pronounced like *h* in Spanish).

Cash and money orders were converted to pesos locally in the post office or shops, or in Santiago, where in 1981 the two largest money-changing houses each reported changing US$80,000 to $100,000 a day. Entire streets of Santo Domingo were also lined with men who announced their desire to change dollars to passersby. Largely through such informal means, an estimated US$230,000,000 to $280,000,000 in remittances was entering the republic annually by the mid-1980s, a sum equivalent to the total budget of the Dominican government (Vega 1987; see also Baez Evertsz and D'Oleo Ramírez 1986:44).

Remittances were one of the most important of the many links Pineros forged between the United States and the domestic community. Sending remittances was the most specific obligation that a migrant had to those left behind. The cultural expectation was that husbands would regularly send enough money to their wives to cover household expenses. Wives, on the other hand, generally did not send regularly to their husbands. Sons and daughters were expected to send remittances to their parents according to their need. The obligation to send to siblings was not so great, and most brothers and sisters of migrants received only occasional sums if they received any cash at all. Remittances were symbolically reciprocated by family members who gave migrants gifts of manoic bread, honey, herbs, rum, and other local products to take back with them (cf. Philpott 1973).

The large flow of remittances into Los Pinos testified to the strength of international migrants' commitments to family members left behind. When migrants sent regular remittances, they were said to "behave well" (*portarse bien*). Who behaved well and who did not was widely noted and commented on in the community; the former received approbation and were regarded as exemplary; the latter were the object of gossip and criticism.

Besides sentiment, cultural expectation, and diffuse social sanction, there were other factors that operated to maintain and even strengthen ties between migrants and those left behind. The fact that migrants' young children might remain in Los Pinos served to strengthen ties between family members. Most often, children were left in the care of the migrant's mother or sister. It was understood that some of the remittances they received would be used to support the household in which the children were residing. Partible inheritance was another factor that worked to maintain a migrant's stake in the home community. As Eric Wolf (1962:19, quoted in Brettell 1986:113) observed for Italy, the practice of impartible inheritance tends to make younger siblings who migrate "socially irrelevant to the family remaining in the village," whereas partible inheritance nurtures the ties between migrants and their kin. In Los Pinos, migrants' land and livestock were left in the care of kin or other members of their networks who were almost entirely responsible for their management.

A final factor reinforcing ties had to do with the fact that migrants regarded the home community as a locus of investment as well as of eventual return. Because migrants operated within a single transnational economic system, they were uniquely situated to take advantage of economic opportunities unequally distributed between the United States and the Dominican Republic. As Portes and Walton (1981:60) have observed, "Opportunities for wage earning are often greater in the center; those for investment and informal economic activity are frequently greater in the periphery." Savings accumulated by working in the United States were often invested in activities that relied heavily on Los Pinos' abundant supply of cheap labor for their profitability. Because migrants were physically absent from their community, however, that profitability was threatened by the unsupervised nature of the labor employed. A common solution was for migrants to employ members of their close personal networks to manage land and cattle and run businesses. Migrants' networks were thus often crucial to the success of their investments and might enhance the possibility of permanent return. When bonds of kinship and confianza were reinforced by remittances and gifts, they were available to be activated economically if the migrant invested in Los Pinos. It must be noted too that clients and customers of businesses were often members of one's network. Maintaining ties with villagers was thus important to many migrants' long-term strategy of return and entrance into the nation's middle class. In short, these multiple considerations worked to reinforce ties with extended family and other network members even though migrants might be absent from the community for years.

That the majority of migrants conformed to cultural expectations and "behaved very well" indeed can be seen from table 4.3, which shows the distribution of amount of remittances received annually by migrant and nonmigrant households in Los Pinos. Nearly three-quarters (73.1 percent) of all migrant households received remittances which averaged an estimated DR$100 or more per month, while almost 40 percent received an average of DR$200 or more per month.[2] These findings comport with those of a recent study of migrant households in Santo Domingo which found that of those sent remittances, some 60 percent received an average of US$115 a month, while another 33 percent received US$350 a month (Baez Evertsz and D'Oleo Ramírez 1986:44–45).[3] Included in the remittances sent by Pinero migrants were the occasional large lump sums for specific expenses such as house improvements and major medical treatment. Sometimes these sums were the pooled contributions of several offspring to cover the medical expenses of an aging parent, such as a prostate or cataract operation. In a country in which quality medical care is privatized, these expenses ran between DR$2000 and $3000.

TABLE 4.3. Annual Remittances Received by Household Type: Los Pinos, 1980–1981

Amount (DR$)	Migrant households		Nonmigrant households		Total	
	N	%	N	%	N	%
0	2	2.2	59	41.8	61	26.1
1–50	1	1.1	25	17.7	26	11.1
51–120	1	1.1	18	12.8	19	8.1
121–600	10	10.8	23	16.3	33	14.1
601–1200	11	11.9	5	3.6	16	6.8
1201–2400	31	33.3	11	7.8	42	18.0
2401–3600	24	25.8	0	0	24	10.3
3601–4800	10	10.8	0	0	10	4.3
4801–6000	1	1.1	0	0	1	.4
6001–7200	2	2.2	0	0	2	.9
Total	93	39.3	141	60.7	234	100.1[a]

[a]Due to rounding.

2. This assumes an average parallel market exchange rate of US$1.00 = DR$1.23 for the period May 1980 to May 1981.
3. Since my research, devaluation of the peso has greatly altered exchange rates. For the sake of comparison, remittance amounts for 1985 are given in U.S. dollars.

Remittances made by U.S. migrants from Los Pinos represented the single largest source of cash income in Los Pinos (figure 4.1). From May 1980 to May 1981, remittance receipts in Los Pinos totaled an estimated DR$229,000, an amount representing approximately 36 percent of total estimated community income from all sources. Remittances averaged $987 for every household in the community. Given such a high volume, it is easy to understand how international remittances both directly and indirectly increased effective demand for a variety of local goods and services.

Some nonmigrant households also received substantial remittances from the United States. Nearly 30 percent of all nonmigrant households received between DR$51 and $600 a year, and another 11 percent received between DR$601 and $2400. Among nonmigrant households receiving the largest amounts were those that were taking care of migrants' children left in Los Pinos. Less frequently, poor households were the recipients of the collective charity of some U.S. migrants. When poor Pineros suffered some calamitous misfortune, such as a serious illness, accident, or the death of the breadwinner,

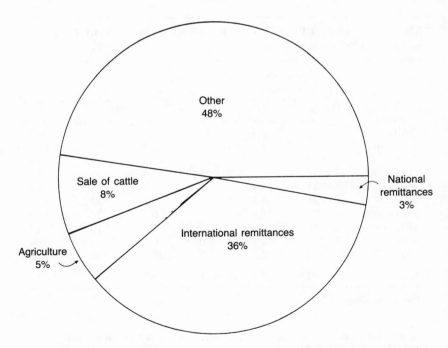

FIGURE 4.1. Percentage Distribution of Total Estimated Community Income, Los Pinos

some migrants in the United States would take up a collection (*una colecta*) and send their pooled contributions, generally U.S.$200–300, to the stricken family (Interestingly, the term *colecta* also refers to welfare subsidies received in the United States, to which a certain amount of stigma is attached. Both usages connote collective charity.) In addition, some nonmigrant women were involved in semiclandestine liaisons with married migrants who sent them remittances. Others were divorced or separated from migrants who sent small sums (between DR$10 and $30 a month) intended to cover their children's basic subsistence expenses, as Pineras put it, "para la leche," only enough for milk money.

The story of one of these women, Sandra Pérez, provides an example of how migration can affect poor women's lives over the course of the life cycle, and of the responses to it that some have been able to fashion. Sandra headed one of the poorest households in Los Pinos. Her father died when she was a small child. Out of necessity, her mother became one of the few Pinera women ever to practice agriculture. At the age of 12, when her mother could no longer afford to feed her, Sandra was sent to Santiago to work as a domestic servant. She returned to Los Pinos four years later. At that time, she became involved in a visiting relationship with Santos Morales, the son of a fairly prosperous mill employee, and bore a son. Shortly thereafter, in 1964, Santos migrated to the United States, where he subsequently married. Three years later, Sandra became involved with another man, Manuel Santana, from a nearby village. She bore a daughter, and again, shortly thereafter, Manuel also migrated to New York. She later entered a consensual union with a landless day laborer which lasted until 1979 and produced three children.

Over the years, Sandra barely kept her family fed by working as a servant in a succession of migrants' and teachers' households in Los Pinos. In 1975, when her eldest son turned eleven, she found she could no longer afford to clothe him and keep him in school. She went to Santos' parents to ask their help but was rebuffed. Because under Dominican Law 2402 fathers must provide support for their minor children, Sandra then threatened to report Santos to the U.S. consulate for violating the law. Santos and his parents relented. Sandra's son moved into their house and Santos began to send money for his expenses. Over the years, as Santos visited his family of origin in Los Pinos, he became fond of the boy and decided to adopt him legally so that he could sponsor his migration to the United States. After the son went to New York in 1981, he began to remit sporadically to his mother.

Sandra attempted to use the same strategy to force her second partner, Manuel, to support their daughter. This time her bluff was called; Manuel refused, and Sandra did nothing and received no remittances. However, Manuel's father, a return migrant who lived comfortably from his social security check and his children's remittances, took the girl into his household. Her grandfather paid her school expenses, and after school the girl performed the bulk of his household chores. In 1980, Sandra entered a semiclandestine visiting relationship with a much older married migrant, who provided roughly half of her total household expenses of DR$950.00 for the year. By 1981, the relationship had ended and she was once again the sole support of her youngest three children.

In her resourcefulness and flexibility, Sandra resembles the poor Dominican women described by Brown (1975:324) for whom a pattern of serial multiple-mating was a "dynamic female adaptation to life under severe poverty." Sandra is also typical of the Dominican women who lodge complaints against ex-spouses under Law 2402. Such complaints are generally made by extremely poor women who have had children by men who are better educated and in a better economic position than they (CIPAF 1985). Living in a migrant community, though, Sandra was also able to negotiate aspects of the migration system to secure some benefits for herself and her children. Other poor Pineras also attempted to gain leverage over fathers remiss in child support payments by threatening to report them. The strategy worked especially well when these fathers did not have proper documents.

The majority of nonmigrant households, however, either received no remittances or only occasional small sums. The small sums received by nonmigrant households often represented the combined contributions of several friends and relatives in the United States. Especially on holidays such as Christmas, Holy Week, and Mother's Day, migrants might send cash to poor friends and neighbors in the community. An extreme example was one well-liked Pinero man in his late fifties who received a total of over DR$250 in 1980–1981 from two nieces, a brother, a godson, a former neighbor, and a former sweetheart. Most nonmigrants receive much smaller sums.

To place the volume of remittances in context, it is instructive briefly to examine the amounts sent by internal migrants. Although the level of internal migration was high, the total remittances sent to Los Pinos by internal migrants were only a fraction of those from international migrants. Between May 1980 and May 1981, remittances sent by migrants within the republic totaled approximately DR$19,218.00 and contributed just 3 percent to the estimated total community income from all sources. This was an average of $81 per household.

Even in El Guano, a community with a high level of internal migration, internal migrants' remittances made only a small contribution to total community income. Although 44 percent of the present population of El Guano consisted of internal migrants, remittances from this group contributed only 4 percent to the total community income. On the other hand, the village's six international migrants, comprising only 3 percent of the present population, sent remittances totalling 14 percent of the total estimated community income (figure 4.2).

Despite the large volume of international remittances sent to Los Pinos—especially when compared to the amount sent by internal migrants—only 61.5 percent of all migrant households reported that the cash they received was sufficient to cover basic household expenses. Indeed, analysis of migrant household budgets and interviews with

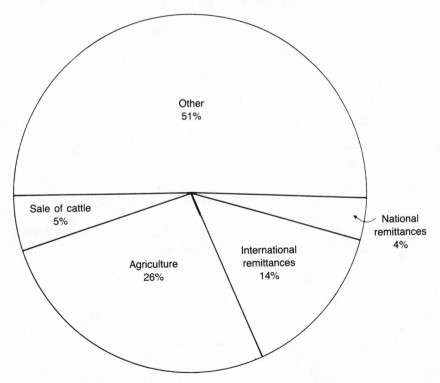

FIGURE 4.2. Percentage Distribution of Total Estimated Community Income, El Guano

remitting migrants suggest the existence of a "subsistence ethic" guiding the calculation of how much to send. That is, there appeared to be a strong inclination to peg remittances just at, or slightly below, the consumption needs of the household. Since most international migrants managed to save, this cannot be explained by appealing to low earnings in the United States. Rather, it appears that the sending of subsistence and sub-subsistence-level remittances was a strategy to circumvent the traditional demands to share resources among members of tightly knit social networks. As the eldest migrant daughter of one household explained:

> When I first went to New York [twenty years ago] I sent my mother and father more money than they needed to eat, and all the neighbors would come to my place to eat and to ask for money. They don't know how hard it is to make money in New York. My mother never refused anyone when they asked her, so my brothers and sisters and I came together and decided to send less. I spoke to a shopkeeper here and told them to give my family all the credit they needed, that I would back them. But we stopped sending so much money each month.

The existence of such an ethic is supported by the detailed budgets collected from three migrant households. For these households, the amount of remittances received did not vary primarily according to the number of household members in the United States. Rather, it appeared to be calibrated to the number of household members in Los Pinos who were dependent upon migrants' remittances and to the amount of income that they were able to generate from their own activities. Thus, for example, one household with ten migrant offspring and a total of eight teenage and adult dependents in Los Pinos received approximately DR$280 each month. This amount was roughly equivalent to the DR$310 per month received by another migrant household. This household, however, had only one member (the husband-father) in the United States. He was the sole support of his wife and their eleven children, ranging in age from 21 to 4 years. A third migrant household, composed of an older couple and their four adult and teenage children, received only DR$800 during the entire year from one migrant son. Since going to New York, this son had invested in a grocery store in Los Pinos which his father managed. The profits from the store, together with the wife-mother's income from sewing and weaving esteras, covered the bulk of this household's subsistence needs during the year.

Because remittances were often insufficient to cover expenses completely, many migrant households had to purchase necessities on credit from local shopkeepers. In Los Pinos, credit was a resource almost as important as cash. It was a resource that migrant households secured with a decided advantage. Even if migrants had not personally assured shopkeepers that they would cover their household's debts, credit was generally extended without question to households with migrant kin who "behaved well."

In their reliance on credit, migrant households behaved like most Pineros, and indeed most Dominicans, for whom debt was an element crucial to survival. The Central Bank's Household Income and Consumption survey conducted in 1976–1977, for example, found that for 66 percent of the households sampled nationally, living expenses outstripped annual income (Soto and Del Rosario 1978). Many Pinero households remained in debt throughout the entire year. Not surprisingly, maintaining credit-worthiness was an important concern. As just noted, households receiving regular remittances were regarded as good risks in Los Pinos, but those that lacked close kin in the United States did not find themselves in such a fortunate position.

Two main strategies were deployed to maintain credit-worthiness. First, Pineros took pains to pay off a bit of their debt every time they went to the store or whenever they were able to do so. This was known as *abondando*—"fertilizing" a line of credit. The *abono*, or fertilizer, of partial repayment nourished the relationship of trust between shopkeeper and client. One Pinera vividly compared this common practice to "feeding corn to the chickens": for just as there was never money to buy enough corn to satisfy the chickens' hunger, but only enough to give a little to each to stop their clamor, so it was with cash and shopkeepers. A second strategy was exemplified by Chuco Reyes. A chronically underemployed semiproletarian with few assets, Chuco maintained an excellent moral reputation in the village. He was a leader in many church-related community activities which involved a considerable investment of time and no remuneration. He was compensated with a good reputation, which in turn made him a good credit risk. Of course, he too was careful to keep his credit line fertilized whenever he could afford to do so.

Although shopkeepers were willing to extend interest-free credit to established customers with whom they had a relationship of trust, the poorest Pineros were often denied. When Martín Pérez was overseer for his neighbor's land, he had easy access to credit. After his fortunes declined and his debts mounted, however, shopkeepers in Los Pinos would no longer extend credit and he had to pay cash. With limited opportunities to earn income, he and his family were forced to cut their consumption. Underconsumption is a feature that inter-mittently or continuously characterized the majority of the poorest Pinero households.

In those cases in which there was a remittance surplus after house-hold expenses had been met, how was it used? Of the fifty-six migrant households that reported remittances sufficient to cover basic needs, only about half, or twenty-nine claimed to experience a surplus reg-ularly. In most cases, the amount of surplus left after covering basic household expenses tended to be quite small. Table 4.4 shows the principal ways in which remittance surpluses were used. Surplus was either saved in a bank or savings cooperative or invested specula-tively to back illegal lottery pools or to make usurious loans. Ap-proximately one-quarter of the households reporting a surplus in-vested in house construction and repair. When the surplus was saved in the community savings and loan cooperative and in Santiago banks, it also became available for income-generating investments, such as construction. Indeed, residential construction was the principal rea-son for requesting a loan from the cooperative in Los Pinos. Despite these instances of productive investment, many households preferred to invest surplus remittances speculatively. Because of this prefer-ence, the small amounts of such savings, and the small number of households involved, on balance surplus remittances do not appear to have contributed significantly to production and job creation in Los Pinos.

Cash remittances were not the only form in which migrant earn-ings were repatriated. A large volume of consumer goods, hand-car-ried to the Republic by migrants on holiday visits, flowed into Los Pinos as well. Every day in the weeks before Christmas, for instance, públicos arrived in Los Pinos packed with men and women, some-

TABLE 4.4. Use of Remittance Surplus by Migrant Households

	N	%
House repair or construction	7	24.1
Savings in bank or cooperative	7	24.1
Loans, savings, and lottery	6	20.7
Making loans	5	17.2
Backing lottery	3	10.3
Luxury consumption	1	3.5
Total	29	99.9[a]

[a]Due to rounding.

times entire families, their trunks, roofs, and back seats crammed with suitcases filled to bursting. Some of the passengers continued on to their hamlets deep in the sección. Their relatives left mules and burros for them in Los Pinos, tethered to the fenceposts of the coffee grove in the center of the village. The men loaded their heavy suitcases onto the mules' backs and stuffed the smaller ones into large *háganas,* saddlebags woven from guano by women of the sección's poorer hamlets.

Shortly after arriving in their villages, migrants would begin to visit relatives and friends. These visits were frequently the occasion for distributing gifts. Gift-giving was another important means of maintaining ties, fulfilling social obligations, and assuring good-will. For example, when one migrant Pinera returned to Los Pinos to visit her fiancé, she brought him a large tape player which thereafter he carried with him on his nightly strolls through the center of the village. Referring to the gift, a friend commented to him, "She must really love you." That such gifts may involve substantial expense to migrants can be seen from the statement of one migrant who told me that on his first trip back to the village, "I spent $400 before I ever stepped foot on the plane." And male migrants often spent a great deal once they arrived in Los Pinos, treating friends to drinks in the bars. Such spending displays were also a way of asserting one's success in the United States and affirming that the process of achieving one's migration project was well under way.

Pineros had a saying that "New York changes people" ("Nueva York hace cambiar a la gente"), referring not only to the obvious changes in clothing and language, but also to the more subtle social distance that migration put between migrants and some villagers. Thus, while on the one hand migrants conveyed a message of success that was potentially distancing, they were often also concerned to show that living in New York had not made them so *comparón* ("stuck-up") that they had forgotten friends and relatives in the village. Migrants made a point of paying visits, however brief and perfunctory, to members of their networks and often used the occasion to reinforce bonds by bringing gifts. Table 4.5 shows the distribution and variety of the most common gifts.

It has been suggested that the display of consumer goods by migrants and their households produces a "demonstration effect" which ultimately increases the demand for these items among non-migrants as well. This increased demand, as noted earlier, might result in a higher import bill, cancel out the foreign exchange benefits that accrue from migrants' remittances, and thereby exacerbate balance of payments difficulties. It is clear that migration does indeed help cre-

TABLE 4.5. Consumer Goods Ever Received as Gifts from
U.S. Migrants[a]

Item	Migrant household		Nonmigrant household		Total	
	N	%	N	%	N	%
Clothing	89	95.7	70	49.7	159	68.0
Towels	68	73.1	31	22.0	99	42.3
Sheets	60	64.5	29	20.6	89	38.0
Shoes	59	63.4	29	20.6	88	37.6
Watches	57	61.3	26	18.4	83	35.5
Television sets	52	55.9	11	7.8	63	26.9
Blenders	31	33.3	7	5.0	38	16.2
Taperecorders	31	33.3	6	4.3	37	15.8
Irons	31	33.3	7	5.0	38	16.2
Stereo sets	10	21.5	4	2.8	24	10.3

[a]This table lists only goods given as gifts; it does not include items Pineros have commissioned and purchased from migrants.

ate new needs among non-migrants for such luxury items as television sets, taperecorders, and designer jeans. In Los Pinos, however, an "informal import trade" conducted by the migrants themselves evolved to fill the bulk of these needs.

All of the items listed in table 4.5 were carried back to the republic by migrants. Goods not given to friends and kin were brought to be sold. Some migrants helped finance their holiday visits in this way. Migrants who worked in factories in the United States often purchased items they produced at reduced prices and took these with them to sell on their next trip. Pineros might write to migrants and commission them to bring back new or used television sets, stereos, watches, and items of clothing sometimes specified by designer. In Santiago, migrant women supplied the many boutiques with the latest fashions in clothing, shoes, and cosmetics from New York. While collecting information in government offices of Santo Domingo, I observed women migrants plying these items to other women workers on paydays. Obviously, this informal import trade did not require foreign exchange and circumvented export duties. However, tips to customs inspectors, to encourage them to waive or reduce import taxes, were an established part of the operating costs.

At the same time, there was evidence that the large influx of consumer nondurables had a deleterious effect on demand for some locally and nationally produced goods. The large amount of clothing given as gifts in Los Pinos is a case in point. Approximately two-thirds of all households received clothing from migrants. Logically, this had an impact on the local production of finished garments. The budget collected from one migrant household, for example, revealed that no item of clothing except school uniforms and some minor items like socks had been purchased during the entire year. Instead, clothing for the migrant's spouse and all eleven of their children was brought from New York by the husband on his annual visits or sent back with his migrant sisters on their visits. Other migrants brought back suitcases full of used clothing which they gave to poorer households.

In Los Pinos, as in other parts of the rural Dominican Republic, tailors and seamstresses still filled much of the community demand for finished clothes. Pinero tailors complained that although migrants brought them many alterations to perform, they had drastically cut into their bread-and-butter business by flooding the community with gifts of pants and shirts. In addition, the migrants themselves fostered new tastes in clothes, tastes which the migrants also helped to satisfy. On their visits to the community, younger migrants almost invariably wore new jeans, preferring specific name brands such as Jordache and Serge Valente, coordinated with crisp pastel shirts and blouses. This "Dominican Yorker" look had become prized by nonmigrants as well. Given the restricted effective demand resulting from low income and the competitive edge of U.S. goods in terms of status, it is not difficult to understand how the informal import trade carried out by migrants posed a threat to local artisans as well as to national industries.

SUMMING UP: INCOME DISTRIBUTION IN LOS PINOS

The migration process set in motion a variety of social and economic crosscurrents in Los Pinos. It also reinforced and intensified processes of change the origins of which were independent of the migration process per se. It is also clear that migration brought with it a mixture of positive and negative economic effects. On the one hand, migrants left job vacancies which nonmigrants had little trouble filling, although initially perhaps not with the same degree of competence. Their investments, although only infrequently in productive aspects of the community economy, nonetheless created additional opportunities for supplemental income-generating activities which were absorbed into the preexisting pattern of occupational multiplicity, particularly for men. The opportunities created for women, in contrast, were far more limited and were restricted primarily to low-paying domestic service or taking care of migrants' children. The massive inflow of remittances increased effective local demand for consumption goods and supported commercial and service activities in an expanding informal sector. On the other hand, increased consumption on the part of migrant households in Los Pinos and the many other communities like it might have contributed to the rise in the rate of inflation experienced nationally in the 1970s. Even if this is indeed the case, which, although it remains to be demonstrated, does not seem unlikely, the question may still be posed, "whether in fact the perceived negative consumption effects of remittances are no different from the results that would have obtained if the poorer members of a developing society had been made better off by some other means" (Russell 1986:687–688). Less ambiguous negative effects include the emergence and establishment of new parasitic roles that preyed on Pineros' aspirations "to progress" through migration, such as the buscón, the tributario, the migration prestamista, and the money changer. The influx of gifts of consumer goods, especially clothing, helped create new preferences which have hurt artisanal production in the community and depressed the business done by tailors and seamstresses.

What, then, can be said of the general consequences of U.S.-bound migration for economic well-being? In particular, what can be said of the effects of these various consequences for the distribution of income in the community? To attempt an answer to this question, it is instructive to compare income distribution in Los Pinos with that of El Guano, where low levels of international migration preclude a substantial inflow of remittances, as well as with that in the republic as a whole. Income distribution is generally regarded as an indicator of progress toward equitable economic development, preferred over other indicators, such as per capita GNP, which are not concerned with equity (Adelman and Morris 1973). Ideally, assessment of the effect of migration-related changes on the present distribution of income in Los Pinos requires longitudinal data which are not available. However, by comparing Los Pinos to El Guano and to the information available for the republic as a whole, we place the community in context and strengthen confidence in the significance and implications of our results.

At this point, it is necessary to clarify what is meant by *income*. As I defined it, household income included wages, salaries, and rent; all income from supplementary activities of the household head or principal breadwinner and spouse; income generated from the sale of livestock and from commercial agriculture; income in kind from subsistence agriculture; and income transfers such as remittances. Income estimates were calculated from data generated by the community census of May 1981, which elicited information on over forty variables pertaining to occupation and income over the preceding year. Recall of income from ancillary sources for both spouses was enhanced by using comprehensive checklists of men's and women's secondary economic activities. The occupations included on the checklists emerged from interviews, observation, and the pretest of the survey. Agricultural production was also elicited by means of a checklist comprising the nine principal crops locally grown. Respondents were asked to recall or estimate the amount of each crop grown, the amount sold, and the price received. Income estimates from subsistence agriculture were calculated by using the average annual market prices for each crop (Chibnik 1976).

It must be emphasized that the figures generated by the community census should be treated as estimates. It is possible that the income of many households was somewhat underestimated. Except for those whose income was derived from monthly paychecks, most Pineros earned income from a variety of more or less irregular activities throughout the year; very few kept records of any sort. Income data may therefore be somewhat more accurate for those who received regular checks than for those who did not. However, reliability of these estimates was enhanced by the cross-checking of census data with intensive interviews conducted with dozens of Pineros. Furthermore, when information obtained by assistants was not clear or did not appear complete, I returned to interview the household a second time.

Table 4.6 presents several measures of inequality which summarize the dispersion in the distribution of income at a given point in time. Measures for the two communities are compared to the information on national distribution obtained from the Central Bank's First National Survey of Income and Expenditures which was made in 1976–1977. Gini coefficients for Los Pinos and El Guano were computed from their income distributions (tables 4.7 and 4.8). The Gini coefficient is derived from the Lorenz curve, which is a plot of percentage of cumulative income versus cumulative households (figure 4.3). The Gini coefficient measures aggregate inequality and ranges in value from 0 to 1, with 0 indicating perfect equality of distribution (Allison 1978). The other measures shown in table 4.6 are more sensitive indicators of the relative income shares received by different segments of the population (Adelman and Morris 1973:149).

On the whole, income was somewhat more equitably distributed

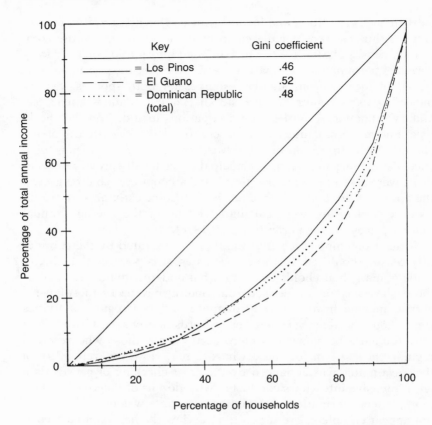

SOURCE: Income distribution for Dominican Republic from Soto and del Rosario (1978).

FIGURE 4.3. Distribution of Annual Income by Household

in Los Pinos than in the non-U.S.–bound migrant community of El Guano or in the republic in general. The top decile of Los Pinos' households received less of the total community income, and the bottom 60 percent slightly more. While the middle quintile of Los Pinos received about the same proportion of income as the national sample, this part of its population received more than its counterpart in El Guano.

That U.S. migration from Los Pinos has been socioeconomically selective might lead quite plausibly to the expectation that preexisting income differentials would be amplified by migration, resulting in a less equitable distribution (e.g., Lipton 1980). However, the information presented above suggests that this has not occurred.

TABLE 4.6. Income Inequality in Los Pinos, El Guano, and the Dominican Republic

	Los Pinos	*El Guano*	*Dominican Republic (total)*
Gini coefficient	.46	.52	.48
Income share of top 10% of households	33.6%	41.0%	38.5%
Income share of bottom 60% of households	28.8%	21.3%	25.6%
Income share of middle quintile[a]	15.3%	10.6%	15.8%

SOURCE: Data on national income distribution for 1976–1977 from Soto and del Rosario (1978).
[a] 10% above and 10% below the median income.

What factors account for the somewhat more equitable income distribution in Los Pinos? They are several. First, as discussed in chapter 3, despite the selective nature of international migration, many individuals from landless and smallholding households had migrated. More importantly, as will be discussed in chapter 5, migrant households had not been immune to the forces operating throughout the republic to splinter landholdings and increase landlessness or to the

TABLE 4.7. Distribution of Income by Household, Los Pinos, 1981

Annual income (DR$)	*Percentage of households*	*Percentage of total income*	*Cumulative percentage*
0	1.3	0	
1–600	15.8	2.3	2.3
601–1200	14.1	4.7	7.0
1201–2400	27.0	18.1	25.1
2401–3600	18.4	19.6	44.7
3601–4800	12.0	18.2	62.9
4801–6000	1.3	2.5	65.4
6001–7200	3.0	7.0	72.4
7201–8400	3.0	8.5	80.9
8401–9600	2.2	7.1	88.0
9601+	2.2	12.1	100.1[a]
Total	100.3[a]	100.1[a]	100.1[a]

[a] Due to rounding.

TABLE 4.8. Distribution of Income by Household, El Guano, 1981

Annual income (DR$)	Percentage of households	Percentage of total income	Cumulative percentage
0	0	0	
1–600	26.7	5.1	5.1
601–1200	33.3	16.2	21.3
1201–2400	20.0	18.7	40.0
2401–3600	6.7	11.2	51.2
3601–4800	3.3	7.8	59.0
4801–6000	3.3	9.9	68.9
6001–7200	3.3	14.8	83.7
7201–8400	0	0	83.7
8401–9600	3.3	16.4	100.1[a]
Total	99.9[a]	100.1[a]	100.1[a]

[a]Due to rounding.

general deterioration of the national economy after 1974. Although at the time of their migration only about one-quarter of all migrants came from landless and smallholder households, by 1981 exactly two-thirds of all migrant households fell into these two categories. Of these, approximately two-thirds (69.4 percent) received between 75 percent and 100 percent of their total annual income from remittances. Annually, remittance income for this grouping averaged DR$1,220 per household, a sum representing 81 percent of the national minimum wage in 1981. A subsidy of this magnitude to those with minimal or no agricultural resources undoubtedly represented an important contribution to increased equality.

Second, there was an inverse relationship between the level of income generated by a household in the republic and the level of remittances received. On an average, the higher the income a household was able to generate in Los Pinos, the lower would be the amount of remittances received. In fact, only 14 percent of Pinero migrant households annually earning DR$4,800 or more from local activities received remittances totaling more than DR$100. It is possible that a subsistence ethic underlay the calculation of remittance amounts and helped level extremes at the higher end of the income scale.[4]

4. In one of the few microeconomic studies of the impact of migration on rural areas, Oberai and Singh (1980) also report that migration exerts an egalitarian effect on the distribution of local income. Their study of internal and international migration from a rural Indian district found that migrants from lower-caste, landless, and nonagricultural households were more likely to remit than those from more privileged households. Because of this tendency, remittances considerably improved the local income distribution.

A third factor is the opening up of jobs for those who remained in the community and the income-generating opportunities created by some migrants' investments, and the tendency of their benefits to spread, albeit thinly, across networks of extended kin, friends, and neighbors.

Of course, other factors not directly related to migration undoubtedly contributed to the way in which income was distributed in Los Pinos. Its size and its political-administrative functions permitted a level of economic activity and occupational diversity not possible in smaller communities like El Guano. In practice, it is extremely difficult to disentangle the multiple factors affecting income distribution in Los Pinos. At the very least, comparison with El Guano and with the national household sample increases confidence that migration had not exacerbated income inequality within Los Pinos, whereas it appears possible that income distribution was improved slightly as a consequence of the reasons just enumerated. The comparison with El Guano does suggest, however, that U.S. migration might have helped exacerbate the historical inequalities between that village and Los Pinos. Thus, although intracommunity income distribution might have improved as a consequence of migration, it is also likely that intercommunity differences had deepened.

I have attempted to illustrate in this chapter how the migration process led to short-term economic improvement for migrants and their households and also for selected nonmigrant members of their networks. Greater community income and increased cash flow lent a boost to the Pinero economy. As one Pinero said, "In Los Pinos there are now more ways to make a peso." With few exceptions, however, the bulk of new income-generating activities created by migrants' investments was situated in the expanding informal sector and, more specifically, in its commercial and service aspects. This type of investment is not surprising: the informal sector in Los Pinos was well-suited to the typically small packages of capital that migrants repatriated for investment; it was a part of the economy about which they had comparatively good information; and, in their absence, it used cheap, unsupervised labor to which they were linked nonetheless by the moral bonds of confianza reinforced by familial or quasi-familial ties and by the glue of remittances and gifts. Although not productive in general, such investments were labor intensive and did provide an income supplement to selected members of migrants' networks. By 1981, however, even informal-sector investment opportunities were becoming glutted, and some migrants were having difficulties finding new outlets for their savings. Some businesses were failing because of increased competition from other migrants, others because of the severe downturn taken by the national economy. On balance, the evidence presented herein indicates that although U.S. migration helped to increase local income and improve the living conditions of many, it was unable to effect deep, structural changes: the productive deployment of repatriated earnings, the infusion of new skills, and the integration of women into the process of growth and change (Food and Agricultural Organization 1984:202).

"Aquí no hay producción"—"Here there is no production"—was one of the standardized responses I heard most often when asking migrants why they left Los Pinos. And it is this highly accurate assessment of the local situation that sheds light on the lack of any fundamental changes in the economy that may be attributed to migration. Students of international migration have sometimes denounced the migration process because it has failed to promote economic development. The example of Los Pinos exposes the somewhat tautological nature of this argument: Pineros migrated because of the lack of meaningful development in the first place. In the absence of policies designed to channel migrants' savings into productive investment, it is naive to expect migrants to behave very differently than they have done.

CHAPTER 5

The Impact of International Migration on the Local Economy

The Agrarian Sector

Once a vital sector of the local economy, agriculture in Los Pinos declined so dramatically in just the past two decades that total production had come to contribute only about 5 percent to aggregate community income. In 1981, it was hard to imagine the high pitch of activity that characterized the tobacco and peanut harvests of the past. The peanut harvest had dropped to a record low of 9,000 pounds, a drastic decline from the harvests of the early 1960s. Only 400 pounds of tobacco were harvested in the entire community that year.

The consequences of international migration for agriculture in sending societies is a question that has generated considerable debate in recent years. At issue are the twin effects of labor loss and repatriated earnings. On the one hand, the local loss of labor might result in higher wages for those agricultural workers left behind, and remittances might be invested productively in agriculture. On the other hand, labor lost to migration might not be replaced at all, with associated declines in production. The assurance that consumption needs will be met by migrants' remittances might encourage the withdrawal of remaining family members from the fields. Perhaps the most significant question to be asked is what effect migration has on the overall process of agricultural production. Answers to these questions are never straightforward: migration is always only one of a complex of pressures affecting agriculture in sending areas. The task is therefore best approached through the use of a combination of analytical foci. By examining the basic components of the Pinero agricultural system as they have evolved over the last two decades, by comparing the community with El Guano, and by looking specifically at the behavior of migrant and nonmigrant households both qualitatively and quantitatively, we may identify with some certainty those changes in agriculture that are directly linked to migration, the subject of this chapter.

AGRICULTURE IN LOS PINOS, 1980–1981: A COMMUNITY-LEVEL ANALYSIS

That agricultural production was much higher in Los Pinos twenty years ago is confirmed by several sources: the records of the peanut agency, the reports of Pineros, and the inspection of aerial photographs. Cash and subsistence crops have suffered this decline equally. Table 5.1 shows estimates of total community and average household agricultural production for Los Pinos and El Guano from May 1980 to May 1981. Average per household production was generally higher, and in specific instances considerably higher, in El Guano than in Los Pinos. It was noted in chapter 4 that more men in El Guano reported agriculture as their primary occupation. As figures 4.1 and 4.2 showed, commercial and subsistence agriculture contributed 26 percent of aggregate community income in El Guano as opposed to only 5 percent in Los Pinos. This was the case despite the fact that soils were poorer—although labor was cheaper—in El Guano. Methods of cultivation were identical in both communities.

Perhaps most striking, however, was the low level of production in both these rural communities. As we have seen, El Guano was an

TABLE 5.1. Aggregate Community and Average Household Agricultural Production Estimates, Los Pinos and El Guano, 1980–1981, in *quintales*[a]

	Aggregate production		Average per household	
Crop	Los Pinos	El Guano	Los Pinos	El Guano
Peanuts	90.0	17.0	.38	.57
Tobacco	38.2	9.3	.16	.31
Coffee	58.1	1.2	.25	.04
Cowpeas	409.6	100.3	1.75	3.34
Sweet Potato	500.5	51.1	2.14	1.70
Beans	70.9	4.0	.30	.13
Corn	246.7	39.8	1.05	1.33
Manioc	1241.0	1162.0	5.30	38.73
Plaintain	616 bunches[b]	120	2.63	4.00

[a]The quintal is the hundred-pound unit of weight widely used in rural areas of the republic.
[b]One bunch (*racimo*) = approximately 50 plaintains.

impoverished village in which alternatives to agriculture were limited and poorly remunerated. Subsistence agriculture was a key component of the survival strategies of the majority of its households. Typically, the fruits of men's labor in the fields and of women's handicraft production of esteras were joined in an attempt to eke out a meager budget. Nevertheless, agricultural production in El Guano fell short of the subsistence needs of the community. A closer look at manioc cultivation may put these figures in perspective. Manioc was the most important dietary staple grown in both El Guano and Los Pinos. In 1980, a family of six—the modal household size in El Guano—relying on manioc as the main staple needed to harvest some fifteen pounds per day. If manioc were eaten each day, annual manioc consumption would total about 55 quintales per household. This is equal to 70 percent of the average household production for El Guano and only 10 percent of that for Los Pinos. Of course, such averages can be misleading. In El Guano, just two largeholding farmers grew over half of all the manioc. Nearly all of their crop was sold to the local factory to be processed into manioc bread. When these farmers are excluded, average household production falls to 18.73 quintales. Thus, the bulk of El Guano's households could not meet even half their annual manioc requirements from their fields. Production levels for other important crops were lower still. Respondents in the two communities concurred that twenty years ago, most households grew enough manioc to fill all or nearly all of their annual consumption needs (see Brown 1975 and Werge 1975 for similar reports for other areas of the republic).

Clearly, there were pressures operating against subsistence and cash crop agriculture in both communities. Nonetheless, the inhabitants of El Guano, lacking the more complex economic and occupational structure that characterized Los Pinos, had few options but to cultivate crops; they simply had to withstand those pressures to a greater extent than Pineros. To produce their crops, however, the farmers of El Guano were literally mining the soil. For example, an ecological study of several Sierran villages including one near El Guano found soil loss from fields sown in food crops to be between six and seventy tons a year per hectare, depending on the conditions of the land and cropping practices—some twenty times the loss from land in pasture (Rocheleau 1984). At such a rate, the resource base of smallholding agriculturalists becomes severely compromised. In fact, the dominance of manioc, a root of low nutrient value, in El Guano's crop repertoire might already have been an indication that "the natural system's positive feedbacks to the soil have been almost completely eliminated" (ibid., p. 263). Thus, the fragility of El Guano's land resources threatened the farmers' ability to continue their comparatively intensive agriculture even into the near future.

To understand more clearly the reasons for the general decline in cash crop production, it is instructive to examine in detail the specific case of peanuts, by far the most important cash crop in the sección and one of the most important food crops in the republic. A discussion of the factors that negatively influenced peanut production will also illustrate more concretely the conditions that affected all aspects of agriculture in Los Pinos as well as, although to a lesser extent, El Guano.

Figure 5.1 depicts the precipitous decline in the sección's total peanut production over the last fifteen years. Between 1969 and 1980, output dropped from 14,552 to 3,285 quintales. Several factors brought peanut cultivation to a near halt. The first and most influential was the steady erosion of profits in the face of sharply increasing input

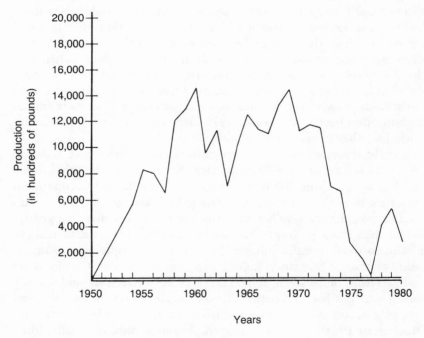

SOURCE: 1954–1977 Records of Sociedad Industrial Dominicana, Santo Domingo; 1978–1980 Records of subagency, Los Pinos

FIGURE 5.1. Total Peanut Production in Los Pinos Sección 1954–1980

costs over the last decade. Table 5.2 shows the costs of all inputs to peanut cultivation in 1970 and 1980. During this ten-year period, the average rate of increase for all inputs was approximately 175 percent. In contrast, the price the local peanut agency paid to farmers rose from DR$9.25/quintal to DR$15.00/quintal, an increase of just 62 percent.

Low prices paid to farmers throughout the 1970s were a result of the state support Dominican industrial capitalists received for their demands for low wages to workers. Through its price stabilization policies, the Balaguer regime ensured that wages were maintained at low levels by freezing the cost of many basic foodstuffs. Low wages were also a key ingredient in the governmental strategies that guided development plans during the 1970s. In the Dominican Republic, peanuts are used to make peanut oil, the principal cooking fat. Peanut oil is used liberally in Dominican cuisine not only for frying but also as a kind of sauce or condiment for many foods. It thus represents an important component of the Dominican diet and budget. The six detailed household budgets collected in Los Pinos indicated that this single item, which made a substantial contribution to a household's caloric intake, accounted for between 8 percent and 17 percent of the total annual food bill. It follows that peanuts were a crop of importance to those concerned with wage stabilization. Nonetheless, low prices paid to farmers led to a 1 percent decrease in national peanut production per year between 1972 and 1978. By the end of this period, production had declined to pre-1970 levels (SEA 1980:78).

Given the importance of peanut oil in determining overall wage policy, the state's neglect of incentives to production appears para-

---

TABLE 5.2. Cost of Inputs to Peanut Cultivation, 1970 and 1980 (DR$)

Item	Cost 1970	Cost 1980	Percentage of increase
Seed	$9.25/qq.	$15.00/qq.	62.2
Plowing	.80/ta.	3.00/ta.	275.0
Fertilizer	7.50	11.50	53.3
Pesticide	3.00	10.84	261.3
Day labor	1.00/day	4.00–5.00/day	300.0–400.0
Sowing seed (men only)	2.00/qq.	6.00/qq.	200.0
Harvest (women and children)	.70–.80/bag[a]	1.50/bag	100.0
Transportation (burros)	.15/bag	.30/bag	100.0

[a]One bag = approximately 100 pounds.

doxical. Such neglect was made possible by adopting a strategy of what may be called "export substitution": by importing cheap "surplus" peanuts and other seeds from the United States under Public Law 480—the "Food for Peace" program—to fill national demand, the bulk of domestic production could be neglected. These imports were made even more competitive by their partial or total exoneration from import duties. In addition to the domestic capitalists who benefited from cheaper inputs, this strategy was also promoted by international capital and by the powerful import sector. Imports permitted the price of peanuts and peanut oil to increase more slowly than the rate of inflation over this period. Planners could thus rationalize ignoring domestic production. This strategy was not limited to peanuts alone but characterized many of the most important food staples, including rice and corn.[1] At the same time, the state exerted an indirect influence on farmers by failing to control the price of key inputs to production (Crouch 1979:103–108). The combined effects of these state strategies presented the Pinero farmer with powerful disincentives to cash crop cultivation. Indeed, as table 5.1 suggests, Pineros withdrew from market relations in agriculture almost entirely.

Environmental factors also contributed to the decline of peanut production. Severe droughts in 1966–67 and again in 1975–76 destroyed crops and ruined many farmers. Apart from such catastrophes, peanuts are highly sensitive to even relatively minor fluctuations in rainfall schedules. A good rain is needed some thirty days after planting or sprouted pods will not begin to fill out. On the other hand, it is vitally important that rain not fall during the harvest: to avoid rot, uprooted pods must have enough time to dry properly in the fields before they are bulked. While Los Pinos was characterized by a generally bimodal annual rainfall pattern, considerable variability existed among and within specific years. In 1979, for example, although total rainfall was close to the average for the decade, no rain fell during the crucial month of May. Consequently, peanuts and other crops could not be planted on schedule.

Declining soil fertility was another environmental factor that negatively affected peanut cultivation. This decline, in turn, was exacerbated by the specific technical requirements of peanuts, such as repeated plowing, rigorous weeding, and considerable soil disturbance during harvest. These requirements intensified runoff and accelerated the depletion of soil fertility. Crop productivity thus inev-

---

1. As a consequence, between 1976 and 1981 the government's food import bill increased from $45,000,000 to $109,000,000 (Grasmuck 1982b:5).

itably declined. Pinero farmers reported that in the 1960s, one bag of seed normally yielded seven or eight bags of peanuts at harvest. Yet the peanut agency administrator in Los Pinos considered the average yield of one to five for the 1980 season "producción fabulosa."

Investment in measures to improve the productivity of land and labor was hampered by the general unavailability of inexpensive credit. In the past, the peanut agency located in Los Pinos regularly extended credit to farmers. By 1981, only the specially treated peanut seed was advanced, to be repaid with an equivalent amount of peanuts at harvest. Only sixteen households in Los Pinos had ever received credit from state sources; they tended be the largest landholders. State loans, administered by the Agricultural Bank and, more recently, through a regional development project, were highly desired for their low interest rates, approximately 11 percent per year. Private lenders, in contrast, might charge that much per month. Recourse was commonly had to these usurious loans because of the difficulty in obtaining state credit. Migrant households tended to finance agricultural production with savings repatriated from the United States. The local savings and loan cooperative organized by Pinero schoolteachers did not make loans for agricultural purposes, although occasionally credit was extended to purchase cattle.

Widely implicated in the decline of agriculture in rural sending regions, loss of labor through migration was a final factor affecting the production of peanuts in Los Pinos. When peanuts were introduced in the early 1950s, Pinero farmers were able to participate in their commercial production by expanding and elaborating the traditional junta system of labor exchange. Juntas became the linchpin in the cultivation of a labor-intensive crop like peanuts, as well as an important strategy for minimizing the risk involved in contracting expensive loans to cover production expenses. With many of Los Pinos' most important farmers and their sons migrating to the United States, the junta system began to unravel. Even as early as 1970, the system could no longer be maintained as it had been prior to migration. Juntas became much smaller, composed of two to five men, and occurred less frequently. Another blow was the early migration of the bueyeros or professional plowers, an economically more privileged group. Specialized juntas of bueyeros had rotated from field to field, initiating the planting season, and preparing the land for the junta of *sembradores*, or sowers, who followed. The loss of these bueyeros hastened the atrophy of the system of reciprocal labor exchange. The undermining of the junta system and the migration of the bueyeros also affected the ability and inclination of Los Pinos' wealthiest landowners to engage in cash crop production. Merchants had relied on the bueyeros to manage their land and oversee production just as they depended on the juntas to provide much of their labor. With the bueyeros' migration, and with the concomitant appearance of new opportunities for investment outside of agriculture, merchants turned away from cash crop production to other avenues that required less management.

In short, it was not so much the absolute loss of labor that was so critical to the continuity of agriculture in Los Pinos, as we shall see in greater detail below. Rather, international migration undermined the traditional organization of unpaid labor—the junta—which had permitted Pinero farmers to produce crops competitively by circumventing high labor costs.

As the preceding discussion suggests, a complex of factors had led farmers to withdraw from agriculture. Disincentives emanating from international and domestic policies, specific crop requirements, local ecological conditions—in addition to loss of labor through migration—all contributed to the decline not just of peanuts, but of a variety of commercial and subsistence crops as well. These same factors also had influenced agricultural production in El Guano, although that community's migration was oriented internally rather than to the United States. Agriculture was in decline in both communities, though clearly more severely in Los Pinos. El Guano, as we have seen, was a poor village with few alternatives to agriculture. It lacked Los Pinos' more complex occupational structure, its patronage networks, and its access to state-funded jobs, educational facilities, and, of course, its international remittances. Nonetheless, although the majority of El Guano men were farmers, agriculture alone could not support most of the households in that community. The cash and credit generated by women's handicraft production as well as the income from logging, gold panning, and other occasional activities represented critical supplements to agriculture that permitted the survival of the household.

One significant development that further helps explain the different levels of agricultural production in the two communities is the large-scale shift to cattle raising in Los Pinos. Deliberately promoted by the Dominican state, this shift was the single most notable change in land use in Los Pinos over the last fifteen years and had affected many other aspects of the agrarian system and the local economy in general. International migrants were active promoters of this shift at the local level, but nonmigrants were involved prominently as well.

CATTLE RAISING

Historically, cattle raising has been an important component of the Pinero economy, a source and symbol of wealth and status. Prior to the Trujillato, cattle were simply branded and left to roam the sección until they were slaughtered. But Trujillo's expropriations in the 1930s greatly decreased the foraging range for Pinero cattle. This situation was aggravated in the 1950s when Trujillo established *La Zona*, a law that called for the enclosure of large livestock and prohibited the customary free foraging. Pineros report that together these two events greatly reduced the number of cattle in the community. During this same period, meat and milk production became yet additional Trujillo monopolies.

After the tumultuous 1965 April revolution and its preceding events were brought to an uneasy end with the election of Balaguer to the presidency in 1966, cattle raising became the object of a vigorous campaign of promotion by the state. Following a policy first developed through a joint effort between the Alliance for Progress and the Dominican government in 1961, but interrupted by the events of 1962–1965, the goal of the Balaguer regime was to promote export-oriented production of meat through the collaborative efforts of private Dominican and large international capital. This process was to be abetted by state institutional supports of various types. These included most prominently a 69 percent reduction in export tariffs, from DR$16.00 per head in 1968 to DR$5.00/head the following year; a reduction in import duties for breeding stock; the establishment of a variety of government institutions designed to assist and promote meat production and exports, especially for the largest cattle raisers; and, perhaps most importantly, a phenomenal increase in the number and value of state-subsidized credits for cattle production (Crouch 1979:192 ff.). Between 1966, the year in which state policies promoting cattle raising were officially promulgated, and 1977, the number of credits granted for cattle raising increased by 80 percent; the value of those credits went up by 265 percent, with the average value exactly doubling (table 5.3).

An additional incentive was provided by the ten-fold increase in export prices over this same period. And as beef production became reoriented toward export and domestic supply shrank, the result was a sharp rise in domestic prices as well (Crouch 1979:195).

In response to these incentives, meat production doubled between

TABLE 5.3. Government Credit for Cattle Raising and Per Capita Beef Consumption, 1961–1977

Year	Number of credits	Value of credits (DR$)	Consumption (lbs/capital)
1961	7	$1,620	13.7
1962	477	1,035,885	10.3
1963	2,926	3,969,112	13.8
1964	3,888	4,652,100	11.4
1965	1,986	3,404,528	11.4
1966	3,056	4,051,019	11.4
1967	2,477	3,938,471	12.8
1968	2,296	4,053,227	12.6
1969	2,493	4,335,285	9.7
1970	2,994	5,015,014	9.2
1971	2,542	4,265,018	12.3
1972	3,136	5,401,005	11.1
1973	4,075	9,031,537	12.2
1974	4,919	13,339,200	13.0
1975	7,080	19,171,100	14.9
1976	5,830	15,664,600	14.6
1977	5,506	14,792,900	16.8

SOURCES: SEA (n.d.), Crouch (1979).

1970 and 1977 (ONAPLAN 1978:93). But at the same time, soaring domestic prices, buttressed by official price support policies, ensured that effective demand remained low. In other words, for the majority of the population beef consumption became increasingly restricted. In fact, it was only after 1974 that annual per capita consumption surpassed the level (14.2 pounds) reached by the end of the Trujillato (SEA n.d., 112). In 1980, when the official agricultural minimum wage stood at DR$3.00 a day, in rural areas of the republic beef cost DR$1.50 per pound. Landless and semiproletarian households in Los Pinos could afford to eat small amounts of beef only two or three times a month.

Incentives to cattle raising and disincentives to agriculture promoted a land use pattern throughout the Sierra in which proportionally more area was in pasture than in commerical and subsistence agriculture. Even as early as 1971, the Sierra had surpassed the nation as a whole in amount of land devoted to pasture, while it trailed in the amount given to agriculture (SEA 1978:29–30).

By 1980, the regional trend toward pasture and away from agriculture had become especially exaggerated in Los Pinos. Analysis of land use from aerial photographs taken in that year revealed that the majority (60 percent) of Los Pinos' land was in pasture and only 7 percent was devoted to commercial and subsistence agriculture, with the remainder in scrub, forest, and coffee. In other words, over eight times as much land was in pasture as in agriculture.[2]

In Los Pinos, the shift from agriculture to cattle raising was encouraged less by preferential credit policies, since only a few Pineros received state loans, and more by the indirect incentive of a favorable price structure. Unlike the stagnant or unstable prices characterizing agricultural products, the secular increase in both domestic and export beef prices was steady and unmarked by reversals. As one Pinero cattleman put it (in the context of 1981 gold prices), "Cattle are like gold; they only increase in value." Credit policy nevertheless might have helped encourage the shift to cattle raising among those with the largest landholdings. Households with the largest herds and the largest landholdings were those most likely to have received low-interest loans from the Agricultural Bank.

There were other incentives to raise cattle as well. Unlike conucos, pasture lands do not require long fallow periods; if they are rested for five or six months of the year, they can be used year after year. Soil conservation was not mentioned by Pineros as a factor encouraging them to adopt cattle raising. Nonetheless, as noted earlier, land sown in pasture grasses tends to have considerably lower rates of erosion than lands sown in food crops (Rocheleau 1984). Converting to pasture, therefore, might be one way to ensure the continued economic viability of landholdings, at least into the near future. Finally, cattle raising also involves lower labor costs than agriculture and reduced managerial requirements. Boys eleven or twelve years old or even younger, were usually in charge of herds. They milked them at dawn, herded them to pasture in the morning, and guided them to the river to drink in the late afternoon. One boy could as easily tend a dozen head as he could only a few.

In sum, there were a variety of reasons why cattle were one of the preferred investments in Los Pinos. Certainly of importance were the low labor demands and the meager managerial requirements. That cattle raising was not so dependent on the vagaries of the rains as agriculture was also an important consideration. For larger land-

2. The work of geographer Gustavo Antonini and his students provides documentation which underscores the recent and massive shift to cattle raising which has taken place in the Sierra. Their analyses of land use change based on aerial photographs and field reconnaissance in one region of the Sierra, Jagua-Bao, reveal that the area devoted to pasture increased by 37 percent between 1958 and 1966, and by another 16 percent between 1966 and 1979 (Antonini et al. 1975; Montero 1979). This increase occurred primarily at the expense of area devoted to short-cycle crops, which decreased by 16 percent in the first period and by 30 percent in the second.

holders, preferential access to cheap government loans might have been influential. In the Sierran context, then, cattle were an economically rational investment, not simply a vestige of traditional preferences. Low risk, steady and secure markets, continually rising prices, comparatively high profit rates, and a dearth of investment alternatives all enticed Pineros to buy cattle and, as a corollary, land for grazing. These same factors induced landholding migrants and nonmigrants alike to pursue this avenue of investment.

Cattle Raising: International Migrant and Nonmigrant Households Compared

In some smaller islands of the English-speaking Caribbean, a shift to cattle raising was a direct response to the large-scale depopulation resulting from migration to the United Kingdom (see, e.g., Frucht 1968; Lowenthal and Comitas 1962). Dominican migration to the United States, in contrast, has always been more restricted, with the visa process posing a significant bottleneck through which only a fraction of aspiring migrants passed. In Los Pinos, population lost through migration was offset by natural increase and by the in-migration of individuals and entire families from neighboring hamlets who were attracted to the community by its educational facilities, electricity, and other amenities. Thus, although migration was heavy, Los Pinos did not experience a major net loss of people, and able-bodied men desiring to work in the fields were by no means in short supply. Nonetheless, cattle raising had become the predominant form of land use in the community.

As just noted, both migrant and nonmigrant households actively participated in this shift. Large landholders parlayed their privileged access to land into an advantage in cattle ownership as well. Partly as a result of the profits they made from the migration process, a few landholders who were also prestamistas were able to avoid migration themselves. Beginning in the late 1960s, these men frequently invested profits from usurious loans to aspiring migrants in more land and cattle, especially in new breeds with superior meat yields. They were also able to acquire land used as collateral for a migration loan when an attempt to enter the United States failed and the loan could not be repaid.

In fact, it was those nonmigrants with the largest landholdings who were also the most important and innovative cattlemen. Rooted in their enterprise, unlike the absentee migrant, they were the Pineros most involved in fattening calves on a relatively large scale. It was they who took the veterary courses offered by government extension agents, built permanent shelters and feed troughs to provide supplements to their cattle, purchased new high-yielding milk and meat breeds, and practiced husbandry with care. It was they, too, who in 1979 organized a cattlemen's association to pressure the regional development project to build a molasses storage tank in the center of the village—the only coordinated effort to improve productivity in Los Pinos over the past two decades. A shortage of pasture was the principal brake on herd expansion. As a result, many fields were overgrazed. High-energy feed supplements such as molasses, a by-product of the island's sugar industry, were one solution to the pasture shortage. This solution was imperfect, however, because molasses supplies were themselves disrupted by periodic shortages that made effective planning difficult. The cattlemen's association thus had two goals: to lower unit prices by buying bulk quantities of feed supplement cooperatively and to permit cattlemen to withstand shortages by laying in a substantial local supply. The effort, despite its organization and energy, did not receive the kind of response the cattlemen felt it needed from the development project; ultimately the effort failed, leaving those involved with a feeling of bitterness.

In contrast to these cattlemen, migrants generally tended to underutilize their resources. Pasture was often in bad condition. For good yields, fields should be reconditioned every year to eliminate invading grasses which compete with high-yielding imported species. Because cattle prefer the more succulent African grasses, they crop those first and leave the less appetizing invaders to proliferate. Some overseers mixed their own herds with the migrants' and milked the cattle too much. By not leaving enough milk for calves, the overseers stunted their growth and reduced output and profits for migrants. When migrants' herds were left in the care of a sibling or parent, they tended to be given greater attention and to yield higher returns. Other migrants had to be content with the random growth of their herds as they grazed practically unattended. Given these circumstances, it is not surprising that among households that owned cattle, the average annual income from cattle sales was significantly higher for nonmigrants than for migrants ($T = 3.075$, $P = .002$).

The Social and Economic Consequences of the Shift to Cattle Raising

The near abandonment of agriculture and the massive shift to cattle raising by better-off farmers had profound community-wide consequences for Los Pinos. In this section, I discuss in some detail two of the most significant: the decline in demand for agricultural wage laborers and sharecroppers and the concentration of landholdings.

The shift to land-extensive cattle raising had greatly diminished the pool of land available for borrowing and sharecropping and was directly responsible for the drastic decline in the demand for agricultural wage labor in Los Pinos. Large landholders began to prepare for the transition to cattle in the mid- and late-1960s by loaning their lands to landless and smallholding farmers; after a season or two, these lands were returned to their owners cultivated in high-yielding African grasses. With this method, by the mid-1970s most of the largest holdings had been converted to permanent pasture. These lands then became unavailable for agricultural use in the future. Even on holdings not yet entirely converted, tenants increasingly came into competition with cattle grazing in areas already in pasture. Knocking down their temporary wooden fences, the cattle invaded conucos and damaged crops. Many poorer farmers stopped borrowing land for this reason. State policies also played a role in the demise of these practices. As part of the agrarian reform project put forth in 1972, the Balaguer regime promulgated a law giving tenants the legal right to claim lands they had cultivated for several years. Fearful of claims, most large landholders stopped loaning land or allowing it to be sharecropped.

It sometimes has been suggested (e.g., Griffin 1976) that the greater relative scarcity of labor resulting from the selective migration of young, productive workers is likely to be translated into higher wages for those remaining in the sending community. For the conjunction of reasons I have just outlined, this had not occurred in Los Pinos. Depending on their skill and reputation, men who worked in the fields in 1980–1981 received between DR$3.50 and $5.00 per ten-hour working day, in addition to breakfast and lunch. This was higher than the official minimum agricultural wage of $3.00, but considerably lower than the wage received in many of the more productive areas of the Cibao Valley, where day laborers in 1981 earned up to $7.00 a day (Rocheleau 1983:27).

During this same period, agricultural workers in El Guano were paid between DR$2.50 andd $4.00 a day. This wage differential between the two communities cannot be attributed to the effects of migration, however. That is, wages were not higher in Los Pinos because migration had drained the community of able-bodied men and led to a scarcity of agricultural workers. On the contrary, there were far more Pinero men willing to work in the fields than there were people who wanted to hire them, and most of these men were chronically underemployed. Rather, wages were exceptionally low in El Guano as a consequence of the noneconomic constraints discussed in chapter 3. Many men in El Guano were bound through debt and a quasi-moral sense of obligation to work for the lower wages offered by their patrons, just as their wives had to sell their esteras at a discount.

The depressed demand for day laborers hit semiproletarian households in Los Pinos especially hard. Out of necessity, wage labor in the fields had become of minor economic importance by 1981. In this regard, the budget collected from the landless household of Daniel Morales, who still considered himself, and was regarded by other Pineros, as a peón or wage laborer is revealing. In 1980–1981, Daniel was able to find only thirty-four days of waged agricultural labor to perform. His work for seven different Pineros contributed only DR$374, or 21 percent of the total household income. In contrast, during the same period, he and his wife were able to earn twice that amount panning gold. By toasting coffee beans for migrant households and weaving esteras his wife also contributed another 16 percent to the family income fund.

In the late 1970s, a new development further diminished opportunities for agricultural wage work in Los Pinos. The overseer of a migrant's farm began to recruit Haitian workers from a sugar mill some distance from Los Pinos to work in the community. Other large landholders, both migrant and nonmigrant, soon followed suit. Haitians were brought to Los Pinos for several weeks at a time to improve pasture lands which had become invaded with weeds and shrubs over the course of the year. Receiving wages approximately one-third the going rate of $4.00 a day, plus food and lodging, the Haitians easily outcompeted local workers. As a consequence, few poor Pineros thereafter were able to find wage labor in the fields. In this, as in other areas, Los Pinos once again reflected societal trends; nationally, the substitution of Haitians for local workers was a well-established pattern in sugar production, and it has become increasingly important in recent years for other crops as well.

The second major consequence of the shift to cattle raising in Los Pinos was the concentration of landholdings. The extensive nature of this enterprise encouraged the largest landowners to expand their holdings pari passu with their herds. The Pinero household with the largest amount of land and cattle, for instance, was exceptionally aggressive in this regard, buying up six parcels totaling over 600 tareas from five farmers since 1965; it also enclosed with barbed wire approximately 1,000 tareas of forested state lands during this period.

At the same time that larger landholders were expanding their holdings, fragmentation encouraged smaller farmers to sell their parcels. Thrown cyclically into de facto landlessness for two or more years at a time while their overworked plots were fallowed, smallholders had come to regard agriculture as an increasingly peripheral part of their income-generating strategies. Plots were most commonly sold to cover emergency expenses, to finance internal migration, or to pay for the high cost of private medical care. Also, as mentioned above, land used as collateral by potential international migrants was sometimes lost to the prestamista if an undocumented entry failed. All of these factors contributed to the increase in the number of landless households, which at the time of fieldwork comprised one-third of all households in Los Pinos (table 5.4).

Land sales were also encouraged by the rampant inflation of land values, which increased approximately eightfold over the last fifteen years. Much of this inflation was attributable to the demand for land generated by the shift to cattle. A portion, however, originated in strong migrant demand for land, especially land near the center of the village on which to build houses and businesses. Migrants were instrumental in fomenting the recent "urban sprawl" in Los Pinos, as new shops and houses spilled from the center of the village into its formerly agricultural outskirts. Inflation also led some migrants to buy land for speculative ends alone.

What consequences did these factors have for the distribution of land in Los Pinos? And, given the complexity of these factors, what can we conclude about the impact of international migration on this distribution? Using the Gini coefficient once again as a summary measure of inequality (figure 5.2), it is evident that the distribution of land was less equitable in Los Pinos (.74) than in the Sierra region in general (.64), or in El Guano in particular (.61), although it was more equitable than in the republic as a whole (.79). The greater equality in the Sierran distribution may be attributed to the fact that historically the forces that promoted the capitalist penetration of the countryside and disturbed land tenure patterns occurred much later and to a far lesser extent than in other areas of the republic. Thus, despite a tendency toward land concentration in recent years, Los Pinos, El Guano, and the Sierra in general continued to maintain a more equitable distribution than the republic as a whole.

The less equitable distribution of land that characterized Los Pinos was a direct result of the factors discussed above. As was seen, investment in cattle had promoted the expansion of landholdings as more pasture was required for increasing herds. This expansion of

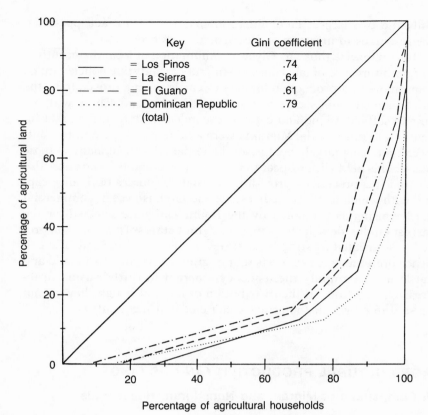

Percentage of agricultural households

SOURCE: Agricultural land distribution for La Sierra and Dominican Republic from SEA (1978).

FIGURE 5.2. Distribution of Agricultural Land by Agricultural Household

landholdings by the largest landholding households—whether migrant or nonmigrant—was one of the principal determinants of the concentration of land in Los Pinos. But by providing an alternative source of capital, international migration had undoubtedly reinforced and exacerbated the shift to cattle raising.

That the Sierra exhibits a Gini value intermediate between that of Los Pinos and of El Guano derives no doubt from the fact that it encompasses a variety of communities, some like Los Pinos, oriented toward international migration and cattle raising, and others like El Guano, dependent on internal migration, subsistence agriculture, and artisanal production. Extreme poverty had prevented nearly all households in El Guano from responding to incentives to raise cattle.

Only the two largest landholders in that village, in fact, possessed the resources to invest in cattle raising.

To summarize thus far: Given a combination of local disincentives to agriculture, loss of labor through migration, and state policies aimed to promote beef production for export, cattle raising proved to be the most lucrative and secure way to invest in the land. Those with access to sufficient land and capital responded to state and market incentives to raise cattle. Migrants were able to participate in the shift to cattle raising largely because of the initial advantage many of those households held with respect to land. Unquestionably, migration also abetted this process by providing alternative sources of finance capital with which to purchase livestock and land. However, commercial cattle raising as promoted by the Dominican state selected for the largest landholders, irrespective of migrant status. This selection process exacerbated existing inequalities in the access to land. The evidence presented here suggests that migrants' investments in land and cattle helped amplify the tendency inherent in cattle raising to increase inequalities in the distribution of land, although they cannot be said to represent the primary cause of that inequality.

AGRICULTURAL PRODUCTIVITY IN LOS PINOS

A Comparison of Migrant and Nonmigrant Households

In order to explore more explicitly and in greater detail the hypothesis that international labor migration is directly responsible for the decline in agriculture in rural sending communities, this section quantitatively examines the differential agricultural behavior of migrant and nonmigrant households. The two types of households are examined with respect to (1) access to land, (2) types of crops produced and agricultural output, and (3) use of wage and nonwage labor.

Production techniques remained primitive in Los Pinos and were identical for migrant and nonmigrant households. There was no evidence that remittances or the repatriated skills of Los Pinos' few return migrants had been used to explore innovations in farming methods—though it must be noted that given a general lack of research and development of innovations technologically appropriate to Los Pinos' conditions, there were in fact few options available to explore. However, migrant households did differ in their access to that strategic productive resource, land. They were far less likely to be landless than nonmigrant households. In 1981, 18.3 percent of all migrant households were landless, representing only about one-fifth of all such households in Los Pinos (table 5.4). Nearly half (48.4 percent) of all migrant households, however, belonged to the smallholding (1–79 tareas) category. That is to say, exactly two-thirds of all migrant households had no land or possessed plots under 80 tareas. In contrast, as seen in chapter 3, at the time of migration, only 4.8 percent and 18.0 percent of all Pinero migrants came from landless or smallholding households, respectively. Partible inheritance and the obligation of parents to provide offspring with parcels upon marriage (even if, as recently, only a small piece of land on which to build a house) had acted as a potent leveling mechanism in Los Pinos. Clearly, migrant households were not immune to these larger pressures fostering the redistribution of land. Nor had their differential access to cash income from remittances been able to stanch these processes. Nevertheless, the average migrant household still possessed one-third more land than the average nonmigrant household, 93 tareas as opposed to 66 tareas.

In Los Pinos, land fragmentation and land sales meant that the total amount of land owned by a household was often divided among two or more nonadjacent plots. All of the largest landholders in the community owned between three and seven plots. Migrant households were more likely to have acquired their first landholding prior to 1961, an association that did not hold for subsequent plots. Once again, it is evident that U.S. migrants overwhelmingly originated in households with superior access to land prior to the onset of migration. Yet even with the increased possibilities for accumulating cap-

TABLE 5.4. Land Distribution in Los Pinos by Migrant Household Status

Size of landholding	Migrant		Nonmigrant		Total	
	N	%	N	%	N	%
0	17	18.3	63	44.7	80	34.2
1–79	45	48.4	56	39.7	101	43.2
80–159	15	16.1	10	7.1	25	10.7
160–799	14	15.1	10	7.1	24	10.3
800–1599	2	2.2	0	0	2	.9
1600–3199	0	0	2	1.4	2	.9
Total	93	39.7	141	60.3	234	100.2[a]

[a]Due to rounding.

ital that migration made possible, most migrant households were unable to acquire landholdings equal to the largest and most prosperous nonmigrant landholders. Only a handful managed to purchase large tracts since migration. It is perhaps fair to conclude that for most migrants investment in land resembled more closely a holding strategy. Nonetheless, many more migrant households slipped into landlessness and near-landlessness than were able to rise out of these categories.

Table 5.5, which indicates size of plots according to year of acquisition, further illustrates this point. Nearly all (95 percent) of the first plots acquired by migrant households after 1961 were under 80 tareas in size. That is, while 21 migrant households managed to move out of the landless category after 1961, 20 of these became smallholders. Of the 7 migrant households that acquired plots totaling more than 80 tareas, 5 already possessed first plots of 80 tareas or larger. Again, expansion of landholdings, for both migrant and nonmigrant households, was occurring among those already possessed of this resource.

Agricultural Production Levels Compared

Were there significant differences in agricultural production between migrant and nonmigrant households in Los Pinos? A little over half of all Pinero households engaged in some form of agriculture, but there was little difference between migrant and nonmigrant households' levels of participation. Almost identical proportions (58 percent and 56 percent respectively) produced some cash or subsistence crops in 1980–1981. Nor did earnings from agriculture differ significantly: migrant households earned an average of DR$377 in cash and kind and nonmigrant households an average of DR$301 over the year. Further, as table 5.6 indicates, when production levels of all major crops grown in Los Pinos are compared, there were no significant differences between migrant and nonmigrant households that farmed, in terms of the kinds or quantities of crops grown.

That migrant and nonmigrant households practicing agriculture did not show significant differences in their average levels of production underscores a basic point of this chapter. Economic pressures emanating from the national level, in combination with local conditions, had had a negative impact on agriculture in Los Pinos as a whole and had induced many Pineros to turn away from agriculture in pursuit of other economic activities characterized by greater returns, reduced risk, or both. But the question remains: how were mi-

TABLE 5.5. Size of Plots by Year of Acquisition by Migrant Household Status

| | Prior to 1961 | | | | 1961 and after | | | |
| | Migrant | | Nonmigrant | | Migrant | | Nonmigrant | |
First plot	N	%	N	%	N	%	N	%
<80 tareas	34	61.8	27	65.9	20	95.2	33	89.2
≥80 tareas	21	38.2	14	34.2	1	4.8	4	10.8
Total	55	35.7	41	26.6	21	13.6	37	24.1
Subsequent plots								
<80 tareas	10	58.8	7	53.9	20	74.1	19	73.1
≥80 tareas	7	41.2	6	46.2	7	25.9	7	26.9
Total	17	20.5	13	15.7	27	32.5	26	31.3

grant households, faced with the loss of the labor of their migrant members, able to produce on the average approximately as much as nonmigrant households?

Domestic labor had always been of great importance to agriculture in Los Pinos, but, as was seen earlier, it had never limited absolutely the household's ability to produce crops. As the above comparison of migrant and nonmigrant levels of production suggests, migrant households were obviously able to compensate for the loss of the labor of their migrant members.

According to the information presented in table 5.7, there were only slight differences between types of labor inputs relied upon by mi-

TABLE 5.6. Average Estimated Production for Households That Farmed by Migrant Status for All Major Crops

Crop (quintales)	Migrant	Nonmigrant	T Score	Probability
Peanuts	8.8	6.6	.82	.44
Tobacco	3.7	6.8	−.67	.55
Coffee	1.8	1.2	.85	.40
Cowpeas	6.8	9.1	−.74	.46
Sweet Potato	9.9	8.7	.08	.94
Beans	3.3	1.3	1.35	.19
Corn	5.7	4.8	.44	.66
Manioc	21.8	21.1	1.75	.11
Plantain[a]	18.9	8.1	.38	.71

[a]Bunches of 50.

TABLE 5.7. Agricultural Household Heads' Use of Labor by Migrant Status

	Migrant		Nonmigrant		Total	
	N	%	N	%	N	%
Uses own labor exclusively						
Yes	7	18.0	13	23.2	20	21.1
No	32	82.0	43	76.8	75	79.0
Type of additional labor inputs used						
Sons	16	50.0	25	58.1	41	54.7
Wage labor	11	34.4	12	28.0	23	30.7
Sharecroppers or Siblings	5	15.6	6	14.0	11	14.7
Total	32	42.7	43	57.3	75	100.1[a]

[a] Due to rounding.

grant and nonmigrant households. However, migrant households were somewhat more likely to hire wage labor to work their fields.

But the kinds of labor inputs used on the farm showed greater variation when households were disaggregated by type of household head, although the differences were not especially marked (table 5.8). In a migrant community like Los Pinos, it is necessary to distinguish not only between male- and female-headed households, but also between those households in which the woman was the head because she was not currently in a union and those in which she was the head because of the absence of her migrant spouse. This is necessary because these

TABLE 5.8. Labor Inputs According to Migrant Status and Type of Household Head

	Household Head											
	Migrant						Nonmigrant					
	Single female		Married female		Male		Single female		Married female		Male	
Type of labor inputs	N	%	N	%	N	%	N	%	N	%	N	%
Sons	2	50.0	6	54.6	8	47.1	6	85.7	1	50.0	18	52.9
Wage labor	0		3	27.3	8	47.1	1	14.3	1	50.0	10	29.4
Sharecroppers or siblings	2	50.0	2	18.2		5.9	0		0			17.7

two types differed considerably in terms of size, composition, income, and locus of decision-making authority, differences that will be explored in greater detail in chapter 6. The households most likely to engage in agriculture were migrant households headed by women whose spouses were in the United States and households headed by men regardless of migrant status. All three types of household were equally likely to rely on the labor of their sons to help produce their crops. It is noteworthy that households headed by women whose husbands were in the United States tended to engage in agriculture in proportions roughly equal to male-headed households, whether migrant or not (37 percent, as compared to 35 percent and 31 percent, respectively). The average incomes they generated from agriculture were also roughly commensurable. Because the division of labor by gender in agriculture was unchanged by migration and the other forces of transformation operating in Los Pinos, women in this position had to rely on the management and labor of male kin. With their husbands in the United States, women depended on their sons, on their own or their spouse's siblings, or on sharecroppers who were most often kin as well. Migrant husbands also maintained direct involvement, writing their wives detailed instructions and sending money to finance production, or overseeing it themselves on vacations in the village. As a corollary, their reliance on male kin meant that these women were less likely to use wage labor than men who headed migrant households. Indeed, male-headed migrant households were most likely to use wage labor. The migrant members of these male-headed households were in almost all cases adult offspring, not wives. Not surprisingly, then, these men tended to be considerably older than the men who headed nonmigrant households. In part due to their age, and in part to the remittances they received from their children, they were much more likely to substitute wage labor for their own than comparable nonmigrant households; they were also less likely to give their land out to be sharecropped. One Pinero farmer in his sixties with several children in New York explained that he hired men to work his fields because "agriculture only serves to break you."

Use of wage labor was more closely associated with the size of landholding than with the migrant status of the household. Over half (54.2 percent) of all households with 80 tareas or more of land employed wage labor at some time during the year, as opposed to only 20.0 percent of those with less than that amount of land. This differential propensity of those with small and large holdings to hire wage labor held for migrants as well as nonmigrants. Yet although the use of wage labor was associated with larger landholdings, larger holdings in turn were more likely than small parcels to be planted in pasture. Conversely, food crop cultivation, a much more labor-intensive use of the land, took place predominantly on plots of less than 80 tareas. In practice, this meant that although households with larger landholdings were more apt to employ wage laborers, fewer days of work were generally required because of the low labor demands of cultivating and conditioning pasture.

CONCLUSION

As the agricultural base of Pinero society disintegrated, the conditions under which Pineros reproduced themselves were increasingly capitalist conditions. Although about half of all Pinero household heads farmed, they produced only a fraction of their families' subsistence needs. Households relied overwhelmingly on cash income from salaries, occasional wages and profits, and credit from shopkeepers to acquire their subsistence needs on a daily basis. And, of course, many migrant households were entirely dependent on remittances from members in the United States. In these circumstances, as Pessar (1982a:359) has observed for another Dominican migrant community, "the international migrant household becomes structurally equivalent to the fully proletarianized household of domestic workers in the core society." In chapter 4, it was noted that the migration of women in numbers equal to men has transferred part of the "renewal function" originally situated in the sending community to the migrants' areas of destination. Given the demise of agriculture, that portion of the renewal function still performed by migrant households in Los Pinos was paid for largely by the wages earned by household members in the United States.

We have also seen in this chapter that as agriculture declined in Los Pinos, it was replaced by cattle raising as the principal way to use the land. Households with the largest landholdings were instrumental in effecting this shift. Encouraged by state and market incentives, this change in land use had deleterious and profound consequences for most poor Pineros. Most significant was the increased inequality in the distribution of land, a result of the drive to expand holdings in order to increase cattle herds. This development was bound to have long-term implications for the economic and social structure of the community. For although income distribution in Los Pinos, dependent as it was on the continued flow of remittances into the community, compared favorably to national trends, distribution of land in the village had become progressively inequitable in a fundamental, structural way—impossible to reverse without profound change in the political economy of the community and, thus necessarily, of the republic.

CHAPTER 6

The Impact of International Migration on Social Organization and Social Structure in Los Pinos

> In the Dominican Republic, there are three kinds of people: the rich, the poor and those who travel to New York.
>
> —Pinera returned migrant woman

The long-term, or semipermanent, nature of most migration from Los Pinos had important implications for the social organization and social structure of the community. Unlike many Mexican migrants, who seasonally go to the United States to harvest crops and regularly return to their communities to live for the remainder of each year, Pineros were not engaged in circular migration; most worked year-round in the United States. They might spend ten to twenty years away from their home communities, paying only brief visits every year or two. The rate of permanent return was low. When migrants did return to the republic to live, they often settled in Santo Domingo or Santiago.

This chapter has two goals: to examine the effects of this kind of migration on family and household organization, with special emphasis on the differential experiences of women and men; and to assess the broader impact on social, political, and ideological structures in Los Pinos.

"FAMILIES DIVIDED": FAMILY ORGANIZATION AND HOUSEHOLD STRUCTURE IN LOS PINOS[1]

Migration had immediate and obvious consequences for Pinero families. Families might divide along generational lines, with parents staying behind, while children migrated one by one to the United States. In other cases, spouses might separate when, as most often

---

1. The term "families divided" is taken from the title of Colin Murray's (1981) book on the consequences of international labor migration for Lesotho.

occurred, the husband left first. As a consequence of the latter pattern, there was a strong tendency for migrant households in Los Pinos to be headed by women (table 6.1). In fact, nearly half (47 percent) of all migrant households were female-headed, as opposed to only 22 percent of nonmigrant households. In chapter 5, I noted that in a migrant community such as Los Pinos, it makes sense analytically to distinguish between those households headed by women in recognized conjugal relationships with absent males and those households headed by women alone. Of course, this distinction is not entirely satisfactory, since some single women were involved in more or less regular but unrecognized visiting relationships. However, for present purposes the distinction is a useful one. In Los Pinos, a large number of the women who headed their households were in recognized unions with men who were in the United States. Some women were also in recognized unions with men who worked elsewhere in the republic, principally in Santiago. In reflection of the increasing "suburbanization" of Los Pinos, some Pinero men worked during the week in stable government or private sector jobs in Santiago, visiting their families on weekends. Others worked elsewhere in the republic as national guardsmen, policemen, or government extension agents and visited less regularly.

In the majority of cases, the separation of spouses was only a phase in the developmental cycle of the international migrant household. Duration of the separation depended most on the legal status of the migrant member. When the wife migrated first, hers was usually a documented entry. Migrant husbands, on the other hand, were much more likely to have entered the United States as undocumented migrants. When the husband migrated first and was undocumented, the family might remain separated for years while he repaid prestamista

TABLE 6.1. Distribution of Sex of Household Head by Migrant Status

	Household Head							
	Women in union		*Single women*		*Men*		*Total*	
Household status	*N*	*%*	*N*	*%*	*N*	*%*	*N*	*%*
Migrant	30	32.3	14	15.1	49	52.7	93	39.7
Nonmigrant	13	9.2	18	12.8	110	78.0	141	60.3
Total	43	18.3	32	13.7	159	68.0	234	100.0

debts and attempted to regularize his legal status in the United States. If the migration was documented from the start, delays still occurred as the husband or wife became established and undertook the paperwork to request visas for spouse and children. These delays were generally shorter than those in which the migrant was undocumented, but in some cases they might also be extensive.

Long delays were largely the result of bureaucratic backlogs, but also of the fact that "business marriages" were common means of regularizing status, causing the United States consulate to cast a suspicious eye on many legitimate marriages as well. Applicants often had to endure waits of more than a year or two while consular staff investigated the nature of the relationship between spouses. These suspicions had also led to increasing consular demands of "proof" of the romantic nature of the bond between a man and woman, such as photographs and love letters. Despite these precautions on the part of the consulate, Pineros were still able to complain that some "business spouses" received visas with little delay, while other men and women who married "for love" had to suffer long separations because of the consulate's doubts. Sometimes, migrants' wives would be denied visas on the grounds that they were considered likely to become wards of the state. To avoid the separation and long wait, two men who were legal U.S. residents even sent their wives the money to migrate illegally.

The psychological burden of separation was often heavy for both spouses. In some respects, though, U.S. migration exacted differential costs from the wives and husbands who were left behind. The dense exchange of information between Pineros in New York and those in the village meant that gossip traveled air mail, and sometimes by satellite. Infractions of community expectations were reported in both directions. Women might hear of their husbands' liaisons in New York and men quickly learned of their wives' behavior in Los Pinos. A husband's behavior, however, was less constrained than his wife's. Censure fell hardest on the women who were viewed as not conforming to norms of proper feminine conduct. Thus, because men were "of the street" and subject to different standards, it was often simply assumed that they would engage in extramarital sex while separated from their wives for long periods. Nonetheless, when Pinero men with wives in the United States established relationships with other women in the republic, they generally tended to do so circumspectly. Such circumspection was not only a product of the respect and the affective ties binding the man to his spouse, but also of the fear that village gossip might reach her and jeopardize his future migration to the United States.

My visit to Los Pinos in 1987 revealed a new psychological cost to U.S. migration. Because of the heavy concentration of cases of acquired immune deficiency syndrome (AIDS) in New York, migrants unwittingly had become a potentially deadly epidemiological link between that city and Los Pinos. Already, one Pinero had contracted AIDS while living in New York was was now dying in a hospital in the capital. This man had made an undocumented migration to New York in the late 1970s, leaving his wife behind. He did not become sick until five years after his return in the early 1980s. Women I spoke with in Los Pinos were now very apprehensive about the disease, worried about their husbands in New York, and worried about themselves.

Most often, the migration of her husband did not increase a woman's autonomy nor enhance her decision-making authority within the household. Indeed, after their husbands left, many married women became more constrained in their movements. In some cases, Pinera women living in Santiago or Santo Domingo returned to Los Pinos to live with their own or their husbands' parents after their husbands migrated. In part, these returns had an economic motivation: it was cheaper to collapse households and to live in the countryside. But such returns also occurred because it was believed that a wife's sexuality would be under greater control if she resided with kin in Los Pinos than if she were left alone in the city. One woman moved from Santiago to her husband's parents' house after he received an anonymous letter in New York alleging that his wife had been unfaithful. To quell the rumors and forestall the separation that her husband threatened, she returned to Los Pinos with her children. There were also occasional exceptions and reversals of this pattern. After her husband migrated to the United States, one young Pinera with a particularly lively personality moved to Santiago to live with her sister. She explained to me that she did this in an attempt to avoid what she felt would be the inevitable gossip about her. Very few Pineras followed this route, however.

In general, women with husbands in the United States were totally, or almost totally, dependent on their husbands' remittances to maintain their families. Thus, although a husband might be physically absent most of the year, typically he remained the breadwinner and the locus of decision-making authority within the household. The absent husband often also continued to determine the uses to which money over and above basic consumption expenses was put. Whether or not to condition pastures, purchase livestock, repair houses, or plant crops was often communicated to wives during visits, in letters, through visiting kin, and occasionally in telephone conversations when wives traveled to the municipal seat or large cities. Interestingly, some husbands made a practice of timing their remittances to arrive on or around the twenty-fifth of every month, payday for government employees throughout the republic; several also sent double the usual remittance in December, mimicking the customary Christmas bonus paid by many employers.

Retention of decision-making authority by absent husbands reflected and was reinforced by the type of union that characterized migrant households. Both migrant and nonmigrant household heads were equally likely to be in a marital union of some kind. But 80 percent of migrant household heads were in church and/or civil marriages, whereas this was true of only 56 percent of nonmigrant households. The rest were in consensual unions. As in other parts of Latin America and the Caribbean, formal marriage ceremonies, especially church weddings ("por la iglesia") were a mark of status and prestige. In Los Pinos, they were associated with ownership of land and cattle and with education. Of course, to a certain extent, both church and civil marriages were encouraged by U.S. immigration regulations. To request a visa for a mate, the migrant had to produce certification of a legal marriage. In some cases, this requisite had resulted in the formal legitimation of unions ten and twenty years after they were formed.

Patrifocal, stable marriages sanctioned by a church wedding or, to a lesser extent, by a civil ceremony embodied community notions of proper unions. As noted earlier, ideally in such unions, women took responsibility for intrahousehold affairs, while husbands were the breadwinners, made all economic decisions, and represented the family in the extrahousehold domain (Brown 1975). Clearly, this normative division of labor by gender was more difficult to maintain in poor households where out of necessity women might participate more widely in extradomestic arenas. In contrast, women with migrant husbands were able more readily to conform to community ideals on two counts: first, because they were more likely to be in proper unions and second, because the steady remittance income they received helped to reinforce traditional patterns of authority within the family and to keep their experience largely confined to domestic concerns.

Despite the stabilizing effect these factors had on marriages, geographical separation inevitably created emotional hardships and strains. It is striking, therefore, that these "families divided" did not exhibit higher rates of divorce and separation than nonmigrant households. Only 9 percent and 10 percent of all migrant and non-migrant household heads, respectively, were divorced or separated.

Apart from attesting the strength of the affective ties bonding many couples, this low rate also reflected the importance of the household unit in the strategy of chain migration. The goal of the overwhelming majority of the Pinero migrants I spoke with was permanent return to the Dominican Republic. Achievement of this goal was hastened by sponsoring the migration of dependents, both wives and children, so that they could work and save as part of the reconstituted household in the United States. In many cases, return migration was made possible only because offspring remained in the United States to work. For these parents, it was the safety net provided by their children's remittances that helped make return a viable option. Thus, the result for many families was a pattern of international "relay migration" (Arizpe 1982) in which children replace their parents in the United States over time. In brief, although the emotional strains of the physical separation of spouses were real enough, there were also strong centripetal pressures emanating from the domestic economy of the international migrant household which worked to hold the family together.

At a point in the chain migration process of many households, family members of working age will all have migrated, and younger children will be left behind in Los Pinos. As noted earlier, some households in Los Pinos assumed the role of caretakers for family members whom migrants temporarily or permanently left behind. Because homemaking, housekeeping, and caretaking were "women's work," the role of guardian of these children fell to them. For many, especially older women, this role could be quite burdensome. In chapter 3, I described the experience of Nina Sánchez, a woman in her sixties left with six grandchildren to look after. She summarized her view of her situation by saying, "I am a prisoner." Some women were able to hire other women to help with domestic chores. However, the extra work load was not the only hardship involved in the caretaker role. This role also entailed a great deal of responsibility. For instance, Yolanda Rodríguez, another grandmother in her seventies, felt obliged to keep a strict vigil over the behavior of her teenage granddaughter whose mother was in the United States. Keeping the girl "off the street" to forestall gossip and maintain her reputation was a heavy responsibility that Yolanda Rodríguez was happy to shed when her granddaughter finally migrated. Thus, as women absorbed a variety of other members into their households for whom they assumed the role of caretakers, their work and responsibility loads often increased.

The twin processes of collapse and consolidation resulting from the chain migration of household members had implications for household structure in Los Pinos (table 6.2). Not surprisingly, migrant households were less likely to be nuclear (one conjugal pair and offspring) than nonmigrant households. This is explained not only by the greater tendency of some migrant households to pare down to female heads and their dependents after the loss of a migrant spouse, but also, as noted, on occasion to expand to include an assortment of additional members from other households. Sometimes, migrant households underwent both processes at once: they lost some members through migration and gained others through consolidation with other households. This tendency is also visible in the fact that three-generation households were nearly twice as common among migrant households.

The following examples illustrate more concretely how the processes of collapse and condensation produced dislocations and rearrangements in household structure in Los Pinos.

1. When I first arrived in Los Pinos, Rosita Rodríguez, divorced for nearly ten years, lived with five of her children in her parents' house. Ten of her siblings lived in New York. Rosita had stayed behind to raise her chidren and care for her aged parents. In 1980, her siblings who were U.S. citizens requested residence visas for her and her two eldest children, who were by now nearly adults. Rosita decided to leave her three youngest children in Los Pinos until she became established in New York. She left one child with her ex-husband's parents, one with a married daughter, and her teenage daughter with her mother, Yolanda.

2. After two unsuccessful attempts, Juana Morales finally succeeded in making an undocumented entry into the United States in 1976. Pregnant at the time of her migration, she gave birth in the United States and subsequently sent her "American" baby back to Los Pinos to be raised by her sister, with whom she had also left her four children from two previous unions. Her sister became a full-time caretaker for these children. For these duties she received remittances on a more or less regular basis from Juana.

3. Hernán and Pinina Pérez are both U.S. residents receiving Social Security benefits. For most of the year, they live in New York, where Hernán works in his son's bodega and Pinina keeps house and provides child care for several of her grandchildren. Their household

TABLE 6.2. Distribution of Type of Household Structure by Migrant Status

Type[a]	Migrant households (N = 93) Percentage	Nonmigrant households (N = 141) Percentage
1 conjugal pair:		
1 conjugal pair	2.2	2.8
1 conjugal pair + S/D	10.8	29.8
1 conjugal pair + S/D + grandchild	7.6	5.7
1 conjugal pair + others	4.3	2.8
1 conjugal pair + S/D + HM/F, WM/F	1.1	2.1
1 conjugal pair + S/D + others	10.8	12.1
1 conjugal pair + S/D + grandchild + others	1.1	1.4
1 conjugal pair + grandchild	4.3	2.1
1 conjugal pair + grandchild + others	1.1	0
2 conjugal pairs:		
1 conjugal pair + S/D + SW/DH + grandchildren	2.2	1.4
1 conjugal pair + S/D + SW/DH	1.1	0
1 conjugal pair + S/D + HZS + HZSW	1.1	0
No conjugal pair:		
M + S/D	18.3	11.4
M + S/D + grandchildren	5.4	2.1
M + S/D + others	15.1	9.2
M + S/D + grandchildren + others	1.1	.7
Woman + grandchildren	3.2	.7
Woman + others	3.2	0
Single woman	0	2.1
Single man	2.2	7.8
F + S/D	0	.7
F + S/D + grandchildren + others	3.2	0
F + S/D + others	1.1	.7
F + others	0	4.3
Total	100.5[b]	99.9[b]

[a]M = Mother   D = Daughter   W = Wife   Z = Sister
  F = Father   S = Son   H = Husband
[b]Due to rounding.

in Los Pinos consists of a mentally disabled daughter and a mute son who repeatedly have been denied resident visas, a married daughter, and her two small children. This daughter lived in Santiago until her husband migrated to the United States in 1978. Because he had been erratic in sending remittances and also because she was needed to care for her parents' house and her two siblings, she moved back to Los Pinos to assume management of the household.

MIGRATION AND SOCIAL DIFFERENTIATION IN LOS PINOS

Class and Status

Until recent decades, possession of land was a key criterion for differentiating among Pineros and for placing them within the local and regional class structure. But, as chapter 5 demonstrated in some detail, the impact of state policies, the structure of markets, the lack of credit, the deterioration of the environment, and the effects of U.S. migration combined to bring agriculture to a near halt in Los Pinos. To an extent, cattle replaced crops as a way to use land productively. However, in general, land ceased to be the sole criterion of differentiation. In the context of widespread destruction of soil and water resources, for example, it became difficult to distinguish the survival strategies of smallholding households from those that were entirely landless. Even large landholders lost much of their ability to dispense patronage and to control the labor of poorer Pineros.

At the same time, new criteria of differentiation emerged, the principal one being access to wage labor or the earnings therefrom, in the form of remittances. Formal education also became a credential increasingly important in determining wage earnings and a person's chances for upward mobility. Thus, by 1981 Pinero society and economy could scarcely be considered to be precapitalist.

The question remains however: how had U.S. migration affected the process of differentiation as it evolved in Los Pinos? Had migration helped amplify differences, level them, or maintain the status quo? In previous chapters, differences between migrant and nonmigrant households in terms of ownership and control of land, labor, and cattle were examined. In the following sections, I examine the position of migrant households in contemporary Pinero society in terms of several other interconnected class-related aspects: life-style, income, occupation, education, and power (Ferguson 1988).

Life-style and Income

U.S. migration had made possible a distinctively high level of consumption among those households with access to the earnings of migrants abroad. Perhaps most emblematic in this regard was housing.

Reflecting aspirations to modernity as well as to social mobility, improved housing is a nearly universal goal of international migrants in most sending communities throughout the world (Graves and Graves 1974; Gmelch 1980), and Dominican migrants are no exception. The primacy of this goal is even reflected in a popular merengue in which a migrant in New York invokes the Virgin of Altagracia, a patron saint of the republic, to help him build his house so that he may return for good:

> *Virgencita de Altagracia,*
> *te estoy hablando desde aquí,*
> *que si consigo mi casa*
> *me largo pa' mi país.*

> Dear Virgin of Altagracia,
> I'm speaking to you from here,
> that if I'm able to get my house
> I'm taking off for my country.

> (Sandy Reyes, Karen Records).

As noted in chapter 4, the construction of new migrant houses and the upgrading and expansion of old ones were continuous activities in Los Pinos. Indeed, nearly all (94 percent) of migrant households owned their own houses, whereas this was true of only about three-quarters (77 percent) of nonmigrant households. Table 6.3 summarizes the characteristics of migrant and nonmigrant houses, listing types of construction materials in descending order of prestige and status, as well as some prestigious amenities, such as indoor kitchens and tanks for water storage.

The Sierra in general had long been known and widely admired throughout the republic for its comparatively large, well-built pine board houses. Migrants, as table 6.3 hints, preferred a style of house quite distinct from the traditional, a style associated with urbanism and hence modernity. Emulating the designs seen in Santiago's middle-class neighborhoods, migrants were more likely to own larger houses with concrete walls, cement floors, indoor kitchens, and metal roofs. That is to say, migrant dwellings were more likely to be constructed of the more expensive materials manufactured outside the community, such as cement and galvanized sheeting, than those produced locally.

Expensive to build, these houses were also hot to live in. They were also responsible for a "keeping up with the Pérez" type of reaction among many community members. This reaction was illustrated in

TABLE 6.3. House Construction by Migrant Household Status

| | \multicolumn{6}{c}{Household status} | | | | | |
| | Migrant | | Nonmigrant | | Total | |
	N	%	N	%	N	%
Wall material						
Cement blocks	39	41.9	37	26.2	76	32.5
Planed wood	47	50.5	63	44.7	110	47.0
Particle board/Pine board	7	7.5	41	29.1	48	20.5
Floor material						
Mosaic	9	9.7	8	5.7	17	7.3
Cement	71	76.3	76	53.9	147	62.8
Wood	12	12.9	27	19.2	39	16.7
Earth	1	1.1	30	20.3	31	13.3
Roof material						
Cement	2	2.2	1	.7	3	1.3
Galvanized metal	85	91.4	79	56.0	164	70.1
Wood	0	0	1	.7	1	.4
Palm thatch	6	6.5	60	42.6	66	28.2
Number of rooms						
1–4	33	35.5	88	62.4	121	51.7
5–9	60	64.5	53	37.6	113	48.3
Indoor kitchen	48	51.6	43	30.5	91	38.9
Water tank	35	37.6	13	9.2	48	20.5

the following quotation from Tonia Sánchez, a Pinera in her early forties. Tonia and her husband Telo, a near-landless Pinero who engaged in a multitude of activities, had a migrant daughter working as a domestic in Puerto Rico. Tonia explained why she and her husband decided to upgrade their modest wooden house:

> We had to build a new kitchen and paint the house now. Dulce has been gone for four years, and we haven't been able to fix the house up at all. It is true that we have debts to pay, but I felt ashamed that our house was unpainted for so long with our daughter in the exterior; and Trina [a neighbor] just painted hers last Christmas, with her husband in New York only a year.

Migrants' improvements thus set a new standard for housing. As Tonia's statement indicates, the Sánchez family felt compelled to meet community expectations and upgrade their housing despite severe budgetary constraints.

Ironically, the most elaborate of the migrant houses in Los Pinos, which took nearly four years to complete at a cost of more than

DR$40,000, was owned by a daughter of Don Pancho Morales, the muleteer-middleman prominent in Pinero society in the 1920s and 1930s. Built only a small distance from the site of Don Pancho's now demolished compound, this elegant Santiago-style house stood as a monument to his former status. To date, however, Don Pancho's daughter, widowed and living alone in New York, had not been able to save enough to return to Los Pinos. Her house remained empty, looked after by an overseer and his wife, although looked over and commented on by all the community.

Although most segments of Pinero society aspired to higher levels of consumption, their superior incomes as well as their ready access to credit made migrant households much more likely to realize them. The superior incomes of migrant households were largely attributable to their claims on the wages earned by members in the United States, as table 6.4 reveals. Indeed, remittances contributed roughly three-fifths of all income at the disposal of the average migrant household. A cash subsidy of this magnitude, together with the many gifts brought from the United States, enabled migrant households to enjoy standards of consumption comparable to the middle-class salaried employees, and substantially higher than the majority of Pineros. Table 6.5 shows that when compared with nonmigrants, they were twice as likely to possess such household amenities as gas stoves and refrigerators, items manufactured and purchased domestically; and they were three times as likely to own television sets, which were in most cases hand-carried to the village by visiting migrants.

Migrants also held an advantage in terms of their ease of access to potable water, a perennial problem in Los Pinos. Over the last decade, Pineros had intensively but unsuccessfully lobbied the government to provide the community with a system of pipe-borne water. Despite these efforts, in 1981 Los Pinos was still without running water. As table 6.5 shows, migrant houses were more likely to have cement tanks to store rainfall runoff for cooking and drinking. These tanks provided the household with a steady and secure supply of water which was rarely exhausted. Those who had metal roofs used them as catchments to collect a more limited amount of rain water; as the rain flowed off the roof, it was channeled into fifty-gallon drums positioned at each corner of the house and kitchen. As was seen in table 6.3, migrant households were also more likely to have metal roofs. Those with thatch roofs, also the poorest Pineros, had to haul water from the river on a daily basis.

Because households with water tanks commonly "loaned" water to poorer neighbors whose houses were covered with thatch roofs, the

TABLE 6.4. Average Annual Income (DR$) for Migrant and Nonmigrant Households

	Migrant	Nonmigrant
Total income	3419.96	2292.30
Remittance income only	2132.16	438.15
Remittance as percentage of total income	62.3	19.1

benefits of this amenity were sometimes spread to nonmigrants as well. Sharing of water among neighbors was reinforced by the fact that they were frequently also kin. Although it is impossible to assign a market value to this form of transfer between migrant and nonmigrant households, the "loaning" of water was of considerable importance to the budgeting of labor and resources in the domestic economy of poor households. The labor of young sons saved by the water loans could be allocated to other useful, and in some cases income-generating, tasks.

Elsewhere in the sección, migrants were responsible for bringing running water to their communities. Where gravity permitted, they used cheap plastic tubing to channel water down to their homes from high mountain streams. Other households could then hook up to this system with their own shorter lengths of tubing. Because Los Pinos is located at a higher altitude than its potable water sources, this method was not feasible there.

Although on the whole migrant households were more likely to enjoy levels of consumption that were high by local standards, there is

TABLE 6.5. Ownership of Consumer Durables by Migrant Househould Status

	Household status					
	Migrants		Nonmigrants		Total	
Item	N	%	N	%	N	%
Radio	92	98.9	121	85.8	213	91.0
Gas stove	67	72.0	46	32.6	113	48.3
Refrigerator	62	66.7	37	26.2	99	42.3
Television set	60	64.6	27	19.2	87	37.2
Water tank	35	37.6	13	9.2	48	20.5
Sewing machine	30	32.3	22	15.6	52	22.2

little question that U.S.-bound migration had increased the demand for certain goods and aspirations to consumption among all sectors of the community. This increase was in large part due to the displays of conspicuous consumption made by the scores of migrants who returned to Los Pinos to visit during holidays. Adorned with gold jewelry, particularly the chains and medallions that have become a sort of "Dominican Yorker" badge, and sporting new clothing often purchased specially for their vacation, young migrants strolled up and down the main street of Los Pinos, listening to their jumbo casette players. The men spent evenings buying drinks for a large coterie of friends and hangers-on, while nearby their children roller-skated to the North American disco music popular at that time. Such displays had an unmistakable demonstration effect on nonmigrants and undoubtedly helped create newly perceived needs throughout the community.

Of course, the positive valuation of consumer goods was promoted continuously through the mass media as well. The great majority (91 percent) of Pineros owned radios. Although only one-third had television sets, those without them regularly viewed many programs in the houses of their neighbors. Still, by bringing cheap sets back to their families (some had color television and in 1987 I saw one satellite dish), migrants helped spread the visual image of middle- and upper-class consumption patterns depicted in commercials and in many programs, particularly the popular evening soap operas. For instance, while I was in the village, the most popular serial was entitled "Los ricos también lloran" ("The Rich also Cry"). So avidly followed was this Mexican soap opera that the English class we taught, a popular social event itself, had to be scheduled not to coincide with it. While the life-styles of the rich were presented in detail on such soaps, intermittantly throughout the year migrant displays brought some of these images concretely if more modestly to life on Los Pinos' main street.

Occupation

Especially in the last two decades, occupation emerged as an important criterion of socioeconomic differentiation in Los Pinos. However, the men and women who headed migrant households in the community exhibited a greater tendency to be without occupation than nonmigrant household heads. Among the men, 16.3 percent reported no employment whatever in 1981, as opposed to only 6.4 percent of the nonmigrants. Roughly three-fifths (61.4 percent) of the women who headed migrant households devoted themselves only to house-work, as compared with slightly less than half (48.4 percent) of the nonmigrant women.

For the men, this difference may be attributed in part to their greater age, an average of 64 years as opposed to only 47 for those who headed nonmigrant households. Yet the women who headed migrant and nonmigrant households had almost identical average ages (48 and 47 years, respectively). Nonetheless, they were also characterized by dif-ferent rates of employment. These findings are very much in line with those of national surveys as well as of other case studies which have found higher levels of unemployment among migrant households (Baez Evertsz and D'Oleo Ramírez 1986; Grasmuck 1985). In Los Pinos, these higher levels derived from a combination of retirement due to ad-vanced age, unfulfilled aspirations on the part of younger individuals to scarce middle-class jobs, and a reluctance to accept low-wage work. In any case, withdrawal from the labor force was made possible largely because of the remittances received by household members.

Generally, for heads of migrant households, occupation was not a source of status and prestige. Two young discretionary return mi-grants were teachers but none of the heads of migrant households were professionals or semiprofessionals by Pinero standards. Except-ing the young returnees, only one had reached the eighth grade. Those women and men with the highest prestige jobs, such as teacher, doc-tor, and nurse, as well as the merchant elite with the most prosperous businesses, generally belonged to nonmigrant households. Thus, the heads of migrant households in Los Pinos, whether men or women, fell outside the higher status echelons of the local occupational hi-erarchy. It was, of course, one of the foremost aspirations of these Pineros that their children would not do so.

Education

In earlier chapters, the increasing importance of education as a cre-dential essential to securing employment in middle-class jobs has often been remarked. Some migrants had attempted to attain additional education for themselves while in the United States. In the main, these migrants attended English and technical courses, believing that these would help them get a better job in the United States and in the re-public when they returned. Most, however, were forced by heavy work schedules and lack of time to abandon their efforts after a while.

Many more migrants pursued the goal of education for their chil-dren. Often involving considerable sacrifice on the part of the parents, and occasionally the larger kindred as well, investment in children's education was viewed as a primary strategy to promote social mobility across the generations. One Pinero migrant who had attended school only to the sixth grade explained why he had placed his two U.S.-born children in a relatively expensive parochial school in New York: "I work for my family and I am proud of this. I want to give my sons a good education because one's children are one's hope." Remittances enabled children from some migrant households to study in Dominican universities and later obtain prestigious jobs as engineers, managers, and doctors. Sometimes, a university education was made possible only through the collective efforts of a network of migrant kin. One Pinero's medical degree was financed with the contributions of his grandfather and four aunts and uncles, all migrants. Another strategy is for parents to finance the education of one child, often the oldest, with the expectation that in turn he or she will take care of the educational expenses of the younger children.

Some migrant children reared in the United States attended universities there, a great many in the city and, to a lesser extent, state systems of New York. It was not at all clear, however, that these children eventually would return to the republic to establish themselves. If parents returned and U.S.-educated children did not, as appeared to be a common pattern, intergenerational mobility would take place outside of the social frame of reference most important to the parents. The status and prestige reflected from children's social mobility thus would be dimmed.

Despite the value placed on children's university education, fewer migrants achieved this goal than managed to build their houses. The exigencies of maintaining households in the republic as well as in New York while attempting to save for the return created pressures to bring family members to the United States where they could be converted from consumers to producers of income. Only a minority of migrant households were thus able to finance the university education of a child. It is clear, nonetheless, that migrant households were able to invest more readily in their children's education than were non-migrant households.

This can be seen most readily at the primary and secondary levels. Children from migrant households in school in Los Pinos were generally able to achieve higher levels of education. On the whole, this advantage held even when controlling for children's age (table 6.6). Proportionally, more school-age children from migrant households were in school; they tended to enter school at an earlier age; and 50 percent more eventually attended secondary school. On occasion, mi-

TABLE 6.6. Distribution of Education of School-Age Children in Los Pinos by Migrant Household Status and Age Group

	Level of education attained					
	0		*1–4*		*5–8*	
Age group	Migrant	Nonmigrant	Migrant	Nonmigrant	Migrant	Nonmigrant
5–9	21.7	40.0	78.3 ·	60.0	0	0
10–14	0	5.0	50.7	52.9	47.9	42.2
15–19	4.7	1.3	6.3	20.6	37.2	56.4

	Level of education attained			
	9–11		*12+*	
Age group	Migrant	Nonmigrant	Migrant	Nonmigrant
5–9	0	0	0	0
10–14	1.4	0	0	0
15–19	29.7	16.7	4.7	5.1

grant families in the United States sent young children back to the republic for their primary and secondary school education. A few were sent to Los Pinos, but more attended private schools in the cities. Some of these parents said they felt that the quality of Dominican education was superior. Others, such as the migrant who told me that "schools in New York damage the youth," wanted their children away from pernicious influences, particularly the easy availability of drugs and, for girls, the permissive attitudes toward sex.

Power: Community Leadership and Migration

After the demise of the Trujillo regime, political life in Los Pinos underwent a profound reorganization. Both at the national and local levels, political power became more widely dispersed. The post-Trujillo years saw the growth of a more systematic state administration in the Dominican countryside. The roles once performed by the alcalde and "Trujillo's men" devolved to individuals who were now directly integrated into the state apparatus as professional bureaucrats. By the early 1980s, the combination of fragmentation and bureaucratization had resulted in the reduction of the influence of former patrons and the emergence of new intermediaries in Los Pinos.

These new intermediaries were almost entirely poor men in their twenties and thirties, by and large small landholders and unemployed youth. Strongly identified with either the PRD or the PR, their principal function was to deliver the vote for their party. On occasion, candidates also made direct appeals to voters in Los Pinos. But party bosses relied heavily on local brokers to rally voters, largely through the mobilization of their extended kin networks and the "clients" for whom they provided access to state resources. In exchange, these petty brokers received small gifts (clothing, a watch) and the promise of a state-sector job if and when their party achieved power. In the day-to-day life of Los Pinos, the brokers functioned primarily as points of access to state services, one of the most important of which was state- or party-supported medical care. They did this either by mediating directly with party bosses in Santiago or, less frequently, with inter-mediate-level bosses in the municipal seat.

The wealthiest Pineros were not involved in this type of brokering. As one man explained, "The rich around here don't waste their time with [local] politics." Only one member of a migrant household and no return migrants functioned as brokers in Los Pinos. The power derived or reflected from state agencies located outside the community was too weak, and the rewards of political brokering too meager, to attract the attention of the Pineros with the greatest access to resources. In any case, their networks often provided informal links to politically influential persons in Santiago or the capital to whom they could appeal directly for patronage.

Nor were they attracted to formal political positions, such as al-calde or municipal delegate, whose principal functions were the resolution of local disputes and the mobilization of community labor for public works projects. For most, the limited recognition and relatively small monthly salaries derived from these positions did not compensate for the responsibilities involved and the certainty that their occupants would arouse the antagonism and ill will of at least some community members.

Political fragmentation in Los Pinos occurred hand in hand with economic fragmentation. As the agrarian foundation crumbled and the economy informalized and became more service-oriented, the local bases of patronage and political power fractured and scattered. Once a source of clients for the large landowners, for example, share-cropping had almost disappeared as a consequence of state legislation and the spread of cattle raising.

U.S. migration was also a significant factor promoting the centrifugal tendencies in the local distribution of economic and political power. The merchant elite's monopoly over commercial activities was eroded directly by migrants' investments in shops and indirectly through their investments in transportation services that allowed Pineros easily to make major purchases in Santiago. Credit sources also multiplied as migrants "put their money to work" as loan capital. Finally, migrants' investments in lottery pools, shops, bars, construction, and públicos deepened the already strong tendency toward informalization of the rural economy. The rise of the informal sector presented employment alternatives which weakened the political hand of the largest landholders. In the face of diminishing stakes, they as well as other better-off Pineros withdrew from the local political game.

The fact that nearly 40 percent of all Pinero households had a migrant member in the United States also decreased the dependence of many on local patronage. In a sense, however, migrants themselves became patrons, on whom the majority of these households now depended for their basic subsistence needs. In some cases, the fact that the migrant patron was also close kin did not always ease the onus of dependency. One widow whose migrant son maintained her household entirely through his remittances told me, "It's a terrible thing to be dependent on others for everything." Another young woman expressed her deep gratitude that her brothers supported her and her mother but also said that this situation made her feel "like a parasite."

As a sort of patron, then, a migrant could and did exert influence over the political behavior of family members in Los Pinos. Dominican politicians were well aware of this influence. During elections, they actively campaigned in New York, even though migrants could only cast their ballots if they returned to the republic. Of course, migration itself might be viewed broadly as a political act: a way of "voting with one's feet," of protesting the existing sociopolitical order by opting out of it, at least temporarily.

At the same time that formal political positions attracted little interest, community associations had proliferated. It is sometimes suggested that migration disrupts institutions in the sending community and fosters the disorganization of community life (e.g., Lowenthal 1972). But in Los Pinos, community participation in a variety of organizations was lively. Several were organized by Pineros themselves, who tended to view them as symbols of progress and modernity. In 1981, Los Pinos had a social club, a food cooperative, and a savings and loan cooperative organized by the best-educated schoolteachers in the community; a cattlemen's association founded by the most prosperous cattle owners; and several other smaller and less active clubs fomented by extension agents from a variety of government community development organs. The Catholic Church was also very active in Los Pinos throughout the 1970s and helped organize several groups. As in many other Sierran migrant communities, migrant donations helped build the church in Los Pinos.

The social club had also received support from international migrants. Completion of the large and modern concrete clubhouse in 1981 was made possible in part by over US $5,000 in contributions from migrants. The balance of $3,000 needed to complete the building was given by the government of the late President Antonio Guzmán, who had been petitioned for assistance by Pinero PRD members during an election year.

Some migrants in New York had organized a charitable association to aid the poor in Los Pinos. For over a decade, this association collected donations from Pineros in New York earmarked for the poorest households in the village. These colectas were made each Christmas and in cases of emergency (loss of a breadwinner, a long and expensive illness). Migrants coordinated the distribution of these donations with some prominent Pinero nonmigrants, in the main merchants and teachers. This association had survived the continual turnover of personnel as the leaders in New York returned to the Dominican Republic and some Pinero members migrated to New York.

It has also sometimes been asserted that return migrants bring with them a counterflow of experience which infuses their communities with new ideas and leadership skills. Did return migrants' experiences abroad enable them in fact to assume positions of responsibility within Pinero associations? With their secure income from kin in the United States, did the members of migrant households use their increased leisure time to tackle these positions? In Los Pinos, leadership roles generally fell to the best educated, and therefore younger, members of the community. Overwhelmingly, these individuals tended to be schoolteachers and health care workers—as noted earlier, members of the community's new middle class. The savings and loan cooperative, for instance, was founded by teachers who copied the model of the teachers' cooperative of the municipal seat. It was the teachers, too, who organized the food cooperative of Los Pinos, to which largely middle-income members of the community belonged. Return migrants and members of migrant households, in contrast, played a prominent role neither as members nor as leaders of associations. In 1981, only one return migrant held a leadership position. Significantly, this was a young secondary school teacher, a discretionary migrant who had briefly traveled to New York in order to save enough to build a new house.

Interestingly, there were no significant gender differences with respect to membership and leadership of voluntary associations in Los

Pinos. With the exception of the cattlemen's association, women participated actively in all of Los Pinos' organizations. That their participation was comparable to that of the men's was probably due to the prominent role that the teachers played in the formation and continued functioning of these associations. In Los Pinos, there were as many women teachers as there were men teachers, and they were as actively involved in the promotion of new ideas and community development. Thus, at least among the younger generation, education and professional status appeared to cut across traditional constraints on women's participation in extradomestic affairs. Also, as appeared to be the case generally in the Dominican Republic (Rosado et al. 1987), experience of the city through an internal move, visits, or stints at school often led rural women to question traditional roles and values.

In short, the information presented in this section suggests that it was the local middle class of younger and better-educated professionals and semiprofessionals that was taking the organizational lead in Los Pinos. In the social context of Los Pinos, it appears that the skills migrants acquired in the factories, hotels, and gypsy cabs of New York were not so relevant to community organization and leadership as those garnered in the schools, universities, and urban centers of the republic. This should not be surprising. Besides, as we shall see in the next section, the most successful migrants returned not to Los Pinos, but to Santiago, where their skills and experience were permanently lost to the community.

RETURN MIGRATION AND SOCIAL MOBILITY

Only 12 percent of all Pinero migrants, or 47 individuals, returned to live in the republic. Although they had not assumed positions of institutionalized or informal leadership in the community, the social status of some return migrants and members of migrant households had unquestionably improved as a consequence of migration. Yet, at least in rural areas such as Los Pinos, the social position of return migrants was far from crystallized. If the socioeconomic characteristics of migrants prior to their migration were diverse, as chapter 3 attempted to show, then it is misleading to speak of return migrants and of migrant households as though they constituted a group. They clearly did not.

Return migrants were heterogeneous both in terms of their experiences in the United States and of their situation after returning to the republic. Some 40 percent of return migrants settled in urban areas, and only 60 percent returned to Los Pinos. In large part, this heterogeneity derives from their differential incorporation into the U.S. labor market and their differential success in regularizing their immigration status. The interplay of these two dimensions had resulted in clearly detectable currents in the stream of return migrants.

One important current was composed of those Pineros who managed to escape the low-wage secondary sector of the U.S. economy and establish small businesses in the Dominican neighborhoods of New York and other northeastern cities. Almost invariably, Pinero entrepreneurs were legal resident aliens for the bulk of their U.S. sojourn. Nearly all Pinero entrepreneurs owned bodegas, grocery stores stocking Dominican staples as well as a variety of other goods. Bodegas could be lucrative ventures, with earnings varying according to the size of the store but, in all the cases that I explored, in excess of US$30,000 a year—over double the annual earnings of a factory worker. In attempting to discover why these men had been able to become bodegueros, I found no pattern that would "preadapt" them to this type of activity. Pinero bodegueros did not differ from other migrants in terms of their education, age, or access to resources in Los Pinos. Two bodegueros could not read or write and relied on their partners to assist them. By and large, Pineros became small entrepreneurs because a relative or close friend had presented them with the opportunity to invest in a bodega. Most often, this opportunity arose because the owner had decided to return to the republic to live. Typically, the business was sold to them on credit, with the loan for the down payment sometimes advanced as well. Despite the potentially high income to be gained, when presented with an offer to purchase a bodega some Pineros nevertheless refused. The principal reason given was fear of violent robbery, the joló, a recognized occupational hazard of the bodeguero. One Pinero was murdered and another very seriously wounded as a result of such attacks.

The comparative lucrativeness of bodegas and other small businesses (most commonly restaurants or garment factories) enabled their owners to return to the republic with accumulated savings ranging from US$35,000 to $80,000—much larger than most other types of migrants. Invariably, these entrepreneurs preferred to settle in the large cities, particularly Santiago, but also Santo Domingo.

In these cities, they owned and operated grocery stores, cafeterias, travel agencies, gas stations, money-changing businesses, and trucks. And, of course, they bought houses. But migrants who returned to the cities often adapted their houses also to serve as locales for small businesses. Most frequently, these were run by women return migrants. The most popular small businesses were the boutiques, in which clothes and cosmetics hand-carried back from the United States were sold; beauty salons run by women who took courses in hairdressing in New York; or pensions, rooms in which were rented to foreign (largely Puerto Rican) students enrolled at the private university in Santiago.

In the largest cities of the republic, entirely new neighborhoods had been built to fill migrant demand for modern housing. This clustering of the migrant population in a city such as Santiago, where it has been estimated that approximately one-quarter of all households had migrant or return migrant members (Grasmuck 1984b:389), also created an environment propitious for many migrant-run businesses. Migrant-operated travel agencies, for instance, did most of their business selling airplane tickets to New York to other migrants. Money changers obviously relied heavily on migrants' repatriated dollars for their livelihood. And the superior cash incomes of migrant households in the cities helped keep the shops and boutiques in business.

Despite the fact that many Pineros were able to establish successful businesses in Santiago, for the majority dependence on international migration did not end with their return to the republic. Few returnees fully escaped a sense of insecurity. This uncertainty arose from a combination of factors: the alarming downturn the Dominican economy had taken by the early 1980s, the increasingly uncertain political environment, and the difficulties of maintaining the middle-class life-style to which most returnees aspired. Ever-increasing competition from new return migrants' enterprises was also a serious problem. For instance, one Pinero explained that in 1971, when he returned to Santiago and established his travel agency, there were only seven other agencies in the city; by 1980, there were over twenty. Forced out of business after nine years by the increased competition, this return migrant used his U.S. residence visa, which he had kept renewed, to travel to Miami and buy shoes to resell in Santiago.

All of these factors helped compel most Pinero returnees to retain their visas and thus spend at least some time each year in the United States. Like the former travel agency owner, Pinero returnees in Santiago commonly traveled to the United States once or twice a year. Husbands and wives seldom traveled together. Rather, they took turns staying behind to take care of the children and manage the family business. Once in the United States, they might work for several weeks to several months in an effort to cover the costs of visa renewal and to supplement their Dominican income. Often, when the wife was in the United States, a kinswoman from Los Pinos would move to Santiago for the duration to care for the household and the children. The following example illustrates this common pattern in greater detail and suggests the degree to which returnees continued to depend on the U.S. migration system.

Alfredo Fernández migrated to New York in 1963 at the age of 24. After sampling a number of low-wage factory jobs in his early months in the country, he found a union job as a janitor in a large metropolitan hospital, where he worked for the next eight years. After two years in New York, he was joined by his wife, Olga, who worked in a series of factories until the birth of their second child in 1969. The expenses of a growing family in New York and the remittances he sent to his parents in the republic prevented Alfredo from saving more than US$4,000 during his first eight years in the United States. In 1971, he used these savings as a down payment and together with his cousin purchased a bodega in Brooklyn from his cousin's brother-in-law. For the next three years, Alfredo ran the bodega with his cousin, working twelve and fourteen hours a day. When he sold his share of the business, his savings and profits totaled approximately US$35,000.

In 1974, eleven years after Alfredo had migrated, he and Olga returned to the Dominican Republic. They and their by now three U.S.-born children settled in one of the new, modern neighborhoods of return migrants in Santiago. Alfredo purchased a pickup truck and began to buy bottled gas and make deliveries in the neighborhood. Olga stayed at home and took customers' orders over the telephone. Alfredo's customers were largely members of other migrant households. Indeed, many of them were from the sección of Los Pinos and neighboring secciones of the municipio, members of his premigration network with whom he had maintained contact in New York and on his return.

Alfredo and Olga lived a solidly middle-class existence in Santiago. He was largely able to support his family with his gas delivery business. Despite the role she played in the business, Olga said she did not work. She employed a servant to do the housework. Their children, like those of many return migrants, attended English classes at the Dominican-American Cultural Institute, where the majority of the institute's teachers were young, bilingual return migrants as well. Despite the success of Alfredo's business, however, both he and Olga had kept their residence visas renewed.

Actually, it was not clear whether the family would have been able to maintain its life-style had Olga not continued to migrate to the

United States. Although Alfredo said Olga traveled to the United States "to renew her visa," unlike Alfredo she stayed two to three months during each visit. While in the United States, she lived with relatives, who had a factory job waiting for her when she arrived. Interestingly, although Olga had disliked working in a factory when she lived in New York, she said she enjoyed these brief visits for the opportunity they gave her to visit friends and relatives and to change her routine. With her earnings, she purchased the family's clothing and household needs for the year and brought back other items, such as clothing and cosmetics, on consignment to sell to neighbors, friends, and kin. Olga claimed that since their return, "Alfredo doesn't know what it is to buy a pair of shoes for the children, or a towel for the house." While their geographic mobility may appear extreme, in fact Alfredo and Olga were fairly typical of Pinero return migrants in Santiago and of return migrants generally. For example, in their sample of over 300 return migrants to Santo Domingo, Baez Evertsz and D'Oleo Ramírez (1986:41) found that 58 percent retained their U.S. legal resident status while another 19 percent were U.S. citizens. They conclude that instability and flux are fundamental features of Dominican return migration.

Migrants like Alfredo and Olga who returned to the urban areas of the republic did not play a direct or significant role in Pinero social life. Occasional visits were paid to the countryside on holidays, but in general they participated very little in Los Pinos' social activities. Ironically, although migrants still living in the United States might be dues-paying members, none of the urban return migrants belonged to a Pinero association. The migrants' charitable association described above is a case in point. This association had survived a continual turnover of personnel, as the leaders in New York returned to the Dominican Republic and the Pinero members migrated to New York. Nonetheless, when members returned to the city to live, they stopped participating in this and in other organized social activities in Los Pinos. Such behavior reinforced the widely held opinion that "New York changes people."

While in the United States, most migrants did maintain a strong allegiance to the community. As noted previously, migrants on holiday in Los Pinos took pains to avoid behavior that would cause Pineros to call them comparón, or conceited. Most returned laden with gifts for friends and kin. Once they returned to Santiago or Santo Domingo, however, this pattern generally changed. The returnees became integrated into the middle-class social life of the city, sending their children to private schools, joining clubs for businessmen, and associating with other return migrants of similar status and aspirations. The composition of their networks changed accordingly. Some had even preferred to bury their parents, who had spent all their lives in Los Pinos, in the middle-class cemetery in Santiago, a practice which was much criticized in the community.

The returned entrepreneurs just described stood in stark contrast to the second current of the Pinero return stream. This current was composed of those who entered the United States as undocumented migrants and were subsequently unable to regularize their status. Most of these migrants eventually returned to Los Pinos to resume their former way of life. Surprisingly, none of these migrants returned because they were apprehended by the U.S. Immigration and Naturalization Service and deported (although many undocumented Pineros had been detained at one time or another). Rather, homesick after four or five years away from their families and frustrated by their repeated and costly failures to regularize their status, the majority simply gave up and came home. Indeed, there were very few Pineros who remained undocumented for more than five years; they either managed to regularize their status or they returned to the republic. Those undocumented Pineros who returned in the 1960s typically had been confident of being able to reenter the United States if they decided to reemigrate. But by the early 1970s, undocumented entry had become increasingly difficult and expensive, and many were unable to finance a second migration.

Nearly all of these migrants returned to Los Pinos. There they invested what savings they had brought back in houses, small shops, land, or públicos, but few managed to improve their economic or social status appreciably. After a while, some were even forced to sell these capital investments to meet household expenses and thus ended up in a social and economic position similar to the one they had occupied before migrating.

Discretionary migrants were the exception to this pattern. They were also undocumented while in the United States, but their migration had a very specific, short-term savings goal. These discretionary migrants had already possessed some wealth prior to migration and went to the United States primarily to accumulate the capital needed to expand their businesses or farms. Unlike the returnees described above, Los Pinos' discretionary return migrants were able to improve their economic and social position substantially, as the stories in chapter 3 revealed. Three of the second-ranking merchants in

Los Pinos fell into this category of return migrants. By 1980, however, the severe deterioration of the Dominican economy had led two of these returnees to emigrate once more.

The final current of return migrants was composed of those who either initially went as documented migrants or who managed to regularize their status in the United States, but who remained in the secondary sector of the economy, or perhaps in the less remunerative areas of ethnic enterprise, such as the nonmedallion or gypsy cab industry in New York. These returnees also tended to settle in Los Pinos. It must be pointed out, however, that the overwhelming majority of migrants with these characteristics were still in the United States.

These individuals conformed most closely to the image commonly held in Los Pinos of a return migrant. This sort of returnee had typically spent ten years or more working in a factory or hotel in the United States. Their documented status had enabled them to sponsor the chain migration of spouse and at least some offspring, all or most of whom worked too. After accumulating savings of between US$20,000–35,000, the migrant returned with his spouse to invest it in the community. Typically, the family became permanently split at this point, as some children remained in the United States to work.

About half of these rural return migrants were retired and received Social Security benefits. A few went to the United States at an already advanced age, sponsored by their adult children. Only one of these retirees had given up his residence card. None of the rest was a U.S. citizen, so they had to travel each year to the United States to renew their resident status. Because of their age and infirmity, some petitioned to receive extensions from the consulate which enabled them to remain in the republic for as long as two years without returning.

Pineros generally recognized and admired the economic security enjoyed by these retirees. But most of them led circumscribed lives and participated little in the affairs of the community. Although in some cases their social status had improved, none, for example, was called *Don*, a title reserved for the largest merchants and landholders of the town and for the most successful of the returnees.

Most of the younger return migrants, on the other hand, had become active and economically important members of the community. They invested their savings in the usual ways—land and cattle, lottery pools, pickup trucks, and públicos—but also in a manioc bread factory and furniture workshops. The following example, that of a returnee considered by many Pineros to be successful, illustrates the rewards of the process of return migration to Los Pinos. It also suggests that rural return migration is no less a complex phenomenon than return to the cities of the republic.

Venero Pérez was a lottery vendor and agriculturalist with about 300 tareas of land. In 1966, his stepmother's sister, Idalia, a U.S. resident, agreed to marry him "sin interés" (without charge) and bring him to the United States. Idalia did this on the condition that he immediately sponsor the migration of his father, Idalia's brother-in-law. Within two years of his arrival in New York, Venero had requested a visa for his father, divorced Idalia, and married the woman with whom he had lived in consensual union for over ten years.

As soon as Venero arrived in New York, his cousin found him a union job as a janitor in a large Manhattan hotel. He worked at this job for the next twelve years. In addition, he sold Dominican lottery numbers to his Hispanic co-workers during the week and on weekends to family and friends, some of whom earlier had been his clients in Los Pinos. After amassing some savings, he began to make high-interest loans to undocumented migrants for migration costs and for bail if they were arrested.

Within seven years of his arrival in New York, Venero had sponsored the migration of his wife, Sonia, and five of their seven children. Not able to achieve the job stability enjoyed by Venero, Sonia worked at a variety of nonunionized jobs in a succession of garment factories. Their son worked with Venero in the hotel, while their daughters worked in factories like their mother. Venero was also indirectly responsible for the migration of ten of his half-siblings. This was because Venero's father in turn sponsored the migration of his children with Idalia's sister. As these half-siblings migrated, they initially came to stay in Venero's large upper Manhattan apartment. By letting rooms to successive waves of kinsmen, he was able to cover the cost of his rent for his entire sojourn in the United States.

In 1977, with savings of approximately US$25,000, Venero returned to Los Pinos to live. Venero stressed that his combination of multiple income-generating activities in New York was crucial to his ability to save enough to return, insisting that "anyone who returns must have something beyond his 'little job' [*el trabajito*]." Back in Los Pinos, he improved his house and purchased an additional 100 tareas of land which he converted to pasture. He also bought fifty head of cattle, all of improved stock. In addition to his investments in land and cattle, while still in the United States he established four small grocery stores in the village and its outskirts, which he left in the hands of Pineros with whom he had a relationship of confianza. He now lived in Los Pinos and managed his herd full time. However, he returned to the United States each year to renew his visa. His wife still spent about half the year in the United States working in a garment factory because she and Venero wanted to be able to request residence visas for their two youngest children when they reached working age. When all their children were in New York, Sonia planed to return permanently to Los Pinos.

The story of Venero Pérez exemplifies several of the strategies used by migrants to meet their goals of saving and return, despite the limitations of low wages earned in the United States and of increasingly high rates of inflation, especially in the New York housing market. One common strategy already noted was the sponsoring of additional family members, whose employment could add to the pool of household income. Another was related to migrants' unique ability to take advantage of investment opportunities and low labor costs in the Dominican Republic even while they were still in the United States. Finally, the story illustrates how migrants had managed to replicate the cultural pattern of occupational multiplicity in the United States in order to supplement earnings from their "little jobs." New York, with its own thriving informal economy and its large concentration of compatriots, had allowed Pineros to use their reconstituted networks to create a variety of supplementary income-generating activities. Like Venero Pérez, migrants might sell lottery tickets to coworkers, let rooms to kin, drive a friend's gypsy cab in the evening, peddle cosmetics to neighbors, bake cakes for sale, care for the children of other migrants, and make loans to potential migrants in Los Pinos, among a host of other activities.

Through the migration process, Venero Pérez had become one of the wealthier cattlemen in Los Pinos, although by no means the wealthiest. There is no doubt that he had improved his economic position in the community. Nevertheless, community recognition was ambivalent. Some poorer people had begun to call him Don Venero. He continued to socialize with the same people as before migrating, his brothers, brothers-in-law, neighbors, and compadres. But his longstanding secondary union with a woman of low social status had negatively affected the way the community regarded him. Moreover, as he himself and other Pineros recognized, it was not clear even after four years whether Venero would succeed in his ventures and be able to remain permanently in Los Pinos. Venero admitted that the remittances his children sent provided a safety net for his economic activities, without which he would feel considerably less secure.

THE "MIGRANT SYNDROME" IN LOS PINOS[2]

That two-fifths of all Pinero households had at least one migrant member meant that nearly everyone in the village had a neighbor, friend, or relative residing in the United States. Through correspondence, through gossip, through the direct presence of migrants in the village during holidays, and more recently through homemade videos as well, nearly all Pineros had some exposure to conditions *allá*, literally and unambiguously, "over there," and the lore of migrants' experiences was widely distributed in the community. Pineros who had made only a few trips to the capital in their lives knew about welfare, drug dealing, and the putative work habits of other immigrant and ethnic groups in the United States. Information about wages, the price of foodstuffs, the dangers of operating a bodega, the relative merits of working in a hotel as opposed to a factory, and a variety of other aspects of working life in New York was widely circulated in the community. Pineros did have a tendency to exaggerate the amount of savings that migrants were able to accumulate in New York, however. Returnees seldom made public the amount they had managed to save, but the discrepancy between what returnees told me thay had saved (checked against the detailed work and wage histories I obtained from them) and the guesses made by villagers were often large. On the whole, however, Pineros had a remarkably realistic view of the migrant's life in New York.

That this view was a rather dark one is reflected in the following merengue about New York:

> *Aquí la vida no vale*
> *una guayaba podrida*
> *si un tigre no te mata*
> *te mata la factoría.*

> Here life is not worth
> a rotten guava.
> If a hoodlum doesn't kill you
> the factory will.

> (Sandy Reyes, Karen Records)

In this merengue, the singer, like many of the migrants I spoke with, acknowledges of New York that "here I was given an opportunity"

2. The term "migrant syndrome" is taken from the title of Joshua Reichert's (1979, 1981) studies of the impact of U.S.-bound labor migration on a rural Mexican community.

("aquí me dieron la oportunidad"). Yet this opportunity was to work very hard at, as one returnee put it, "all the dirty jobs" ("todo lo sucio"). Thus, Pineros had few illusions about what conditions they would find once they migrated. This is further illustrated by the example of one young and robust Pinero who was about to acquire his residence visa. Because he had heard from his brothers how hard life was in New York, he quit his job in a Santiago factory several months before migrating to return to Los Pinos to rest and gather his strength. This lack of illusions is also seen in the comment a Pinera made to me on her first visit back to Los Pinos after migrating: "New York isn't the hell I expected it to be."

Obviously, Pineros had absorbed an array of factual information—and occasional misinformation—about life in the United States. But the migration experience had also permeated their lives and their perceptions in other, often subtle, ways. The local lexicon was one example. It had expanded to include a variety of new words as well as new meanings for old words. The use of the word *viaje* or "trip" is a case in point. When unmarked by destination, *viaje* unambiguously referred to U.S. migration: "Ella está de viaje" ("she is in the United States"), "él la está haciendo viaje" ("he is sponsoring her U.S. migration"). When the marked form was used, the meaning changed quite radically: "Ella está de viaje a Santiago" ("she is visiting Santiago"). It is noteworthy that both the marked and unmarked uses of *viaje* usually connote a temporary stay. English words had also been borrowed for referents outside the normal sphere of Pinero experience, such as welfare, disability, and social security. And other words had entered the local vocabulary. I heard some nonmigrant Pineros refer to sympathetic people as "nice" (pronounced "nai," as final *s* is most often dropped in Dominican Spanish) and to formidable men as "muy heavy."

But the influence of migration extended beyond the domain of linguistic loans. Migration in fact often appeared to be the central concern of the broadest array of Pineros, the daily and endless subject of discussion on público rides to the city and in social gatherings at grocery stores and bars. There were many instances, sometimes arresting, of this overwhelming absorption with migration among all age groups in the community. When a teacher asked her first-grade class what they would do with a million dollars, for example, a seven-year-old boy answered that he would buy an airplane and go to New York. At the funeral of a very old Pinera, an old man who had never migrated gave a eulogy in which he compared God to a Great Consul who issues visas to the next life: "Nena's visa was finally issued by the Great Consul. This is one visa we will all get; one *viaje* we will all make."

Another less dramatic indicator of the pervasiveness and deep-rootedness of Pineros' concern with U.S. migration was the high percentage of household heads who indicated that they wanted to migrate to the United States. Despite the lack of illusions concerning living and working conditions in New York, most migrant and non-migrant Pineros shared a positive view of U.S. migration, especially of its economic aspects and its effects for Los Pinos. Slightly over three-fifths (62 percent) said that they wanted to migrate, and nearly all (97 percent) said that they wanted members of their family to migrate. As table 6.7 shows, the principal reasons household heads gave for not wanting to migrate themselves were old age (24 percent) and poor health (25 percent).

Many Pineros, from all but the very poorest sectors of the community, viewed migration as a possible, if not necessarily a desirable, event in their lives. As table 6.8 shows, when those Pineros who had said that they wanted to migrate to the United States were asked why, the majority of nonmigrant household heads said they desired

TABLE 6.7. Reasons Reported by Household Heads for Not Wanting to Emigrate by Migrant Status of Household

	Migrant		Nonmigrant		Total	
Reasons	*N*	*%*	*N*	*%*	*N*	*%*
Health won't permit	18	36.0	4	10.3	22	24.7
Too old to go	10	20.0	11	28.2	21	23.6
Doesn't want to leave children/mother in D.R.	12	24.0	7	18.0	19	21.4
Doesn't want to live in a foreign country/ prefers D.R.	6	12.0	7	18.0	13	14.6
Doesn't like what has heard about U.S.	2	4.0	6	15.4	8	9.0
Already went and didn't like it	2	4.0	0	0	2	2.3
Afraid of airplane	0	0	2	5.1	2	2.3
Afraid of people in U.S.	0	0	2	5.1	2	2.3
Total	50	56.2	39	43.8	89	100.2[a]

[a]Due to rounding.

TABLE 6.8. Reasons Reported by Household Heads for Desire to Emigrate, by Migrant Status of Household

	Migrant		Nonmigrant		Total	
Reasons	N	%	N	%	N	%
To improve life situation[a]	9	20.0	62	60.8	71	48.3
To be with rest of the family	19	42.2	6	5.9	25	17.0
To make more money	1	2.2	12	11.8	13	8.8
To educate children	1	2.2	4	3.9	5	3.4
To see U.S.	3	6.7	6	5.9	9	6.1
To renew visa	7	15.6	0	0	7	4.7
Life is easier in U.S.	0	0	3	2.9	3	2.0
To help out spouse in U.S.	2	4.7	0	0	2	1.4
To improve health	0	0	2	2.0	2	1.4
To build a house	0	0	2	2.0	2	1.4
To help out family in D.R.	1	2.2	2	2.0	3	2.0
Likes Americans	0	0	1	1.0	1	.7
To be independent of parents' resources	0	0	2	2.0	2	1.4
To make residence for children	2	4.4	0	0	2	1.4
Total	45	30.6	102	69.4	147	100

[a]The Pineros who gave similar responses such as "To progress," "For a better future," "To live a better life," and so on have been included here.

emigration "to improve their life situation." Heads of migrant households cited this and a desire to be with their family members most often as reasons for wanting to migrate. Although education was widely perceived as the most desirable means to a good and secure job, and hence to upward social mobility, it was also recognized that not all of those who became educated would be able to find such jobs. But everyone who migrated to the United States, in contrast, was perceived to have an equal opportunity to work, save, and return. Because the sense of insecuriy which characterized the lives of most Pineros could only persist or worsen, it is likely that most Pineros would continue to view migration as a viable option.

THE CONSEQUENCES OF INTERNATIONAL MIGRATION FOR PINERO SOCIAL STRUCTURE

Since the onset of intensive U.S. migration in 1961, Los Pinos' social structure had experienced considerable diversification. At the same time, there had been some notable continuities with the premigration period.

At the top of Pinero society in terms of wealth and prestige, the merchant elite had experienced remarkable stability over the last twenty years. In one sense, the members had profited directly from the migration system by providing low-risk, high-interest loans to potential migrants. They had also benefited indirectly from the higher levels of consumption made possible by migrants' remittances to their families. On the other hand, they had suffered increased competition from migrants' own investments in usurious loans and in commercial activities. The transportation boom promoted by migrants had altered shopping patterns, helped weaken Pinero dependency on local merchants, and undermined their former ability to fix prices at levels considerably higher than those in Santiago. The net result of these countervailing effects on the merchants' ability to extract profits was a stabilization of this group. Indeed, plot histories revealed that the great bulk of their property was amassed by the mid-1960s—that is, before the migration process gained momentum. Since then, the merchants' aggressive expansion had been checked, and they had neither bought nor sold an appreciable amount of land.

Although demonstrating longevity and stability in Los Pinos, the merchant elite was a group whose social orientation ultimately lay outside the community. The richest merchant family, for example, had never joined the Pinero social club. Instead, this family continued to belong to the club of its natal town, some thirty kilometers from Los Pinos, a town they left over forty years ago. The children, of course, left Los Pinos years ago to establish themselves as professionals and entrepreneurs in the city. The parents, too, planned to retire to Santiago, where they were building a house in a prestigious neighborhood.

This elite was an aging group. Their children, who had found middle-class niches in the republic's largest cities, would not return to Los Pinos to assume their families' businesses. Therefore, it is possible that in the future the merchant elite might be replaced by some of the return migrants who had been successful in their pursuit of commercial activities in Los Pinos. At the time of fieldwork, however, no migrant or return migrant household had been able to approach the wealth and status of the merchant elite. None had educated as many of their children as highly or placed them so well. None was called *Don* by nearly everyone in the community. And none had managed to create networks with links to as many prominent and wealthy individuals in the urban centers of the republic.

Another significant feature of Pinero social structure was the already noted expansion of the number of households that fell within the middle sectors of the community. Many Pineros lived in what, in the rural Dominican context, might be called middle-income households. This middle-income sector had expanded in large part as a result of the remittances of money and consumer durables to migrant households. It had also grown as the number of relatively well-remunerated (by local standards) state employees increased as a consequence of national policies. As we have seen, the most important members of this category in Los Pinos were the schoolteachers, who, along with the members of many migrant households, had become the local vanguard of consumption. With their up-to-date housing and household amenities, fashionable style of dress, urbane recreational preferences, and superior access to education for themselves or for their children, these two groups were the driving force behind modernization in Los Pinos. It was the teachers, however, who had taken the lead in the attempt to bring Los Pinos more in line with urban and modern directions in community organization.

While the teachers already enjoyed considerable prestige, many of the migrants and their families were engaged in attempts to jockey with one another for status within Los Pinos' social order. Conspicuous consumption, especially of housing—which was continuously achieving new heights of sophistication—was one tactic.

Another was found in the annual fiesta of Los Pinos' patron saint, San Gerónimo. It was among migrants and their kindreds that the most intense competition occurred to have a young kinswoman occupy the position of queen of the fiesta, or, to a lesser extent, of princess in her court. In the past, the patron saint's fiesta was primarily a religious celebration, often used as the occasion for pilgrimages in which supplicants requested special favors of San Gerónimo. In more recent years, in contrast, the fiesta had become almost totally secularized. Increasingly, it was becoming a migrant holiday. The priest still visited Los Pinos to celebrate a special mass. But it was the secular festivities that attracted the migrants from New York and people from the surrounding countryside to the community. A series of competitive games, such as scaling greased logs and racing mules, engaged young men from poor households in competition for the bags of groceries awarded as prizes.

But it was the election of the queen and her court and her coronation at a gala dance at which a band from Santiago played merengues until very late at night that capped the fiesta and attracted the most attendance and attention. Election conferred recognition and status on the young women as well as on their entire families. These young women were not elected on the basis of personal or aesthetic attributes alone, however. Rather, candidates competed by selling votes, and individuals might buy as many votes as they wished. The money raised in this fashion was used for a specific community project; in 1980, this was the completion of the social club. Four of the five candidates in that year came from migrant households and nearly all of the siblings of both parents of the fifth were in the United States. Some migrants spent hundreds of dollars buying votes in the hope of electing their daughter, granddaughter, or niece as queen.

Despite attempts such as these to augment the prestige of migrants and their families, the ambivalent status of many migrant and return migrant households continued. Their superior standard of living, improved housing, and greater access to household amenities and luxuries were admired, to be sure. Yet, as noted earlier, many did not enjoy the prestige of the teachers, and none that of the merchant elite. It may be that significant improvement would have to await the next generation, as migrants' children graduated from the universities and found their solidly middle-class niches in the urban centers of the republic—that is, unless they, too, migrated as opportunities contracted in the years to come. Six years after their election to the court of San Gerónimo, for instance, the queen and three of her five princesses had migrated to New York, where some were working in factories. In any event, if migrants' offspring did manage to achieve social mobility, the arena would not be Los Pinos. Most likely, such improvement would confer only a reflected prestige on their families in the village.

Since intensive migration began, the number of landless and near-landless Pineros had also grown. But at the same time that access to land for subsistence and commercial purposes became increasingly restricted, new opportunities in the service, commercial, and artisanal sectors appeared. Poorly remunerated for the most part, the majority of these occupations were not full time. Nonetheless, their appearance had permitted poorer households to survive and reproduce themselves, if only barely in some cases. The sons of landless and near-landless households had become part-time carpenters and masons, chair craftsmen, illegal lottery vendors, contraband loggers, público drivers, and shop clerks. The daughters had become domestics and providers of child care to better-off households. Some had migrated to urban areas of the republic where they engaged in similar activities. Thus, while the shift to cattle raising and the resulting inflation of land values redistributed land away from poorer households and drastically decreased the demand for agricultural laborers, Pinero society simultaneously experienced the growth of nonagricultural employment opportunities, principally in service and commercial aspects of the informal sector. Migrants' investment patterns helped promote both of these trends in Pinero society. However, their fundamental determinants, as we have seen, lay outside the community.

It is difficult to imagine in retrospect what Pinero society would have looked like had there been no period of U.S.-bound migration. But as the example of El Guano suggests, Los Pinos would probably not have been an agriculturally self-sufficient community. Most of the households with middle-sized and large landholdings that joined the international migrant stream undoubtedly would have experienced economic decline as family land became divided and state and market incentives to agriculture diminished. Their offspring would have become either small farmers necessarily enmeshed in a variety of other occupational strategies or full-time members of the community's (or Santiago's or Santo Domingo's) informal sector. In short, U.S. migration had enabled many initially better-off households to maintain their social standing in the community while improving their standard of living. Moreover, as the case of El Guano also suggests, communities not caught up in the international migrant stream also experienced intensive population loss, directed internally to the urban and rural áreas of the republic. It is likely that in the absence of U.S. migration, Los Pinos would have experienced much higher rates of internal migration. The example of El Guano showed that internal migration, like the international form, drew from the most productive age cohorts in rural society. Unlike the latter, however, it did not generate an appreciable couterflow of remittances.

In an important sense, then, U.S. migration had enabled a portion of Pinero households to maintain a kind of dynamic stability. Migrants and their families had not displaced local elites, nor had they slipped into the pauperized sectors of Pinero society. This apparent lack of mobility obscures an important point which must be made explicit: without migration, many no doubt would have fallen into poverty and lost their standing in Pinero society. Migration thus enabled many households to hold on to their middle-level status in a context of a drastically deteriorating national economy which had resonated with special force in the countryside.

It also must be emphasized that if most migrant households continued to occupy the same relative social positions in the community, this was a similarity with a difference. Migrants and many of their family members lived, as Dominicans put it, with "one foot here and the other there" ("un pie aquí y el otro allá"). Both through their social networks and their economic strategies, many walked on two legs—a posture that straddled international boundaries and in the process articulated both the migrants and Los Pinos with the ideologies and life-styles of the North American metropolis. Yet despite the fact that U.S. migration had thoroughly penetrated Dominican popular and national culture, this migrant posture created anomalies. Contrary to ideals of proper union, migrants' households were divided; the migrants were only intermittently present in their communities; and their return, even after a decade or two abroad, was uncertain. Returnees were often no less anomalous: few gave up their residence visas, and most still spent part of each year working in the United States. It is no wonder, then, that the Pinera return migrant quoted at the beginning of this chapter placed migrants in a category by themselves. The rich and the poor in the Dominican Republic had their distinctive features which set them apart. But even after two decades, migrants were a group in flux; they negotiated a transnational way of life partly of their own making, and their future remained unclear.

CHAPTER 7
Los Pinos in Cross-Cultural Context

At the same time that external forces impinged on and transformed the Dominican countryside, inhabitants of Los Pinos used their cultural resources to mount a response to these processes. Once state restrictions on international movement were removed, a self-recruiting and self-financing migration system, complete with its own institutions and roles, evolved to help shuttle large numbers of women and men out of the declining rural sector to the comparatively higher wage areas of the world economy, overwhelmingly to New York. Constraints imposed by geography and U.S. immigration law conditioned the general contours of the Pinero migrant stream. Where the provisions of the latter failed to coincide with Pineros' cultural expectations, however, they were challenged and partially offset by relations of kinship, friendship, patronage, and community. These relations came to span international boundaries, articulating Los Pinos and New York into a single transnational social field. With time, the migration system that Pineros devised also turned back on the community to exert a strong reciprocal effect on its social and economic life. In this final chapter, I review and summarize several of the most significant migration-related changes that have taken place in Los Pinos and examine these in the context of what is presently known of other Dominican sending communities, the nation as a whole, and prevailing patterns in other such societies elsewhere.

REMITTANCES

In the literature on international migration, perhaps the greatest degree of agreement exists regarding the contribution of migrants' repatriated earnings to improving the standard of living of their family members in the sending society. In Los Pinos, remittances annually provided roughly one-third of the estimated income of the community. Remittances were directed primarily to members of migrant households. In some three-quarters of those, the amounts received pushed household income to levels at or above the national minimum wage in 1981. Given the progressive stagnation of the rural economy, it is highly unlikely that the majority of these households would have been able otherwise to generate incomes even approaching the minimum levels.

The large amount of remittances flowing to selected Pineros was not unusual for migrant households generally in the Dominican Republic. In a sample of 129 households receiving remittances, 60 percent received an average of US$115 per month in 1985, and another 33 percent received an average of $350 (Baez Evertsz and D'Oleo Ramírez 1986:445). Eighteen percent of a sample of Santiago families received regular remittances averaging DR$150 in 1980 (Grasmuck 1985:155). In Los Pinos, some nonmigrants also received remittances, although on a much smaller scale than members of migrants' households. Kin who took care of migrants' children, women who were involved with married migrants, and women separated from migrants with children to support received modest sums on a more or less regular basis.

At the community level, the relatively large concentration of households receiving regular remittances, together with the income-generating opportunities created by migrants, had given Los Pinos a somewhat more equitable distribution of income than that of a nearby community with a low level of U.S. migration or that of the republic as a whole. In the Cibao migrant town of Licey, a modest increase in equity as a result of remittances has also been suggested, although the sizable return flow of entrepreneurial migrants to that town may have had the opposite effect (Castro 1985:448). An egalitarian impact has been noted for India (Oberai and Singh 1980), Pakistan (Burki 1984; Gilani et al. 1981, cited in Russell 1986:688) and for some areas of Mexico (Cornelius 1980:79). But other studies of Mexican sending communities have reported exacerbated inequality as a result of migration (Reichert 1979). Differences in the preexisting socioeconomic characteristics of migrants, the nature of their communities, and the intensity of migration and return migration, among other factors, complicate comparison and may lead to variable effects on equity among distinct sending areas. Such variability negates attempts to decide the effects of international migration on an a priori basis and argues for a holistic analysis of particular cases.

At the national level, there is widespread agreement as to the importance of remittances as a source of foreign exchange and a means to improve the balance of payments. A lack of official statistics prevents precise calculation of the total inflow of remittances to the republic as a whole. But careful estimates placed the amount between US$230,000,000 and $280,000,000 in the mid-1980s (Baez Evertsz and D'Oleo Ramírez 1986; Vega 1987). This sum is equivalent to 10 percent of GDP in 1984 and close to the $288,000,000 earned from the republic's principal export, sugar. Remittances represented 33 percent of the value of all exports and 23 percent of the value of all imports in 1984 (Values of imports and exports are from World Bank 1986). At such high levels, the contribution of remittances to the Dominican balance of payments was considerably greater than in some other major Caribbean sending nations, such as Jamaica and Barbados (Hakim and Weintraub 1985; Marshall 1985b).

That remittances are one of the principal benefits derived from migration is a belief that is widely held not only popularly, but by many government officials as well. However, because remittances have been converted largely on the "parallel market," fiscal and monetary authorities lose control over the division of this source of foreign exchange between consumer and investment goods imports (see Stahl 1982:875). Ultimately, private interests decide how remittances will be used. In the Dominican Republic, there were no explicit state policies to direct the patterns of remittance allocation to specific development goals (Morrison and Sinkin 1982).

Studies of remittance use in the Dominican Republic confirm the pattern found in Los Pinos and hint that migrants in general tend to be guided by a "subsistence ethic" when determining how much to send. In Los Pinos, less than one-third of migrant households reported regularly having some money left over after covering basic household expenses. Among migrant households surveyed by Baez Evertsz and D'Oleo Ramírez (1986:45), food accounted for 63 percent of remittance expenditures and education for some 20 percent. Relatively large sums of U.S. earnings also are repatriated from time to time. Most often, these are spent on housing.

Housing is the most visible manifestation of the migrant project:

even while the migrant is physically absent for long periods, the house serves as a kind of place marker in the community's social and economic hierarchy. For migrants who buy in urban areas, houses are also a secure and profitable way to invest savings in an inflationary environment. In fact, worldwide, housing is the migrant investment par excellence (Gmelch 1980). In a survey of Turkish returned migrants, for example, the purchase of a house or house plot was the most popular large expenditure of savings (Paine 1974:118). In Port-au-Prince, Haiti, migrants' investments have contributed to the housing boom in that city (Fass 1978). Similar observations have been made in areas as diverse as rural Mexico (e.g., Massey et al. 1987), rural Hong Kong (Watson 1975), and Pakistan (Burki 1984).

Migrants' investments have helped ameliorate to some extent the severe housing bottleneck in the Dominican Republic. The bulk of the huge housing shortfall has been filled by the informal sector, which provided some 85 percent of all new housing between 1970 and 1980. Much of this housing, however, was of very low quality (Tatis 1985:26). Because of the skewed distribution of income in the Dominican Republic, only a small fraction (about 15 percent) of the population qualifies for housing loans from financial institutions (p. 28). The crunch in middle-income housing has been partially alleviated by the availability of migrants' dwellings which would otherwise lie vacant for years. The fact that the rent received is generally sufficient to meet monthly note payments helps make this an attractive form of investment, especially in a context of scarce alternatives. Inflation also increases the appeal of purchasing a house. In a circular and self-reinforcing fashion, strong migrant demand undoubtedly has made an important contribution to the inflationary pressure on housing.

EMPLOYMENT

A second significant and much debated question is the impact of international migration on employment in the sending society. In Los Pinos, it was seen that migrants' investments created a few opportunities for full-time employment as público drivers, store managers, and lottery vendors and that most of these jobs were filled by poorer Pineros. Migrants also generated a variety of part-time opportunities that permitted nonmigrants to supplement household income from other sources. The vacancies created by the exodus of employed migrants also opened some employment possibilities. High effective demand by migrants for goods and services injected a degree of liveliness into the Pinero economy that it would otherwise have lacked. On the other hand, migrants' disinterest in agriculture contributed to the decreased demand for agricultural workers. Overall, there had been a shift from productive activity to employment in the expanding informal sector, a trend with national parallels.

Information from other sending communities in the Dominican Republic provides somewhat contrasting pictures. In the Sierran village of Juan Pablo studied by Pessar (1982a), migrants had not created new income-generating opportunities. At the same time, opportunities for wage labor in agriculture had decreased drastically, in large part as a result of migrants' purchase of cattle and abandonment of agriculture. In contrast, the agrotown of Licey studied by Castro (1985) experienced a modest increase in the number of people employed in the businesses established by migrants, although, as in Los Pinos, the wages they received were low. Because migrants from Licey were notably more likely to cultivate crops and to cultivate more of their land than nonmigrants, they also were more likely to hire agricultural wage laborers (Grasmuck 1984b:392). Los Pinos displayed some features found in each of these communities. Variation among the communities is best explained by their different ecology, infrastructural characteristics, and the regional roles they play. Licey enjoyed fertile valley soils, easy access to the nearby Santiago labor and commodities market, and many infrastructural advantages lacking in Juan Pablo and Los Pinos (see Castro 1985). The latter two shared a precarious and deteriorating ecology. Unlike Juan Pablo, however, Los Pinos had electricity and, with its easier access to Santiago, was less isolated. Additionally, Los Pinos' position as the commercial entrepôt and political and administrative center for its hinterlands and, perhaps even more importantly, its historical role as a central node in the local network of exploitation had made possible investment opportunities in commerce, transportation, and service.

What can be said of migrants' impact on employment at the national level? Employment is one of the most serious problems facing the Dominican Republic. Half of the population is unemployed or underemployed, and in the present economic climate chances for improvement appear remote. In 1980, the difference between the economically active population and the number of jobs was 522,000. By 1990, it is projected that the difference will have nearly doubled to 916,000 (Ramírez, Tatis and Germán 1983, cited in Larson 1987b:84).

In the long run, international migration may play an indirect role in reducing unemployment through its effect on the rate of population growth. In 1965, the Dominican Republic had one of the highest annual growth rates in the world—some 3.5 percent. The intensity of the drop, to 2.6 percent in 1980, surprised even demographers (Ramírez 1984:178). While increased rates of urbanization, higher levels of education, and family planning programs were also responsible, the strong participation of women in the United States migration stream was an important contributor to declining birth rates on the national level (de los Santos et al. 1981), as it was in Los Pinos. However, the decline has not been as sharp as in the smaller Caribbean nations with high levels of migration (e.g., Jamaica, Barbados), and the Dominican Republic still maintains a high rate of population increase.

Dominant sectors of Dominican society today generally regard migration as the principal solution to the unemployment problem (Cassá et al. 1986:79; Morrison and Sinkin 1982:824). Unfortunately, to date there have been no studies of the effects of international migration on the labor force. Nevertheless, it seems likely that several considerations might qualify this sanguine perception, so widely held. First, there is the sheer magnitude of the problem. At best, international migration can provide only a modest degree of relief for the close to 60 percent of the economically active population expected to be unemployed or underemployed by 1990.

Second, it is possible that the migration of highly skilled and professional workers has a number of consequences which may adversely affect employment nationally. Although the Dominican exodus to the United States cannot be classified as a brain-drain migration, there does exist an important current of highly educated workers. For instance, Castro (1985:139) has calculated that from 1969 to 1974, 5,125 Dominicans were admitted to the United States with the intention of working in professional, managerial, administrative, or related jobs. This number was the equivalent of some 45 percent of the output of Dominican higher institutions of learning during that period. In Latin America, on a per capita basis, only Cuba sent more professionals and managers to the United States. Clearly, U.S. migration has skimmed a substantial proportion of the republic's educated cream.

A portion of those employed in skilled occupations prior to migration would be replaced by the ample annual output of the expanded Dominican educational system. This was the case in Los Pinos where, despite a considerable rural brain drain, replacements for relatively well-educated migrants such as schoolteachers were abundant and easy to find. But in urban centers of investment and accumulation, the untrammeled migration of skilled and experienced workers in their prime might create a bottleneck that would act as a brake on investments that, in turn, would open up new positions for unskilled workers. (See Stahl 1982 for a general statement and Ebiri 1985 for the case of Turkey.) For example, such has been the experience of other Caribbean sending nations such as Haiti and Dominica (Pastor and Rogers 1985:323). Furthermore, although workers with formal credentials similar to those of the migrants might be available, their lack of experience might critically hinder such investment. In some jobs, migration can create a revolving door as those with experience continuously leave for the United States and are replaced by inexperienced and less efficient newcomers.

On the whole, migrants' investments probably have created few employment opportunities nationally. The most important exception is housing. Migrants' investments have helped create new opportunities for unskilled and semiskilled employment in the labor-intensive construction industry and its allied crafts. Largely because of such investments, the construction industry, which boomed under Balaguer and flagged with the economic downturn, has been able to regain some of its momentum (Baez Evertsz and D'Oleo Ramírez 1986:45; cf. Grasmuck 1985:167). After the Dominican government prohibited the importing of bricks and cement in the latter part of the 1970s, national production of these construction materials increased over fourfold (Tatis 1985:24). The increased demand for these national products also undoubtedly created jobs for those with few formal skills.

Other than in housing, however, migrants' investments probably have created few jobs. Because the majority of migrants' investments in business tend to be on a small scale, as was the case in Los Pinos, they can do little more than provide a living for the return migrant and an occasional employee or two. In a small community like Los Pinos, migrants' investments could exert a more intense influence. Furthermore, at both the local and national levels, such opportunities as are created are overwhelmingly situated in the informal sector. Very few are of a productive nature.

The migrant custom of bringing suitcases full of consumer goods when visiting the republic may have adversely affected national employment. This vigorous informal import trade has flooded the country with high-status "American" clothing, among other items. Quite often, this traffic manages to circumvent official channels and thus avoid the burden of import taxes. The vulnerability of national industries is no doubt increased by the competition, and employment may be affected adversely as well.

Perhaps the most important adverse effect on employment is the widespread perception among the dominant sectors of Dominican society that U.S. migration is the major solution to massive unemployment. In fact, a concern has been how to increase the rate of migration (Cassá et al. 1986). As Morrison and Sinkin (1982:824) have observed, it is possible that this attitude "has enabled the government and influential private interests to avoid undertaking serious economic policy reforms to encourage greater employment generation in the Dominican Republic."

AGRICULTURE

Agriculture in Los Pinos had experienced a serious decline that coincided with the accelerated pace of U.S. migration from the community. Beginning in the early 1970s, the departure of large numbers of men was responsible for the rapid unraveling of the system of reciprocal labor exchange that had undergirded the commercial cultivation of the labor-intensive crop, peanuts. Although the demise of the junta was a blow, the reasons for agricultural decline must be situated more generally in the operation of markets, state policies, and a drastically deteriorating local ecology. In the face of a battery of disincentives to agriculture on the one hand and state and market incentives to cattle raising on the other, those Pineros with access to sufficient land responded by changing their patterns of land use from short-cycle food crops to permanent pasture for cattle raising. Migrant households were able to join large landholding nonmigrants in effecting this shift as a result of their originally greater access to land and because of the capital from the repatriated earnings of their members in the United States. By largely abandoning the pattern of cultivation that produced twenty-five times as much soil loss as pasture (Rocheleau 1984:273), migrants and other Pineros ensured their continued ability to use the land, at least into the near future. Smallholders, who did not have this option, practiced an extractive form of cultivation that eventually might permanently destroy their land.

However, the overall productivity of cattle raising was low. Nor had this form of land use been able to create more than a few part-time jobs. Its extensive nature, together with strong migrant demand for land, also contributed to the inflation in land values in Los Pinos.

The net impact was increased inequality in the distribution of landholdings.

A similar pattern of agricultural decline was found in the Sierran migrant community of Juan Pablo (Pessar 1982a), as noted earlier. But studies of other Dominican sending communities suggest that such decline is not always an inevitable result of migration. In Licey, migrants were more likely to have the resources to take advantage of new technologies to increase production relative to nonmigrants (Castro 1985:429). In another Cibao migrant community studied by Bray (personal communication), production of cacao, the principal cash crop, appeared to have remained stable and even to have increased. That cacao was an implanted tree crop whose relatively low labor demands could be met by the local supply was in part responsible for maintaining production levels. Also important was the crop's export context. These examples notwithstanding, the case of Los Pinos and comparative information from other sending regions suggest that the most likely consequence of migration for agricultural production is the exacerbation of decline.

Given that migration from rural areas is most often a response to deteriorating agrarian conditions, it is not surprising that decline is subsequently exacerbated by migration. This has occurred especially in those sending areas dependent on the cultivation of ecologically marginal or depleted lands. Perhaps the most extreme case is the village of San Tin, in rural Hong Kong. The collapse of prices for the low-grade rice that was that village's specialty was one of the main factors that prompted large-scale migration to England in the 1960s. Once migration got under way, agriculture in the brackish-water fields surrounding the village was abandoned entirely. Ultimately, this resulted in deflation of the value of the community's agricultural land, a situation highly unusual in an international sending community (Watson 1975).

Another factor exacerbating decline is an absolute loss of labor in areas where migration is massive. When migration levels reach a critical threshold, agricultural production sometimes may be drastically reduced or simply abandoned. This occurs perhaps most frequently in small sending societies, such as Nevis (Frucht 1968) and Oman and Yemen, where intensive labor migration has led to the dilapidation of terrace and irrigation systems, which in turn further intensified agricultural decline (Birks and Sinclair 1980:89–90; Richards and Martin 1983). In other cases, labor-intensive crops may be replaced with others that require little attention. In Sicily, for example, loss of population has led some migrant households to replace labor-intensive viticulture with the casual cultivation of wheat (Vivolo 1984). In parts of Yemen, coffee has been replaced by the less-demanding qat tree (Birks and Sinclair 1980:91).

In other sending regions, particularly those in which women are responsible for all or some of the agricultural tasks and migration opportunities are open primarily to men, the remitted wage earnings of migrant sons and husbands are one of the most important sources of agricultural capital. Such is the situation in many parts of Africa (Meillassoux 1981). In Lesotho, which has experienced intensive male emigration to South Africa beginning in the early decades of this century, successful farming depends on access to cash income, the primary source of which is migrants' remittances (Murray 1981; Spiegel 1980). Similarly, rural Jamaican women oversee farming operations financed by remittances sent by the migrants who seasonally travel to Florida to cut sugar cane (Griffith 1985). However, in neither case has this type of investment led to innovation, increased productivity, or meaningful agrarian development. Indeed, as a consequence of its historic incorporation into the South African economic system, Lesotho has gone "from granary to labor reserve," from a net exporter to a net importer of food (Murray 1981). Jamaican cane cutters' remittances essentially permit the reproduction of their households and to a lesser extent those around them, as the increased demand for hired labor creates some employment opportunities for nonmigrant men. But on the whole, remittances have served to maintain production levels, not to expand them.

Although, in the majority of cases, international migration is associated with declining agricultural production and in some areas with approximate stabilization, there are a few instances in which migrants have acted as innovators and contributed to expansion. Portugal offers one instance. In the coastal towns of its Algarve region, a tourist boom in the 1970s created new demand for fruits and vegetables. Migrants responded by purchasing land from local elites who were looking for capital to invest in tourism. They dug wells for irrigation and sponsored the migration of their sons to Germany in order to acquire more capital to purchase fruit trees. In response to the new markets created by tourists, the production of fruits and vegetables expanded on a large scale (Gregory and Pérez 1985:253). A similar situation is reported by Baucic (1972:17) for Yugoslavia. There, too, demand from coastal tourist resorts prompted rural Dalmation return migrants to invest their savings in new techniques for growing fruits and vegetables. In the rural Mexican communities studied by Massey et al. (1987), migrant households were less likely to cultivate their land than other community members. But those migrant households that did farm were in a better position to take advantage of state-subsidized green revolution techniques to produce new cash crops, such as sorghum. Migrant households that farmed were characterized by greater productivity than nonmigrant households and a greater tendency to sell larger portions of their product on the market (pp. 247–249). Interestingly, the more years of experience a person had as a migrant, the more likely he was to use modernized techniques of production. A similar finding is reported for migrant communities in Illocos, the Philippines, where once again it was the long-term migrants who were most likely to adopt green revolution techniques for growing rice (McArthur 1979).

The case of Los Pinos and this review of recent research suggest the need to elucidate clearly the multiple relationships that mediate between migration and agricultural production. Where new techniques of production, new markets, and/or state policies amend to some extent unfavorable terms of exchange for the rural sector, migrants may participate in expansion, or even promote innovation. Where such conditions are lacking and the deterioration of natural resources continues unabated, agriculture most likely will decline, as it has in Los Pinos. This kind of comparative analysis is essential to break out of the tautology characterizing many evaluations of the putative impact of migration on rural sending communities: most are areas of institutionalized agrarian stagnation which migrants leave largely because of structural barriers to meaningful development. These same structural barriers present formidable obstacles to productive investment of migrants' remittances and savings.

WOMEN'S ROLES AND GENDER RELATIONS

In Los Pinos, U.S. migration had done very little to challenge traditional gender roles. Rather, it strengthened them in two related ways. First, when a woman's husband "behaved well"—that is, remitted regularly—the higher standard of living her household enjoyed removed the economic necessity for her to work. Indeed, women who headed migrant households in Los Pinos were less likely to work for pay than nonmigrant women. The fact that they did not need to perform remunerated work was a sign of status. At the same time, a secure income from remittances served to bind these women more tightly to the domestic circle in conformance with the norms of proper feminine conduct. For the older Pinera, there was the satisfaction that her reputation for propriety was enhanced by such behavior. But for some younger women, such confinement was often a chafing obligation observed at least in part out of fear of gossip. Second, regular remittances perpetuated the dominance of husbands in household decision making. Despite their absence, by remitting regularly men retained and reinforced their position as principal decision makers within the household. Thus, U.S.-bound migration was not a source of change in the structure of gender roles in Los Pinos. Rather, it reinforced existing norms of conduct which perpetuated the subordination of women left behind in the community.

Similar findings have been reported for a number of other sending regions. In rural Lesotho, women's experiences ranged broadly from security to extreme vulnerability, depending on the regularity of remittances. When these were regular, the balance of authority was maintained "firmly in favor of the husband" (Murray 1981:159). The lives of the Chinese women left behind in San Tin became more sheltered than those of women in nonmigrant communities. When their husbands migrated to establish restaurants or work in the restaurants of other immigrants in London, these rural Hong Kong women were often left behind with their in-laws, whose vigilance ensured that they behaved according to rules designed to restrict severely their contacts with men outside the household (Watson 1975:181). Similarly, in rural Michoacan, Mexico, young wives of migrants lived in the houses of their mothers-in-law, who directly received the remittances of their sons (M. de Alarcón 1983, cited in Wilson 1985:1023). In Portugal, migrants' wives were an important vehicle for displaying success and social mobility. Wives "dress traditionally [in black], stay in the house, do not work the land, they crochet and embroider, following traditional conceptions of what seems proper" (Serra-Santana 1984:56).

At the level of the community, Pinera women had benefited less than men from the economic consequences of migration. The better-paying work opportunities created by migrant investments in Los Pinos had gone disproportionately to men. Those work opportunities created for women were in the main simply low-paying extensions of their domestic roles as housekeepers and child care providers. There is unfortunately little comparative information regarding the gender distribution of migrant-created work opportunities in other sending communities. The little information available suggests that other patterns might be found elsewhere. In rural northwest Pakistan, for example, women entrepreneurs have become the drivers of migrant-owned vans which they use to market produce in urban areas. Burki

(1984) reports that the "Suzuki revolution" of recent years has resulted largely from government policies that have allowed migrants to send vehicles back to their families as gifts. The highly mobile vans have helped clear the rural economy of serious marketing bottlenecks and have boosted the income and status of some rural women.

It must be emphasized that the discussion in this section has focused on rural women. It is possible that the effects of migration on women's role and status may vary from rural to urban contexts, where expanded opportunities for women may exist. For instance, the largest Pinero return migrant business, a garment factory that employed fifteen workers, was established and operated by a woman who settled in Santiago. It is also important to note that patterns described for Pinera women may begin to change when they migrate to the United States. Pessar's studies of Dominican women in New York (1984) indicate that wage work outside the home could result in a more egalitarian division of labor within the household and more equitable control over domestic resources, although it did not alter fundamentally women's primary identities as mothers and wives.

THE SOCIAL CONSEQUENCES OF INTERNATIONAL MIGRATION

In over two decades, mounting U.S.-bound migration from Los Pinos had not fundamentally altered the community's social structure. Beginning in the 1940s and 1950s, the increased commercialization of local society propelled a handful of merchant-usurers into economic prosperity and enhanced their social standing in the community. Several decades later, although approaching retirement, these same merchants remained the elite of Los Pinos. Migrants' remittances were largely responsible for maintaining a large number of households in the middle-income sector of Los Pinos society. The subsidized lifestyle of most migrant households placed them squarely within the community's middle class, otherwise composed of state employees and a few middle-tier merchants.

But although migration had indisputably permitted higher levels of consumption, it had changed the relative social standing of only a few local households. To be sure, over time the criteria for placement in the local social hierarchy had changed from size of landholding to access to cash income from wages and profits. But migrants originated largely in households that were privileged with regard to the former criterion and subsequently to the latter as well as a consequence of migration. U.S. migration had thus helped stabilize the social standing of migrant households. Perhaps most importantly, it had prevented the downward economic and social slide that would have been inevitable for most. This is not to say that real social mobility had not occurred for some migrants and their families; it had, particularly for those ethnic entrepreneurs who returned to urban areas of the republic. For others, the credential of a university education for a child purchased with U.S. earnings held the promise of substantial intergenerational mobility. For most, however, migration represented a holding strategy in a rapidly deteriorating economic environment, a means of skirting the impoverishment that afflicted the bulk of nonmigrants.

The large exodus of Pineros to the United States had not led to the disorganization of community life. In fact, over the last decade, local organizations of many kinds had proliferated and flourished. Migrants had organized a charitable association and periodic collection drives for specific community projects. However, it was the growing number of better-educated members of Los Pinos' middle class (particularly its teachers), not the migrants and their families, who had taken the organizational lead in Los Pinos.

It is a widely held perception in the Dominican Republic that migrants have been responsible for the introduction of socially undesirable practices. Drug use and crime are often cited. These were not apparent in Los Pinos and may be more evident in urban areas of the republic. A more insidious social effect of migration was the increased competitiveness among Pineros in terms of material display, the "keeping up with the Pérez" syndrome. In Pineros' eyes, the display of improved housing and stylish clothing was regarded as an indication that a family was improving itself and progressing. Such so-called progressive consumption affirmed the membership of many migrant households in the local middle class. But because the social progress achieved by migration is by nature an individual, not a collective phenomenon, it is perhaps more aptly characterized as conservative.

Other Dominican sending communities for which there is information differ from Los Pinos in some ways. Hendricks' early (1974) study of a village near Santiago suggested a socially disruptive effect as local leadership was drained by the especially massive migration that characterized that community. In Licey, a town considerably larger and more urbanized than Los Pinos, migration appeared to

have eroded local cooperative efforts. In addition, migrants' introduction of evangelical Christianity had injected a politically conservative ideology into the local society (Castro 1985:449–450).

That migration, despite its reinforcement of modernizing trends,
promotes the continuity of traditional structures of rural life has often
been reported for other sending regions. For many migrants, the home
community represents the "cultural hearth" (Rhoades 1978:143) and
remains the social frame of reference in which improved status and
mobility are affirmed. The community is also a locus of economic
investment and security, a fact that additionally reinforces the migrants' stake in its values and institutions. In some cases, migrants
may even attempt to recreate the idealized village of their youth by
supporting expensive traditional celebrations of increasing elabo-
rateness, as had occurred in rural Hong Kong (Watson 1975:215). In
other communities, migrants try to ensure future security by participating in cultural institutions that verify their membership and stake
in local society. Mixtec migrants from Mexico to the United States,
for instance, continue to serve in the civil religious complex of their
village and may return specifically to make appearances at fiestas.
Indeed, in an apparent paradox, massive migration has been responsible for the village's ability to retain its "closed, corporate" nature
(Stuart and Kearney 1981:27). Similarly, in the context of labor migration in southern Africa in the 1950s, participation in traditional
society and preservation of its values were important aspects of migrants' strategy for long-term social security, a situation reinforced
and promoted by the policies of colonial administrations (Van Velsen
1961). In the face of palpable change, even if only "modernization
without development" (Schneider and Schneider 1974), the social effect of international migration is often conservative or, perhaps more
accurately, preservative.

An intriguing counterexample to this generalization is found among
Andalusian migrants, the majority of whom were rural proletarians
and casual laborers before leaving Spain. Experience abroad generated among migrants a new social and political awareness of the value
of their time and labor. On return, this enhanced consciousness was
translated into electoral opposition to the centralist party and greater
support for leftist parties than shown by other regions of Spain. Return migrants also played a prominent role as leaders of many of the
new "free syndicates" in rural areas. This enhanced activism is in
sharp contrast to other sending regions in which peasant agriculture
predominates (Gregory and Pérez 1985). Interestingly, these differ-

·ences partially echo contrasts found at the turn of the century among different regions of Italy, Slovakia, and Transylvania. Areas in which capitalist relations of production were more advanced and class differentiation more markedly polarized tended to be characterized by low rates of emigration to the United States but high rates of participation in militant agricultural organizations. On the other hand, sending regions tended to be characterized by peasant farming. For peasants from these areas, emigration represented a response to threats to their way of life and a means to attempt to preserve it (Barton 1975:29ff.).

MIGRATION AND DEVELOPMENT

Migration from the Dominican Republic has been private, fragmented, and, in sociopolitical terms, spontaneous. Because migrants' investment decisions share these characteristics, they are unlikely to pose a challenge to the basic social and economic structures of Dominican society, the same structures that helped promote migration in the first place. In the earliest stages of the post-World War II upsurge in immigration, the notion that migrants could be a force behind meaningful development may have been useful in providing ideological justification for the massive transfer of people from the peripheral to the advanced capitalist nations. However, after the experience of some two decades, such a notion no longer appears tenable. As Reyneri and Mughini (1984:35) have wryly noted, migrants have behaved rationally, even if the same cannot be said of the economists and politicians who expected them single-handedly to promote development. It has become increasingly clear, however, that the pursuit of individual, private objectives, no matter how rational, is not necessarily congruent with broader social goals (Stahl 1982:870).

The Dominican Republic, in common with most sending nations in the world, had done nothing to channel the potential benefits of migration into more productive, employment-generating directions. Lacking any policy initiative, with no institutions to provide orientation and assistance, migrants had to fend for themselves. In deciding how to invest their capital, they once again turned to that most valuable cultural resource, their informal networks, for information, advice, assistance, and credit. However, as Penninx (1982:802) noted of Turkish migrants, rather than innovation, this pattern often leads to investments that imitate the successful decisions made by others—

the "me too" effect that results in a sometimes self-defeating proliferation of certain kinds of small enterprises, a portion of which inevitably fail.

A strong desire for independence or a preference for self-employment is often adduced as the reason returnees invest their hard-earned savings in the often redundant shops, bars, and cafeterias that make little productive contribution to the economy (Gmelch 1980:150; cf. Piore 1979). Yet the case of Los Pinos suggests that the propensity to such investments is also often the outcome of the interplay of several additional factors: the migrants' own characteristics, particularly the generally modest levels of education and skill acquired before migrating; the nature of their insertion into the U.S. labor market, which limited opportunities to acquire new skills and amass substantial savings; the increased importance of credentials and connections to securing desirable jobs in the Dominican Republic; and recent trends in the Dominican economy toward the growth of services and contraction of productive sectors. Given a paucity of relevant skills and training, the moderate size of most migrants' savings, and a dearth of alternatives, investing in a small business is one of the few options that provides the returnee with a degree of status and an income superior to the average wage of a worker or low-level bureaucrat (see Castro 1985). Typically, the limited size of migrants' savings ensures that the business will have little potential for creating employment.

Although this pattern may be the most frequently encountered, there were some migrants who were highly educated before leaving; there were others who managed to acquire valuable skills and training in the United States; and there were some whose entrepreneurial ventures enabled them to amass substantial savings. Yet, the Dominican government has maintained a passive attitude with respect to return migration. The result is a lack of substantive policies to attract skilled and entrepreneurial migrants home and to assist them in finding jobs and employment-generating investment opportunities. Among those who do return spontaneously to the Dominican Republic, skills and capital can be easily dissipated and readily channeled by existing social and economic institutions into less than optimal directions.

From the onset of large-scale emigration to the United States, the Dominican government has adopted a laissez-faire stance toward the process. In times of perceived crisis, however, it becomes evident that migration is in fact regarded as an important part of a solution to the republic's social and economic ills; it is not seen as part of a problem. The most recent instance occurred as a result of the passage of the Immigration Reform and Control Act in 1986. Concern over its consequences, particularly the possibility of massive repatriation of undocumented Dominicans, for the republic was made manifest in a number of statements by high-ranking officials, including one by the newly reelected president, Joaquín Balaguer to President Ronald Reagan. This generalized view that migration is an unmitigated social benefit constitutes an important obstacle to the critical rethinking that must precede the design of measures aimed at minimizing the costs of migration and augmenting its benefits.

There is an emerging recognition in the Caribbean as in other sending regions of the need to formulate national policies that will enable both individuals and their societies to capture the potential benefits of the migration process (Pastor and Rogers 1985; Chandavarkar 1980; Richards and Martin 1983; Birks and Sinclair 1980). Because the majority of Dominicans enter the United States under family reunification provisions, there is a potential for long-term planning lacking in other sending nations that must rely on uncertain temporary worker programs. Thus, despite the increasingly exclusionist trend in U.S. immigration policy, chain migration from the Dominican Republic will probably continue to be fairly steady in the years to come. No matter what its consequences, migration is a fact of life in the Dominican Republic.

Efforts to increase the potential benefits of migration will inevitably be constrained by the larger development environment. Options are limited, especially in the present climate of economic crisis. This only makes more urgent the need to turn the migration process to best account. In order to capture and amplify potential benefits in a systematic way, a migration policy must be part and parcel of a more comprehensive development policy. Specifically, this study suggests that policies must be formulated that would encourage migrants to invest in an agriculture using locally appropriate labor-intensive technology and geared toward food production. In the Dominican Republic, several regional development programs already have initiated research and extension efforts in an attempt to formulate regionally specific responses to agricultural stagnation. In high-migration areas like the Sierra, projects could be designed that would explicitly integrate the locally appropriate knowledge and experience garnered over time with the material and human assets of the migrants. While U.S. migration is recognized as a salient feature in several areas of the republic, regional programs have not included specific components that would use migrants' assets to best advantage. To optimize the chance of success, the planning of such components must include the participation of the migrants themselves.

On the national level, the foreign exchange generated by U.S. migrants could be put to better use if encouraged to flow into institutions that function to promote development. Pastor and Rogers (1985:334 ff.) have explored in some detail the possibility of creating national or regional remittance banks. These banks would identify and target for investment certain development projects that would be labor-intensive and productive and that optimally would contribute to economic diversification and social equity. They also would serve to attract matching funds from the United States and international institutions. Given the transnational nature of the migration process, efforts to promote local development have the best chance of exerting a positive impact if they receive bilateral and multilateral support.

Policies to encourage the return of skilled and experienced migrants are also needed. The ideology of return is strong among migrants. As Pastor and Rogers (1985:332) have noted, given sufficient incentives, such as specific jobs and housing, some professionals would be likely to return. It is recognized that it is less difficult and less expensive to retain new graduates. However, the ability to hold onto professionals will depend on changes in government policies which at present, by keeping wages low, encourage their migration.

The microcosm of Los Pinos as described in this book reveals some of the pitfalls as well as the possibilities inherent in international migration. This migration is a social process not easily characterized in zero-sum terms. Effects interact in complex ways that may shift over time. Assigning a single valence to migration's impact on complex economic, social, political, and cultural changes is further complicated by the reality that migration is only one force of change among many. Not surprisingly, the outcome of such evaluations frequently depends on the political lens through which the researcher regards the migration process. Neglect of such considerations can obscure the kind of nuanced understanding of migration's effects that is essential to the formulation of policy, which, if it is to have any success, must include the voices of the women and men whose own hopes and desires have propelled them into the flux of a transnational way of life.

References

Abu-Lughod, J. 1982. Review of *International Migration and Development in the Arab Region*, by J. S. Birks and C. A. Sinclair. *Economic Development and Cultural Change* 30(2):448–452.

Adelman, I. and C. Morris. 1973. *Economic Growth and Social Equity in Developing Countries*. Stanford: Stanford University Press.

Albuquerque, A. 1961. Títulos de los terrenos comuneros de la República Dominicana. Ciudad Trujillo: Impresora Dominicana.

Allison, P. 1978. Measures of Inequality. *American Sociological Review* 43(6):865–880.

Ameringer, C. 1974. *The Democratic Left in Exile: The Antidictatorial Struggle in the Caribbean, 1945–1959*. Coral Gables, Fla.: University of Miami Press.

Amin, S., ed. 1974. *Modern Migrations in Western Africa*. Oxford: Oxford University Press.

Antonini, G., K. Ewel, and H. Tupper. 1975. *Population and Energy: A Systems Analysis of Resource Utilization in the Dominican Republic*. Gainesville: University of Florida Press.

Arizpe, L. 1982. Relay Migration and the Survival of the Peasant Household. In H. Safa, ed., *Towards a Political Economy of Urbanization in Third World Countries*, pp. 19–46. Delhi: Oxford University Press.

Arrighi, G. 1973. Labor Supplies in Historical Perspective: A Study of the African Peasantry in Rhodesia. In G. Arrighi and J. Saul, eds., *Essays on the Political Economy of Africa*. New York: Monthly Review Press.

Bach, R., and L. Schraml. 1982. Migration, Crisis, and Theoretical Conflict. *International Migration Review* 6(2):320–341.

Baez Evertsz, F. and F. D'Oleo Ramírez. 1986. *La emigración de dominicanos a Estados Unidos: determinantes socio-económicos y consecuencias*. Santo Domingo: Fundación Friedrich Ebert.

Banco Central. 1962. Estadísticas económicas. Santo Domingo, Dominican Republic.

Barton, J. 1975. *Peasants and Strangers: Italians, Rumanians, and Slovaks in an American City*. Cambridge, Mass.: Harvard University Press.

Baucic, I. 1972. *The Effect of Emigration from Yugoslavia and the Problems of Returning Emigrant Workers*. The Hague: Nijhoff.

Bell, I. 1981. *The Dominican Republic*. Boulder, Col.: Westview Press.

Bendezú Alvarado, G. 1982. La realidad campesina dominicana y sus posibilidades de desarrollo. *Forum* 3:93–138.

Benería, L. and M. Roldán. 1987. *The Crossroads of Class and Gender: Industrial*

Homework, Subcontracting, and Household Dynamics in Mexico City. Chicago and London: University of Chicago Press.

Birks, J. and C. Sinclair. 1980. *International Migration and Development in the Arab Region.* Geneva: International Labour Office.

Black, J. 1986. *The Dominican Republic: Politics and Development in an Unsovereign State.* Boston: Allen and Unwin.

Bohning, W. 1975. Some Thoughts on Emigration from the Mediterranean Basin. *International Labor Review* 111(3):251–277.

Boin, J. and Serullé, J. 1979. *El proceso de desarrollo del capitalismo en la República Dominicana, 1844–1930,* vol. 1. Santo Domingo: Ediciones Gramil.

——1980. *La explotación capitalista en la República Dominicana.* Santo Domingo: Ediciones Gramil.

——1981. *El proceso de desarrollo del capitalismo en la República Dominicana, 1844–1930,* vol. 2. Santo Domingo: Ediciones Gramil.

Bonó, P. 1968. *El Montero.* Santo Domingo: Julio D. Postigo & Sons.

Bosch, J. 1983. *Composición social dominicana: historia e interpretación.* Santo Domingo: Alfa y Omega.

Bray, D. 1983. "Dependency, Class Formation and the Creation of Caribbean Labor Reserves: Internal and International Migration in the Dominican Republic." Ph.D. dissertation, Brown University.

——1984. Economic Development: The Middle Class and International Migration in the Dominican Republic. *International Migration Review* 18(2):217–236.

——1987. The Dominican Exodus: Origins, Problems, Solutions. In B. Levine, ed., *Caribbean Exodus.* New York: Praeger.

Brettell, C. 1986. *Men Who Migrate, Women Who Wait: Population and History in a Portuguese Parish.* Princeton: Princeton University Press.

Brown, S. 1975. Love Unites Them and Hunger Separates Them: Poor Women in the Dominican Republic. In R. Rapp, ed., *Toward an Anthropology of Women.* New York: Monthly Review Press.

Burawoy, M. 1976. The Functions and Reproduction of Migrant Labor: Comparative Material from Southern Africa and the United States. *American Journal of Sociology* 81:1050–87.

Burki, S. 1984. International Migration: Implications for Labor-Exporting Countries. *The Middle East Journal* 38(4):668–684.

Calder, B. 1984. *The Impact of Intervention: The Dominican Republic during the U.S. Occupation of 1916–1924.* Austin: University of Texas Press.

Cassá, R. 1979. *Modos de producción, clases sociales y luchas políticas (República Dominicana, Siglo XX).* Santo Domingo: Alfa y Omega.

——1980. *Historia social y económica de la República Dominicana,* vol. 2. Santo Domingo: Alfa y Omega.

——1982. *Capitalismo y dictadura.* Santo Domingo: Alfa y Omega.

Cassá, R., D. Ortiz, R. González, and G. Rodríguez. 1986. *Actualidad y perspectivas de la cuestión nacional en la República Dominicana.* Santo Domingo: Editora Buho.

Castells, M. 1975. Immigrant Workers and Class Struggles in Advanced Capitalism: The Western European Experience. *Politics and Society* 5(1):33–66.

Castles, S. 1984. *Here for Good: Western Europe's New Ethnic Minorities.* London: Pluto Press.

Castles, S. and G. Kosack. 1973. *Immigrant Workers and Class Structure in Western Europe.* London: Oxford University Press.

Castro, M. 1985. "Dominican Journey: Patterns, Context and Consequences of Migration from the Dominican Republic to the United States." Ph.D. dissertation, University of North Carolina at Chapel Hill.

Chandavarkar, A. 1980. Use of Migrants' Remittances in Labor-Exporting Countries. *Finance and Development* 17(2):36–39.

Cheng, L. and E. Bonacich, eds. 1984. *Labor Immigration Under Capitalism: Asian*

Immigrant Workers in the United States before World War II. Berkeley: University of California Press.

Chibnik, M. 1976. The Value of Subsistence Production. *Journal of Anthropological Research* 34(4):561–576.

CIPAF (Centro de Investigación para la Acción Femenina). 1985. *Paternidad responsable (un estudio sobre la ley 2402).* Santo Domingo: Taller.

Comitas, L. 1973. Occupational Multiplicity in Rural Jamaica. In L. Comitas and D. Lowenthal, eds., *Work and Family Life in the West Indies,* pp. 157–74. New York: Anchor Press.

Cornelius, W. 1976. *Mexican Migration to the U.S.: The View from the Rural Sending Communities.* Cambridge: Migration and Development Study Group, Massachusetts Institute of Technology.

—— 1980. Mexican Immigration: Causes and Consequences for Mexico. In R. Bryce-Laporte, D. Mortimer, and S. Couch, eds., *Sourcebook on The New Immigration: Implications for the United States and the International Community,* pp. 69–84. New Brunswick, N.J.: Transaction Books.

Crassweller, R. 1966. *Trujillo: The Life and Times of a Caribbean Dictator.* New York: Macmillan.

Crouch, L. 1979. "Desarrollo del capitalismo en el campo dominicano." Santo Domingo, manuscript.

Deere, C. and A. de Janvry. 1981. Demographic and Social Differentiation Among Northern Peruvian Peasants. *Journal of Peasant Studies* 8(3):335–66.

Deere, C. and M. Leon de Leal. 1981. Peasant Production, Proletarianization, and the Sexual Division of Labor in the Andes. *Signs* 7(2):338–360.

Deere, C. and R. Wasserstrom. 1980. "Ingreso familiar y trabajo no agrícola entre los pequeños productores de América Latina y El Caribe." Paper presented to Seminario Internacional sobre la producción agropecuaria y forestal en zonas de ladera en América Latina. Turrialba, Costa Rica.

de Janvry, A. 1981. *The Agrarian Question and Reformism in Latin America.* Baltimore and London: Johns Hopkins University Press.

del Castillo, J. and W. Cordero. 1980. *La economía dominicana durante el primer cuarto del siglo XX.* Santo Domingo: Fundación García Arévalo, Inc.

de los Santos, A., M. Holina, M. Montero, and D. Santos. 1981. Tendencias demográficas y problemas socio-económicos en la República Dominicana. Santo Domingo: CONAPOFA, mimeograph.

Díaz, M. 1987. La tensión crece entre ilegales criollos en Puerto Rico. *Ultima Hora,* May 5, p. 17.

Díaz Santana, M. and M. Murphy. 1983. The 1982 National Elections in the Dominican Republic: A Sociological and Historical Interpretation. *Caribbean Occasional Series,* No. 3. Rio Piedras, Puerto Rico: Institute of Caribbean Studies.

Dore y Cabral, C. 1979. *Problemas de la estructura agraria dominicana.* Santo Domingo: Ediciones de Taller.

—— 1981. *Reforma agraria y luchas sociales en la República Dominicana 1966–1978.* Santo Domingo: Editora Taller.

Duarte, I. 1980. *Capitalismo y superpoblación en Santo Domingo.* Santo Domingo: CODIA.

Duarte, I. and F. Pou. 1983. "Patrones características de fuerza de trabajo migratoria en la República Dominicana." Paper presented at the Seminar on Dominican Migration to the United States, Museo del Hombre Dominicano, April 28, 1983.

Ebiri, K. 1985. Impact of Labor Migration on the Turkish Economy. In R. Rogers, ed., *Guests Come to Stay: The Effects of European Labor Migration on Sending and Receiving Societies,* pp. 207–229. Boulder and London: Westview Press.

Edwards, R., M. Reich, and D. Gordon, eds. 1975. *Labor Market Segmentation.* Lexington, Mass.: D. C. Heath.

Emmanuel, A. 1972. *Unequal Exchange: A Study of the Imperialism of Trade.* New York: Monthly Review Press.

Encarnación, S. 1982. La producción de alimentos y las posibilidades de abastecimiento de la agricultura dominicana. *Forum* 3:13–29.

Fass, S. 1978. Port-au-Prince: Awakening to the Urban Crisis. In W. Cornelius and R. Kemper, eds., *Metropolitan Latin American Urban Research*, 6:155–180. Beverly Hills: Sage.

Ferguson, R. 1987. "When Do Classes Make History? A Perspective from the South Coast of Puerto Rico." Paper presented at the meetings of the American Ethnological Society, April 30–May 3, San Antonio, Texas.

—— 1988. "Class Transformation in Puerto Rico." Ph.D. dissertation, Columbia University.

Fernandez-Kelly, M. 1985. Contemporary Production and the New International Division of Labor. In S. Sanderson, ed., *The Americas in the New International Division of Labor*, pp. 206–225. New York: Holmes & Meier.

Fitzpatrick, J. and D. Gurak. 1979. *Hispanic Intermarriage in New York City: 1975.* New York: Hispanic Research Center, Fordham University. Monograph No. 2.

Food and Agricultural Organization of the United Nations. 1984. Migration and Rural Development. In *Population Distribution, Migration, and Development: Proceedings of the Expert Group on Population Distribution.* International Conference on Population. New York: United Nations.

Friedlander, S. 1965. *Labor, Migration and Economic Growth: A Case Study of Puerto Rico.* Cambridge, Mass.: MIT Press.

Frucht, R. 1968. Emigration, Remittances and Social Change: Aspects of the Social Field of Nevis, the West Indies. *Anthropologica*, n.s., 10(2):193–209.

Gabb, W. 1881. On the Topography and Geology of Santo Domingo. *Transactions of the American Philosophical Society*, n.s., 15:49–260.

Garrison, V. and C. Weiss. 1979. Dominican Family Networks and United States Immigration Policy: A Case Study. *International Migration Review* 13(2):264–283.

Geertz, C. 1963. *Peddlers and Princes: Social Development and Economic Change in Two Indonesian Towns.* Chicago: University of Chicago Press.

Geffroy, J. 1975. "Political Leadership and Factionalism in a Dominican Municipio." Ph.D. dissertation, University of New Mexico.

Georges, E. 1984. *Ethnic Associations and the Integration of New Immigrants: Dominicans in New York City.* Occasional Paper No. 41, New York Research Program in Inter-American Affairs.

Gleijeses, P. 1978. *The Dominican Crisis: The 1965 Constitutionalist Revolt and American Intervention.* Baltimore: Johns Hopkins University Press.

Gmelch, G. 1980. Return Migration. *Annual Review of Anthropology*, B. Siegal, ed., 9:135–59. Palo Alto, Calif.: Annual Reviews.

Gomez, L. 1979. *Relaciones de producción dominantes en la sociedad dominicana, 1897–1975.* Santo Domingo: Alfa y Omega.

Gonzalez, N. 1961. Family Organization in Five Types of Migratory Wage Labor. *American Anthropologist* 63(6):1264–80.

—— 1970. Peasants' Progress: Dominicans in New York. *Caribbean Studies* 10:154–171.

—— 1973. Patterns of Dominican Ethnicity. In J. Bennet, ed., *The New Ethnicity: Perspectives from Ethnology.* Seattle: Proceedings of the American Ethnological Society.

—— 1976. Multiple Migratory Experiences of the Dominican Worker. *Anthropological Quarterly* 49(1):36–44.

Grasmuck, S. 1982a. Migration Within the Periphery: Haitian Labor in the Dominican Sugar and Coffee Industries. *International Migration Review* 16(2):365–77.

—— 1982b. *The Impact of Emigration on National Development: Three Sending Com-*

munities in the Dominican Republic. Occasional Paper No. 33, New York Research Program in Inter-American Affairs.

——1984a. Immigration, Ethnic Stratification, and Native Working Class Discipline: Comparisons of Documented and Undocumented Dominicans. *International Migration Review* 18(3):692–713.

——1984b. The Impact of Emigration on National Development: Three Sending Communities in the Dominican Republic. *Development and Change* 15:381–403.

——1985. The Consequences of Dominican Urban Outmigration for National Development: The Case of Santiago. In S. Sanderson, ed., *The Americas in the New International Division of Labor*, pp. 145–76. New York: Holmes & Meier.

Graves, N. and T. Graves. 1974. Adaptive Strategies in Urban Migration. In B. Siegal, ed., *Annual Review of Anthropology*, 3:117–151. Palo Alto, Calif.: Annual Reviews.

Gregory, D. and J. Pérez. 1985. Intra-European Migration and Regional Development: Spain and Portugal. In R. Rogers, ed., *Guests Come to Stay: The Effects of European Labor Migration on Sending and Receiving Societies*, pp. 231–61. Boulder, Col.: Westview Press.

Griffin, K. 1976. On the Emigration of the Peasantry. *World Development* 4:353–361.

Griffith, D. 1985. Women, Remittances and Reproduction. *American Ethnologist* 12(4):676–690.

Gudeman, S. 1978. *The Demise of a Rural Economy: From Subsistence to Capitalism in a Latin American Village.* London: Routledge & Kegan Paul.

Gurak, D. 1982. Immigration History: Cubans, Dominicans and Puerto Ricans. In *Hispanics in New York: Religious, Cultural and Social Experiences*, 2:95–129, New York: Office of Pastoral Research, Archdiocese of New York.

——1987. Family Formation and Marital Selectivity Among Colombian and Dominican Immigrants in New York City. *International Migration Review* 21(2): 275–297.

Gurak, D. and M. Kritz. 1982. Dominican and Colombian Women in New York City: Household Structure and Employment Patterns. *Migration Today* 10: 14–21.

Guyer, J. 1981. Household and Community in African Studies. *African Studies Review* 24(2 and 3):87–137.

Hakim, P. and S. Weintraub. 1985. Economic Development, U.S. Economic Policy, and Migration: Establishing the Connections in the Caribbean. In R. Pastor, ed. *Migration and Development in the Caribbean: The Unexplored Connection*, pp. 371–394. Boulder and London: Westview Press.

Hart, K. 1973. Informal Income Opportunities and Urban Employment in Ghana. *Journal of Modern African Studies* 11:61–89.

Hendricks, G. 1974. *Dominican Diaspora: From the Dominican Republic to New York City—Villagers in Transition.* New York: Teachers College Press.

Herman, E. and F. Brodhead. 1984. *Demonstration Elections: U.S.-Staged Elections in the Dominican Republic, Viet Nam and El Salvador.* Boston: South End Press.

Hoetink, H. 1982. *The Dominican People: 1850–1900.* Baltimore: Johns Hopkins University Press.

Houstoun, M., R. Kramer, and J. Barrett. 1984. Female Predominance in Immigration to the U.S. since 1930: A First Look. *International Migration Review* 18(4):908–963.

Hume, I. 1973. Migrant Workers in Europe. *Finance and Development* 10(1):2–6.

Immigration and Naturalization Service (INS). 1966–1981. Statistical Abstracts. Washington, D.C.: G.P.O.

——1961–1980. Annual Reports. Washington, D.C.: G.P.O.

——1989. Provisional Legalization Application Statistics, May 12. Statistical Analysis Branch, Office of Plans and Analysis. Mimeograph.

Instituto Agrario Dominicano (IAD). 1963. *Bienes e inversiones de Trujillo, esposa y hijos.* Santo Domingo.

International Labor Organization (ILO). 1974. *Generation of Employment in the Dominican Republic.* Geneva.

Jones, R. 1984. Introduction. In R. Jones, ed., *Patterns of Undocumented Migration: Mexico and the United States,* pp. 1–12. Totowa, N.J.: Rowman and Allenheld.

Justo Duarte, A. 1979. *Las luchas de clases en República Dominicana.* Tomo 1. Santo Domingo: Alfa y Omega.

Kayal, P. 1978. The Dominicans in New York, Part 1. *Migration Today* 6:11–15.

Kearney, M. 1986. From the Invisible Hand to the Visible Feet: Anthropological Studies of Migration and Development. In B. Siegal, ed., *Annual Review of Anthropology,* 15:331–361. Palo Alto, Calif.: Annual Reviews.

Kim, I. 1981. *New Urban Immigrants: The Korean Community in New York.* Princeton, N.J.: Princeton University Press.

King, R., J. Mortimer, A. Strachan, and M. Viganola. 1985. Back to Bernalda: The Dynamics of Return Migration to a South Italian Agro-Town. In G. Van der Knaap and P. White, eds., *Contemporary Studies of Migration,* pp. 155–171. Norwich: Geo Books.

Koch, J. 1987. The Incomes of Recent Immigrants: A Look at Ethnic Differences. *Social Science Quarterly* 68(2):294–310.

Kritz, M., and D. Gurak. 1983. "Kinship Networks and the Settlement Process: Dominican and Colombian Immigrants in New York City." Manuscript.

Kryzanek, T. 1979. Diversion, Subversion and Repression: The Strategies of Anti-Regime Politics in Balaguer's Dominican Republic. *Caribbean Studies* 19(1 and 2):83–103.

Larson, E. 1987a. Patterns of Labor Absorption by Occupation in the Dominican Republic. *International Journal of Sociology and Social Policy* 7(4):67–77.

——1987b. "International Migration and the Labor Force: A Study of Members of Migrant Households versus Members of Domestic Households in the Dominican Republic." Ph.D. dissertation, University of Texas at Austin.

Larson, E., and W. Opitz. 1988. "Sex Ratio-Based Estimates of Emigration from the Dominican Republic." Paper presented at the Conference on Dominican Migration to the United States, sponsored by the Fundación Friedrich Ebert and the Fondo para el Avance de las Ciencias Sociales, March 21–23, Santo Domingo.

Larson, E., and T. Sullivan. 1987. "Conventional Numbers" in Immigration Research: The Case of the Missing Dominicans. *International Migration Review* 21(4):1474–1497.

Lipton, M. 1980. Migration from Rural Areas of Poor Countries: The Impact on Rural Productivity and Income Distribution. *World Development* 8:1–24.

Lomnitz, L. 1977. *Networks and Marginality: Life in a Mexican Shantytown.* New York: Academic Press.

Long, N. and B. Roberts. 1984. *Miners, Peasants and Entrepreneurs: Regional Development in the Central Highlands of Peru.* Cambridge: Cambridge University Press.

Lowenthal, D. 1972. *West Indian Societies.* New York: Oxford University Press.

Lowenthal, D. and L. Comitas. 1962. Emigration and Depopulation: Some Neglected Aspects of Population Geography. *Geographical Review* 3:195–210.

Lozano, W. 1985. *El reformismo dependiente.* Santo Domingo: Editora Taller.

——1987. *Desempleo estructural, dinámica económica y fragmentación de los mercados de trabajo urbanos: el caso dominicano. Documento Base.* Santo Domingo: Fundación Friedrich Ebert.

Mangin, W. 1967. Latin American Squatter Settlements: A Problem and a Solution. *Latin American Research Review* 2:65–98.

Marshall, D. 1985a. International Migration as Circulation: Haitian Movement to the Bahamas. In R. Prothero and M. Chapman, eds., *Circulation in Third World Countries*, pp. 226–240. London: Routledge & Kegan Paul.

—— 1985b. Migration and Development in the Eastern Caribbean. In R. Pastor, ed., *Migration and Development in the Caribbean; The Unexplored Connection*, pp. 91–116. Boulder and London: Westview Press.

Martin, J. 1966. *Overtaken by Events: From the Death of Trujillo to the Civil War.* New York: Doubleday.

Marx, E. 1986. Migration and the Labour Market. *Anthropology Today* 2(6):17–19.

Massey, D., R. Alarcon, J. Durand, and H. Gonzalez. 1987. *Return to Aztlan: The Social Process of International Migration from Western Mexico.* Berkeley: University of California Press.

McArthur, J. 1979. The Effects of Overseas Work on Return Migrants and Their Home Communities: A Philippine Case. *Papers in Anthropology* 20:85–104.

Meillassoux, C. 1972. From Reproduction to Production. *Economy and Society* 1: 93–105.

—— 1981. *Maidens, Meal and Money: Capitalism and the Domestic Community.* Cambridge: Cambridge University Press.

Mies, M. 1982. The Dynamics of the Sexual Division of Labor and Integration of Rural Women into the World Market. In L. Benería, ed., *Women and Development: The Sexual Division of Labor in Rural Societies*, pp. 1–28. New York: Praeger.

Mines, R. 1984. Network Migration and Mexican Rural Development: A Case Study. In R. Jones, ed., *Patterns of Undocumented Migration; Mexico and the United States*, pp. 136–55. Totowa, N.J.: Rowman and Allenheld.

Mones, B. et al. 1987. Proletarización feminina y el limitado mercado laboral agrícola. In F. Pou et al., eds., *La mujer rural dominicana*, pp. 169–194. Santo Domingo: CIPAF.

Montero, V., 1979. *Diseño de un sistema de manejo agroforestal para el plan Sierra; República Dominicana.* Gainesville: Center for Latin American Studies, University of Florida.

Morokvasic, M. 1984. Birds of Passage are also Women. *International Migration Review* 18(4):886–907.

Morrison, T. and R. Sinkin. 1982. International Migration in the Dominican Republic: Implications for Development Planning. *International Migration Review* 16(4):819–836.

Moser, C. 1978. Informal Sector of Petty Commodity Production. *World Development* 6(9/10):1041–1064.

Moya Pons, F. 1980. *Manual de historia dominicana*, 5th ed. Santiago: Universidad Católica Madre y Maestra.

Murphy, M. 1987. The International Monetary Fund and Crisis in the Dominican Republic. In R. Tardanico, ed., *Crisis in the Caribbean Basin*, pp. 241–259. Beverly Hills: Sage.

Murray, C. 1981. *Families Divided: The Impact of Migrant Labor in Lesotho.* Cambridge: Cambridge University Press.

NACLA. (North American Congress on Latin America). 1975. *Fruits of the Invasion: U.S. Interests in the Dominican Republic Ten Years Later.* New York.

Nash, J. 1981. Ethnographic Aspects of the World Capitalist System. In *Annual Review of Anthropology* B. Siegal, ed. 10:393–423. Palo Alto, Calif.: Annual Reviews.

Nevadomsky, J. 1983. Economic Organization, Social Mobility and Changing Social Status among East Indians in Rural Trinidad. *Ethnology* 22(1):63–79.

Nikolinakos, M. 1975. Notes Towards a General Theory of Migration in Late Capitalism. *Race and Class* 17:5–17.

Oberai, A. and H. Singh. 1980. Migration, Remittances and Rural Development: Findings of a Case Study in the Indian Punjab. *International Labor Review* 119(2):229–241.

ONAPLAN. (Oficina Nacional de Planificación). 1978. *Indicadores Básicos*. Santo Domingo.

——1980a. *Participación de la mano de obra haitiana en el mercado laboral: el caso de la caña y el café*. Santo Domingo.

——1980b. *Hacia una política del empleo en la República Dominicana*. Santo Domingo: Editora del Caribe.

ONAPLAN-ONE (Oficina Nacional de Planificación y Oficina Nacional de Estadística). 1981. *La situación del empleo en Santo Domingo y Santiago en noviembre de 1979*. Santo Domingo: Oficina Nacional de Planificación.

Orlansky, D. and S. Dubrovsky. 1978. *The Effects of Rural-Urban Migration on Women's Role and Status in Latin America*. Paris: UNESCO.

Ortiz Fernández, F. 1947. *Cuban Counterpoint; Tobacco and Sugar*. New York: Knopf.

Paine, S. 1974. *Exporting Workers: The Turkish Case*. London: Cambridge University Press.

Pastor, R., and R. Rogers. 1985. Using Migration to Enhance Economic Development in the Caribbean: Three Sets of Proposals. In R. Pastor, ed., *Migration and Development in the Caribbean: The Unexplored Connection*, pp. 321–347. Boulder and London: Westview Press.

Penninx, R. 1982. A Critical Review of Theory and Practice: The Case of Turkey. *International Migration Review* 16(4):781–818.

Pérez, G. 1981. "The Legal and Illegal Dominican in New York City." Paper presented at the Conference on Hispanic Migration to New York City: Global Trends and Neighborhood Change. The New York Research Program in Inter-American Affairs at New York University, December 4.

Pérez, J. 1972. *Geografía y sociedad*. Santo Domingo: Editora del Caribe.

Perlman, J. 1976. *The Myth of Marginality: Urban Poverty and Politics in Rio de Janeiro*. Berkeley: University of California Press.

Pessar, P. 1982a. The Role of Households in International Migration and the Case of U.S.-Bound Migration from the Dominican Republic. *International Migration Review* 16(2):342–364.

——1982b. *Kinship Relations of Production in the Migration Process: The Case of Dominican Emigration to the United States*. The New York Research Program in Inter-American Affairs at New York University, Occasional Paper No. 32.

——1984. The Linkage Between the Household and Workplace in the Experience of Dominican Immigrant Women in the United States. *International Migration Review* 18:1188–1211.

Petras, E. 1980. Toward a Theory of International Migration: The New Division of Labor. In R. Bryce-Laporte, ed., *Sourcebook on the New Immigration: Implications for the United States and the International Community*, pp. 439–452. New Brunswick, N.J.: Transaction Books.

Philpott, S. 1973. *West Indian Migration: The Monserrat Case*. New York: Humanities Press.

Piore, M. 1979. *Birds of Passage: Migrant Labor and Industrial Societies*. Cambridge: Cambridge University Press.

Portes, A. 1978. Toward a Structural Analysis of Illegal (Undocumented) Immigration. *International Migration Review* 12(4):469–484.

Portes, A. and R. Bach. 1984. *Latin Journey: Cuban and Mexican Immigrants in the United States*. Berkeley: University of California Press.

Portes, A. and J. Walton. 1981. *Labor, Class, and the International System*. New York: Academic Press.

Ramírez, N. 1984. Planificación familiar, crecimiento demográfico y condiciones de vida en la República Dominicana. Planteamientos para una política de población y desarrollo. In F. Moya Pons, ed., *Población y pobreza en la Repúlica Dominicana*, pp. 175–198. Santo Domingo: Forum.

Rapp, R. 1977. Claude Meillassoux: "Femmes, Greniers et Capitaux." *Dialectical Anthropology* 2(4):317–324.

——1983. Peasants into Proletarians from the Household Out: An Analysis of the Intersection of Anthropology and Social History. In J. Mencher, ed., *Social Anthropology of the Peasantry*, pp. 32–47. Bombay: Somaiya Publishers.

Reichert, J. 1979. "The Migrant Syndrome: An Analysis of U.S. Migration and Its Impact on a Rural Mexican Town." Ph.D. dissertation, Princeton University.

——1981. The Migrant Syndrome: Seasonal U.S. Wage Labor and Rural Development in Central Mexico. *Human Organization* 40(1):56–66.

Reichert, J. and D. Massey. 1979. Patterns of U.S. Migration from a Mexican Sending Community: A Comparison of Legal and Illegal Migrants. *International Migration Review* 13:599–623.

Reimers, D. 1985. *Still the Golden Door: The Third World Comes to America*. New York: Columbia University Press.

Rey, P. 1973. *Les Alliances de Classes*. Paris: Maspero.

Reyneri, E. and C. Mughini. 1984. Migration, Co-operation and Development: An Examination of a Pilot Project in Portugal. In D. Kubat, ed., *The Politics of Return: International Return Migration in Europe*, pp. 31–36. Proceedings of the First European Conference on International Return Migration, Rome, November 11–14, 1981. New York: Center for Migration Studies.

Rhoades, R. 1978. Intra-European Return Migration and Rural Development: Lessons from the Spanish Case. *Human Organization* 37(2):136–47.

——1979. From Caves to Main Street: Return Migration and the Transformation of a Spanish Village. *Papers in Anthropology* 20:57–74.

Richards, A. and P. Martin. 1983. The Laissez-Faire Approach to International Labor Migration: The Case of the Arab Middle East. *Economic Development and Cultural Change* 31(3):652–674.

Richardson, N. 1978. *Foreign Policy and Economic Dependence*. Austin, Texas: University of Texas Press.

Rivière d'Arc, H. 1980. Change and Rural Emigration in Central Mexico. In D. Preston, ed., *Environment, Society, and Rural Change in Latin America*, pp. 185–193. New York: Wiley.

Rocheleau, D. 1983. "The Combined Application of Ecosystems and Farming Systems Analysis to Agroforestry Production in the Sierra, Dominican Republic." Paper presented to the Conference of Latin American Geographers, Santo Domingo, October 12, 1983.

——1984. "An Ecological Analysis of Soil and Water Conservation in Hillslope Farming Systems: Plan Sierra, Dominican Republic." Ph.D. dissertation, University of Florida.

Rogers, R., ed. 1985. *Guests Come to Stay: The Effects of European Labor Migration on Sending and Receiving Societies*. Boulder and London: Westview Press.

Rosado, T., B. Fernández, and I. Hernández. 1987. Ideología y subordinación. In F. Pou et al., eds., *La mujer rural dominicana*, pp. 197–207. Santo Domingo: CIPAF.

Rose, A. 1969. *Migrants in Europe: Problems of Acceptance and Adjustment*. Minneapolis: University of Minnesota Press.

Ross, E. and R. Rapp. 1981. Sex and Society: A Research Note from Social History and Anthropology. *Comparative Studies in Society and History* 23(1):51–72.

Russell, S. 1986. Remittances from International Migration: A Review in Perspective. *World Development* 14(6):677–696.

Sassen-Koob, S. 1978. The International Circulation of Resources and Development: The Case of Migrant Labor. *Development and Change* 9:509–545.

——1979. Formal and Informal Associations: Dominicans and Colombians in New York City. *International Migration Review* 8(2):314–332.

Schneider, P. and J. Schneider. 1974. *Culture and Political Economy in Western Sicily*. New York: Academic Press.

SEA (Secretaria de Estado de Agricultura). 1978. *Plan de desarrollo, La Sierra*. Santo Domingo.

——1980. *Diagnóstico del Sector Agrario*. Santo Domingo.

——n.d. *Diagnóstico del Sub-Sector Pecuario*. Santo Domingo.

Serra-Santana, E. 1984. Return of Portuguese: Economic Goals or Retention of One's Identity? In D. Kubat, ed., *The Politics of Return: International Return Migration in Europe*, pp. 55–56. Proceedings of the First European Conference on International Return Migration, Rome, November 11–14, 1981. New York: Center for Migration Studies.

Shanin, T. 1978. The Peasants Are Coming: Migrants Who Labour, Peasants Who Travel, and Marxists Who Write. *Race and Class* 19(3):277–288.

Silfa, N. 1983. *Guerra, traición y exilio*. Barcelona: Manuel Girón.

Smith, M. 1981. "Nutrition and Public Health in the Dominican Republic." Plan Sierra unpublished document.

Soares, G. 1977. The Web of Exploitation: State and Peasants in Latin America. *Studies in Comparative International Development* 12:13–24.

Soto, R. and G. del Rosario. 1978. *El presupuesto de la familia dominicana: ingreso y consumo familiar*. Santo Domingo: Banco Central.

Spengler, J. and G. Meyers. 1977. Migration and Socioeconomic Development: Today and Yesterday. In A. Brown and E. Neuberger, eds., *Internal Migration: A Comparative Perspective*, pp. 11–35. New York: Academic Press.

Spiegel, A. 1980. Rural Differentiation and the Diffusion of Migrant Labour Remittances in Lesotho. In P. Mayer, ed., *Black Villagers in an Industrial Society*, pp. 109–168. Cape Town: Oxford University Press.

Stahl, C. 1982. Labor Emigration and Economic Development. *International Migration Review* 13(4):869–899.

Stone, C. 1980. *Democracy and Clientelism in Jamaica*. New Brunswick and London: Transaction Books.

Stuart, J. and M. Kearney. 1981. *Causes and Effects of Agricultural Labor Migration from the Mixteca of Oaxaca to California*. La Jolla: Program in U.S.-Mexican Studies, University of California, San Diego.

Swanson, J. 1979. The Consequences of Emigration for Economic Development: A Review of the Literature. *Papers in Anthropology* 20:39–56.

Tatis, A. 1985. Situación actual del sector vivienda: sus características y sus causas, 1970–1980. In F. Moya Pons, ed., *Situación de la vivienda en la República Dominicana*, pp. 21–31. Santo Domingo: Forum.

Ugalde A., F. Bean, and G. Cardenas. 1979. International Migration from the Dominican Republic: Findings from a National Survey. *International Migration Review* 13(2):235–254.

Van Velsen, J. 1961. Labour Migration as a Positive Factor in the Continuity of Tonga Tribal Society. In A. Southall, ed., *Social Change in Modern Africa*, pp. 230–241. Chicago: University of Chicago Press.

Vega, B. 1987. Ventajas e inconveniencias de la emigración de los dominicanos. *Listín Diario*, February 18, p. 6.

Vicens, L. 1982. *Crisis económica 1978–1982*. Santo Domingo: Alfa y Omega.

Vicioso, C. 1976. Dominican Migration to the U.S.A. *Migration Today* 20:59–72.

Vincent, J. 1977. Agrarian Society as Organized Flow: Processes of Development Past and Present. *Peasant Studies* VI(2):56–65.

Vivolo, R. 1984. Emigration and Agriculture in a Sicilian Village. In D. Kubat, ed., *The Politics of Return: International Return Migration in Europe*, pp. 73–78. Proceedings of the First European Conference on International Return Migration, Rome, November 11–14, 1981. New York: Center for Migration Studies.

Waldinger, R. 1985. Immigration and Industrial Change in the New York City Apparel Industry. In G. Borjas and M. Tienda, eds., *Hispanics in the U.S. Economy*, pp. 323–349. Orlando: Academic Press.

Walker, M. 1972. *Politics and the Power Structure: A Rural Community in the Dominican Republic*. New York: Teachers College Press.

Wallerstein, I. 1979. The Rise and Future Demise of the World Capitalist System: Concepts for Comparative Analysis. *Comparative Studies in Society and History* 14(4):387–415.

Wallerstein, I., W. Martin, and T. Dickinson. 1979. Household Structure and Production Processes: Theoretical Concerns Plus Data from Southern Africa and Nineteenth Century United States. Binghamton, N.Y.: Fernand Braudel Center. Mimeograph.

Warren, R. 1988. "The Role of Statistics in Shaping U.S. Immigration Policy." Paper presented at the annual meetings of the American Statistics Association, New Orleans, August.

Warren, R. and J. Passel. 1987. A Count of the Uncountable: Estimates of Undocumented Aliens in the 1980 United States Census. *Demography* 24(3):375–393.

Watson, J. 1975. *Emigration and the Chinese Lineage: The Mans in Hong Kong and London.* Berkeley: University of California Press.

Weist, R. 1973. Wage-Labor Migration and the Household in a Mexican Town. *Journal of Anthropological Research* 29:180–209.

—— 1979. Anthropological Perspectives on Return Migration: A Critical Commentary. *Papers in Anthropology* 20:167–188.

Werge, R. 1975. "Agricultural Development in Clear Creek: Adaptive Strategies and Economic Roles in a Dominican Settlement." Ph.D. dissertation, University of Florida.

Whitten, N. 1965. *Class, Kinship and Power in an Ecuadorean Town: The Negroes of San Lorenzo.* Stanford, Calif.: Stanford University Press.

Wilkie, J. and A. Perkal. 1984. *Statistical Abstract of Latin America*, vol. 23, Los Angeles: UCLA Latin American Center Publication.

Wilson, F. 1985. Women and Agricultural Change in Latin America: Some Concepts Guiding Research. *World Development* 13(9):1017–1035.

Wolpe, H. 1972. Capitalism and Cheap Labour-Power in South Africa: From Segregation to Apartheid. *Economy and Society* 1:425–456.

Wood, C. 1981. Structural Changes and Household Strategies: A Conceptual Framework for the Study of Rural Migration. *Human Organization* 40(4):338–344.

—— 1982. Equilibrium and Historical-Structural Perspectives on Migration. *International Migration Review* 16(2):298–319.

World Bank. 1978. *Dominican Republic: Its Main Economic Development Problems.* Washington, D.C.

—— 1980. World Development Report. Washington, D.C.

—— 1986. World Development Report. New York: Oxford University Press.

Yanigasako, S. 1979. Family and Household: The Analysis of Domestic Groups. B. Siegel, ed., *Annual Review of Anthropology* 8:161–205. Palo Alto, Calif.: Annual Reviews.

Index